SING TO THE COLORS

A Writer Explores Two Centuries at the University of Michigan

James Tobin

D1569929

University of Michigan Press
Ann Arbor

ISBN-13: 978-0-472-03857-2 (print)
ISBN-13: 978-0-472-12906-5 (ebook)

2024   2023   2022   2021   4   3   2   1

Contents

Prologue

One afternoon in June 2020, I took a chair on the back porch of an old friend, Francis Blouin, the historian and archivist who served the University of Michigan for more than thirty years as director of the Bentley Historical Library.

The Bentley Library—unassuming in its low, dark-brick disguise at the edge of North Campus—is in fact the University's treasure chest. Inside are the University's own rich records and an enormous collection that documents the history of the entire state. Over the years, I had dipped into that storehouse often enough to draw out some 150 stories about the University's history. Now I wanted to assemble some of them to make a book.

Fran Blouin was the one to ask for advice. He knew as much about the University's history as anyone alive—more than I did, certainly. He was also a friend who had figured in my life for many years, not least by recruiting the young woman I would later marry to enroll in U-M's master's program in archives administration. (When I showed up for the first day of Professor Shaw Livermore's "Jeffersonian America" in the fall of 1978, she was sitting in the back row. Good course. Some girl.)

Fran had read my brief proposal to the University of Michigan Press. He was for it, but with a proviso. Any such book, he said, should be more than just a collection of pieces already published. I had been on a journey through the University's past, stopping here and there to stare at lost scenes. A reader would want to know what I had learned along the way. Where had I been inspired? Troubled? What did I think after these years of studying the place?

I saw his point. But what *did* I think, after all?

✣ ✣ ✣

Fran and I were talking to each other at a discreet distance of eight feet. We were four months into the COVID-19 pandemic. We traded impressions of the plague's frightening effects on two campuses—the one in Ann Arbor, where both of us live and where I had gone to college as an undergraduate and graduate student, where my parents, my wife, and our two daughters had gone; and the one in Oxford, Ohio, where I teach narrative nonfiction at Miami University.

We had been thinking along the same lines. The coronavirus had chased students and professors out of real classrooms into the shallow, unsatisfactory sphere of "digital learning." Now, suddenly, the whole long enterprise of the American university seemed to be trembling on its foundations. Maybe that was just a panicky passing thought. Maybe not.

For centuries, there had been no way to go to college but to literally *go*. Fledgling students who made the journey from home to a specific portion of ground—a campus with familiar buildings and idiosyncratic traditions, each with its own deeply felt sense of place—passed from childhood to adulthood on that ground. In the dormitories and the boarding houses, they met friends and lovers. In the classroom they met teachers who, if they were lucky, transformed their minds. And it was not only students who depended on being together in the flesh. Scholars and scientists searching for truths and creating new knowledge did their work through close contact with others—in the library and the laboratory, at the conference table.

Now, in a twinkling, a virus had erased all that, at least for a long moment. The students suddenly were gone. The campuses were empty and silent.

But the residential experience of college was endangered by more than a rampant virus. For years, skeptics had questioned the value of that experience. The enterprise had become far too costly, they said, and the internet was rendering it obsolete, anyway. A thousand faculties teaching essentially the same courses on a thousand campuses? Why, the whole thing could be done online with a fraction of the personnel at a fraction of the cost. Now the pandemic was proving it! Just look—millions of college students were still going to class, but in the safety of their homes!

In fact, I thought the virus was demonstrating how much would be lost if the residential campus were consigned to history. I had to look no further than the depressed and digitized faces of my own students, suddenly attending their classes through glass screens.

Until the pandemic, I had not thought very hard about why I wrote stories about U-M's history—apart from the fees I got from the editors of University publications. (I was, after all, a freelance writer for part of every working week.) I thought of these stories as something more than a hobby but less than a writerly calling. They provided a good excuse to satisfy my curiosity, and if I did the work well, then my fellow Michigan alumni might enjoy a little pleasurable reading.

But now, suddenly, the task of telling the University's old stories struck me as more important than that, even urgent. And as I pondered Fran's suggestion—to reflect on what I had learned, what these stories amounted to when summed up—I began to see that this work meant more to me than I'd realized. As I went back through the stories I'd written, I thought about how deeply my life was entwined with the place, like a thin green vine twisting up the trunk and limbs of an old oak.

I saw the campus for the first time at the age of seven or eight, in the mid-1960s. My parents, who graduated from the University in the spring before Pearl Harbor, would drive out from Detroit with my brother and sister and me to see football and basketball games and to stroll here and there. I remember only snapshots of these visits—college guys standing on the sagging roof of a front porch, shouting at passing cars; the great Cazzie Russell on the basketball floor at Yost Field House; the dimly lit pool hall at the Union.

In our basement at home, on a big wall map of the state of Michigan, I spotted what struck me as an odd, two-word name for a city. Then in a flash I realized this must be how you spelled the lyrical syllables I had heard my parents speak so often, as if they were run together in a single word, just as one of the city's founders, John Allen, had spelled them long ago—*Annarbour*.

I enrolled as a freshman in 1974. Technically, I majored in history, but my true major was the *Michigan Daily*. Like any good college journalist, I may have skipped one in three of the classes I was supposed to attend, not so much to report stories as to hang out with my pals in the glorious old newsroom of the Student Publications Building at 420 Maynard.

I loved the *Daily*. But soon after graduation, I decided I wanted to be a historian. So I re-enrolled, this time for a PhD. I met my wife and we started a family.

I loved the time I spent as a doctoral student. But after a while, I sensed that I was not cut out to be an academic historian.

So, doctorate in hand, I flipped back to journalism, raising puzzled eyebrows among family and friends. For twelve years I went to work every day as a reporter at my hometown newspaper, the *Detroit News*. For four of those years I covered higher education and wrote many stories about U-M. In this role I was supposed to bury my loyalties and study the place with a journalist's critical eye.

I roasted the University of Michigan more than once. For example, in 1992, I wrote an extended portrait of intellectual alienation among undergraduates living in South Quad. In the course of my interviews, the chair of the English Department conceded on the record that he would not want his own son to enroll at Michigan. After the stories were published, the professor—now very unhappy with me—informed my employers at the *News* that he did not recognize the "misshapen caricatures" I had written about. "We love these students," he said. "They are the reason most of us would never leave."

Actually, a couple years later, he did leave. Come to think of it, he left not long after he helped to deep-six U-M's century-old curriculum in journalism. Coincidence?

My view of the place had grown more complex. But I never found a reason not to believe that of all our society's embattled institutions, the college and the university embody our best hope of living in a dominion of reason and perpetual renewal.

After the *News* I went on my own as a freelancer. I wrote in the genre where my two paths, history and journalism, converged. The genre is called popular history—narratives built out of careful research but intended for readers who want to read about the past simply as a story, not as a pitched battle between arguing academics.

I wrote books about people distant from me in time and space—the great war correspondent Ernie Pyle; the Wright brothers and their rivals in the early days of human flight; Franklin Roosevelt and his struggle with polio.

But my home turf beckoned, too.

For *Michigan Today*, the digital monthly that goes to Michigan's global throng of alumni, I wrote a story about Avery Hopwood, the tortured playwright who founded Michigan's Hopwood Awards. It was fun to write that story. So I went to John Lofy, my friend and *Michigan Today*'s editor, and asked, "How about if I write a monthly piece about U-M history?" I would avoid the usual rah-rah stuff, I said. I would look for stories no one knew or for fresh angles on familiar tales.

"Sure," John said, "let's try it."

Story followed story, year after year.

When the University's 2017 bicentennial began to peek over the far horizon, I met with another friend, Kim Clarke, a veteran journalist who had joined the University's staff as an in-house writer. (She served, among other roles, as speechwriter to President Mary Sue Coleman.) Kim asked me to help her plan a new digital publication to be called the University of Michigan Heritage Project. Under her editorship, I began to write much longer stories than my articles in *Michigan Today*, though I kept writing for *Michigan Today*, too, now run by a new editor, Deborah Holdship.

Some pieces had a sharp edge of self-criticism—sharp enough that the occasional alumnus asked why the University would publish such a thing on its own websites. But all three editors—John, Kim, and Deborah—believed as I did that frank reporting about the University's past, including its dark moments, would win more favor among its constituents than any sugary diet of feel-good chatter. Anyway, I wasn't writing to help or hurt the University's reputation. I just liked telling the stories.

✢ ✣ ✢

Time had to pass before I could say exactly why I chose not to be an academic historian. Finally I understood. Scholarly historians are in the business of analysis. They amass evidence, then construct arguments about cause and effect. And I was not much of an analyst. I had few big ideas. My talent as a writer, such as it was, was to tell true stories—to say (a) happened, then (b), then finally (c), with a reflection or two along the way. I prefer not to be the one who tries to explain what it all means.

So I've decided that my response to Fran Blouin's questions—What had I learned? What did all this work add up to?—can only be to show that many of the stories I've written grew from some fragment of my own entanglement with the place. This may give a reader some sense of how one student's life can be so profoundly shaped by a university, and of how grateful one ought to feel for the long work of the many generations who envisioned and built and sustained the place, whatever its imperfections and errors.

Thinking about all this, I remembered something that one of my writer-heroes, the essayist and author E.B. White, said in a letter to a young reader of *Charlotte's Web*. She had asked what White was trying to say in his novel about a spider who saves the life of a young pig. He replied: "All that I hope to say in books, all that I ever hope to say, is that I love the world. I guess you can find that in there, if you dig around."

That's my answer to my friend Fran, who asked what I'd learned about the University of Michigan—simply that I love the institution on which I've spun much of the web of my life, and that I hope it will survive and thrive to nourish more lives to come. I guess you can find that in here.

PART I: THE PLACE ITSELF

On any street corner around the campus, I can look here or there and suddenly feel as if I'm looking down through layers of time—my own time, my family's time, the University's time.

Say I'm at the corner of Hill and Washtenaw, standing by the Rock. Across Washtenaw, behind some trees, there's a stone house with a tower. Henry Simmons Frieze used to live there. He was the popular professor of Latin who stepped in as president of the University when James Burrill Angell was on leave as U.S. minister to China in 1880—1881. Frieze did more than anyone else to make music a central part of life at Michigan. I see the house and then I see Professor Frieze.

If I pivot to look across Hill Street, I see the rambling house where John Sinclair's Rainbow People lived when Sinclair went to prison for possession of two joints, and "Free John" became a pro-marijuana rallying cry. That was in 1969. I see the house and then I see that crazy bunch of hippies.

Up the long slant of Washtenaw Avenue is the Phi Delta Theta house, where my dad was set up on a blind date with my mom, who lived a few blocks away at Kappa Kappa Gamma. That was in 1938. Kitty-corner from the Kappa house, in 2013, I dropped off my younger daughter to start her freshman year at East Quad, where I had started my own first year in 1974. I see us all.

Or say I'm at the corner of State and South University. I turn and see John F. Kennedy on the steps of the Union, asking a crowd of students: "How many of you who are going to be doctors, are willing to spend your days in Ghana? Technicians or engineers, how many of you are willing to work in the Foreign Service and spend your lives traveling around the world?" That was very late one night in the fall of 1960.

1

Then I turn and look at the Law School and see the sculptors who carved the comic stone heads for the main archway of the Lawyers Club. That was in 1924. One of those heads is a likeness of Henry Philip Tappan, who lived across the street in the President's House, the only building still standing from the original campus. He stayed from 1852 until the Regents fired him in 1863, though he was the one who envisioned the University we know today. I see him, too.

At the corner of North University and East University, I see a building no longer there, Waterman Gymnasium, where I stood in line to register for classes in the 1970s. In the fall of 1945, my father was standing in line on the same wood floor to register for his first term in the Law School when he heard a familiar voice shout from across the room: "Hey, Tobin, you son of a bitch!" It was the voice of his best friend, Charlie Ross. Both had survived combat in World War II, and now here they were, back in Waterman Gym.

The University of Michigan has never been renowned for its architecture. It grew as a hodgepodge to serve utilitarian needs. Despite touches of beauty in this building or that, even a charitable outsider would say that any overall theme is, at best, "vigorous eclecticism."

But I am not a visitor. I feel attached to the place—the physical, concrete place—not because of its architectural graces. What I feel as I walk around the campus is akin to what I feel when I go back and look at the house and the yard where I grew up. When I see late-afternoon light on the dark brick of the Michigan League, or the girth of the Tappan Oak by the north wing of the Harlan Hatcher Graduate Library, a sense stirs that I belong to this ground and the ground belongs to me.

The past can be understood as our companion. It lends us a system of echolocation, a way of knowing where we are in time and thus of knowing who we are. That's a comfort in any era, and certainly in this one, with so much in flux. The physical place of the campus is an irreplaceable embodiment of a student's connection to the long phenomenon of the University as an idea and a mission. I don't believe there can really be a college without a campus.

1: A Different Diag

One day as I entered the Diag at its northwest corner—State Street and North University—I saw U-M groundskeepers preparing to cut down a big tree. It occurred to me that this was very likely one of the trees planted during the Civil War by Professor Andrew Dickson White, the great historian who, as a young man coming to Michigan, missed the elms of Yale, his alma mater. I called John Lofy at *Michigan Today*. He dispatched a videographer to film the laborious cutting-down. Then I did a little video story about how the University manages its trees, which number some 14,000 on the central campus alone.

For that story I spoke with Jane Immonen, one of U-M's foresters, who offered a reason why human beings may feel so deeply drawn to landscapes like the Diag, with trees widely spaced across expanses of grass. She said these places resemble the savannahs of Africa, where early humans lived. I thought that was a delightful insight. She also told me that in spots along the Huron River, the natural habitat—nearly vanished in the 21st century—is known among biologists as an oak savannah.

That winsome blend of trees and grass, I learned a little later, was the very thing that caught the eyes of two canny entrepreneurs as they explored the sparsely settled lands west of Detroit in the early 1820s.

One June day long ago, when Ann Arbor was a frontier town not yet 15 years old, two lawyers and a politician were given the job of recommending exactly where to build the campus of the new University of Michigan.

They had two sites to look at, both of about 40 acres.

One was at the north end of State Street. It spread across the promontory that offers a fine view to the northeast across the valley of the Huron River.

The other site was a flat farm field half a mile back from the river. At the north end the visitors saw the burned-down ruins of a log cabin. They also had a good view of a swampy, snake-ridden ravine.

Naturally, the men recommended the pretty spot overlooking the river. They could imagine a day when a campus built on this spot might be like Oxford on the Thames or Harvard on the Charles. Students walking to classes in the morning would look east to the sun rising over the river. And from the valley below, the campus would beckon like a city on a hill.

But it didn't turn out that way.

✤ ✤ ✤

To understand why, we must start with the first two settlers of Ann Arbor, the ones who had seen a good place for a town at this particular bend of the Huron. They had an eye out for natural beauty, but not for the sake of sheer aesthetic appreciation. They were thinking of the land as a commodity for sale.

They were John Allen, 29, a big, ambitious Virginian, and Elisha Walker Rumsey, a New Englander ten years older. In the spring of 1824 they happened to meet in Detroit, and they soon discovered common ground. Both had made financial messes back East, and both had fled West in search of a path out of their troubles.

Elisha Rumsey had been struggling for years, and apparently not very nobly. Not long after his wife died in 1820, he left five children behind in Bethany, NY, and ran to Canada, then Michigan, with "a woman of remarkable beauty" named Mary Ann Sprague, called Ann by family and friends. Hauled back to New York to settle bad debts, Rumsey found life in Bethany uncomfortable and soon departed again for the Michigan frontier with Ann Sprague, who either had become or would become his second wife.

With Elisha Rumsey, his partner, John Allen set out from Detroit in search of land deals that might bail them out of business troubles back east. In oak savannahs along the Huron River, they spotted opportunity. (*Bentley Historical Library*)

John Allen, also widowed at a young age, had remarried, too. His new wife was also an Ann. Her upright family disapproved of the marriage, since Allen's own family had recently plunged from feast to famine. His father, a well-to-do farmer and slaveowner near Staunton, Virginia, had lost his fortune in bad investments. Attempting a rescue, John, the eldest son, had done some risky borrowing. With the loan he bought a herd of cattle in Virginia, then sold the herd at a profit in Maryland. But instead of paying off his creditor, he headed to Buffalo, then Detroit.

He had a big plan.

Rumsey and Allen had fled West with the same idea, and now they joined forces. They would buy raw federal land at low prices, draw a new town on the map, promote it, then sell lots to eager settlers and come out rich. About the first of February 1824, they left Detroit together in a horse-drawn sleigh, heading west on the Sauk Trail in search of a likely spot for a town.

They were in the grip of what soon would be called "Michigan Fever"—a rush for land that would drive the territory's population from fewer than 9,000 in 1820 to nearly 90,000 by 1834, all but ensuring statehood. It was the same all across the territories of the Old Northwest—Ohio, Indiana, Illinois, Wisconsin. The promoters of Chicago would become only the most spectacular winners among hundreds of visionaries who foresaw small investments in cheap land spawning a new metropolis. But you didn't need to build a Chicago to get rich. All you needed was a suitable stretch of land holdings, some claim to distinction, and a few advertisements in Eastern newspapers. Then you'd be flooded with buyers hungry for farms or a plot to start a mill or a store.

In a day or two Allen and Rumsey reached a tiny settlement called Woodruff's Grove, just across the Huron River from the site where another hamlet, Ypsilanti, would be built a year later. They pressed on ten more miles and came to a place where gentle glacial ridges rose up on either side of the river and tall bur oaks grew in a pattern called oak openings or oak savannahs. These were lovely expanses where tall, broad trees grew not in a dense forest but apart from each other, with grass between them. The effect was not unlike that of a classic college campus. A farmer could graze livestock in an oak opening or plant crops with a minimum of clearing. And an oak opening was a nice spot to build houses.

Allen and Rumsey liked the look of it: a pleasant landscape, fairly close to Detroit without being overshadowed by it, with water, timber, and some open spaces, all conducive to settlement.

So they hurried back to the U.S. land office in Detroit. Rumsey paid $200 for 160 acres. Allen put down $600 in cash for 480 acres. Then they went to see Lewis Cass, governor of the Michigan Territory, and urged him to designate their unnamed, nonexistent town the seat of the new Washtenaw County. That would seal the town's status as a local hub of government and commerce. Cass appointed a commission that approved the request.

Now the founders needed a name for their town. One or both of them apparently thought of the oak groves and their wives' first names, and this led to a minor but memorable fragment of poetry: "Annarbour." (This was soon changed to "Ann Arbor," though Allen always used the original spelling.)

Then they drew streets on paper and divided their holdings into half-acre town lots for sale. Allen's property was mostly north of the new Huron Street, Rumsey's south of it.

That spring and summer, others came quickly. One of them was Andrew Nowland, "a very enterprising man; in heart and action, benevolent to a marked degree," according to a friend. Another was Elisha Rumsey's brother Henry, a lawyer soon known as Judge Rumsey. Nowland bought acreage at the north end of what would become State Street, on the heights overlooking the Huron. Judge Rumsey took over part of his brother's land just east of the village. Ten years later, these two properties would suddenly compete for primacy.

Elisha Rumsey died young in 1827, but John Allen lived and prospered. By the early 1830s the half-acre lots he had bought for 75 cents each were selling for hundreds of dollars. He paid off his bad debts back in Virginia, moved his parents to Ann Arbor, built stores and mills, bought thousands more acres, and enjoyed his prestige as founder and patriarch of a local empire. Around him the town thrived.

In the 1830s, talk of statehood for Michigan was buzzing in Ann Arbor. The town might become the seat of the state capital, a virtual gold mine for the place that landed the prize. Of course Ann Arbor wasn't the only contender. But there would be another big prize to contend for, too.

In 1817 an effort had been made to establish a territorial university in Detroit. But by the 1830s, that experiment had fizzled. Now the new state constitution envisioned another try at education, this one a statewide network of schools with a new university at its head. Whatever town became the headquarters would undoubtedly become a leading city in the state, with good things to come for those who had land and services to sell there.

The historian Daniel Boorstin once noted the bewilderment of European tourists who discovered many more colleges on the sparsely settled frontier of the United States than on the populous Eastern seaboard. Boorstin traced the sprawl of higher education in the West to two sources. One was the eagerness of Protestant churches to attract followers among "Nothingarian" settlers who had dropped their old religious ties. The other was the urge of many a frontier town to convince prospective settlers that it was a rising metropolis with fine institutions of culture and learning. The frontier craze to build colleges was nearly as powerful as the craze to buy and sell land, and the two were often linked. Many good schools grew up as a result. But the drive to get them built often had little to do with a thirst for learning.

Michigan's citizens voted for statehood in 1835, but actual admission to the Union hung fire during a long struggle with Ohio over where to draw the border. This allowed time for Ann Arbor entrepreneurs to plan for the opportunities that statehood would bring.

Things began to move fast in the summer of 1836, when the new state legislature prepared to choose locations for the state capital and the new state university. At this news, two merchants, Daniel Brown and Augustus Garrett, hustled to set up a new Ann Arbor Land Company in league with four other men with money—Edward Morgan; Charles Thayer; William Maynard; and Samuel Denton, one of the physicians in town. These six put together $2,000 and bought up all the available lots they could afford. It was Augustus Garrett—the only out-of-towner of the original six—who urged the master stroke: The company should promise to donate a suitable parcel to the state as a location for either the capital or the new university.

The company bought up tracts that extended for twenty or so hypothetical city blocks to the east and south of the original village, which had its center at about the corner of Huron and Main. These projected blocks pushed into Judge Rumsey's property, with the names of Land Company members given to hypothetical streets on a map published in 1836—Maynard, Thayer, Denton, Morgan, and Fletcher (named for William Asa Fletcher, the judge who joined the original partners). The map left one block open for a projected "State House Square" and "Public Square."

In Detroit, Charles Thayer's brother-in-law, a well-connected lobbyist in political circles, pushed Ann Arbor hard for state capital. In the end, the capital was given to Lansing, which was closer to the Lower Peninsula's geographic center. But the legislators agreed to put the university in Ann Arbor.

Now the Ann Arbor Land Company set about marketing its properties with the new university uppermost in its promises. In a poster advertising a "Splendid Sale of Real Estate in Ann Arbor," the company touted the virtues of the coming seat of higher learning. "Everything connected with the institution will doubtless be conducted upon a scale of unparalleled munificence," the promoters promised, "and nothing will be omitted which taste, science, and wealth can do to embellish the Town, improve the society, and make it the most desirable residence in the Great West, for persons of Literature and refinement, while the great Agricultural, Manufacturing, and Commercial advantages of the place . . . will afford ample employment for the capitalist and man of business. Similar inducements can never again be offered to purchasers in Michigan."

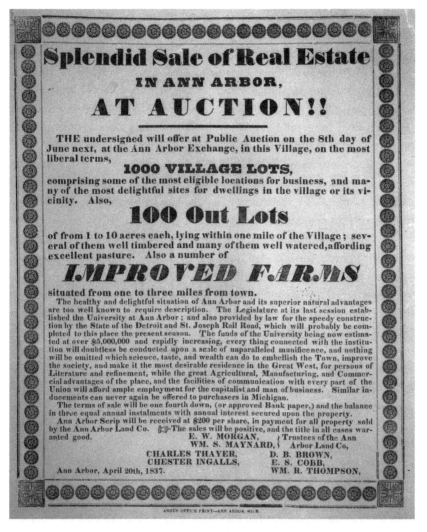

The decision to place the University in Ann Arbor was intimately tied to the buying and selling of real estate. The Ann Arbor Land Company promised prospective investors everything that "science, taste and wealth can do to embellish the Town." (*Bentley Historical Library*)

The question of precisely where the campus would be located would be up to the University's brand new Board of Regents, appointed by 25-year-old Stephens T. Mason, Michigan's "boy governor" and an Ann Arborite himself.

But two of the Regents, as it happened, were also members of the Land Company—William Asa Fletcher and Samuel Denton, the local doctor. In the ethical light of later times, their position would have been delicate, to say the least, since they stood to profit if the campus was placed on the Rumsey property, smack in the center of the company's land holdings.

The Regents gathered in the first week of June 1837 for three days of meetings in Ann Arbor. The question of locating the campus was among their first items of business. For some reason, Judge Fletcher was absent. But Dr. Denton was very much on the scene.

Of the 18 appointed Regents, 11 attended this first set of meetings, plus Governor Mason, who presided, and Lt. Gov. Edward Mundy, yet another Ann Arborite.

Three Regents were appointed as a committee to recommend the best site for the campus. They went right to work, touring the town with the other board members tagging along.

They looked chiefly at two sites. One was the farm parcel that lay just east of the village along State Street—the Rumsey property. Judge Fletcher owned property just north of it; in fact, it was Fletcher's old log house that had burned down where the properties adjoined.

The second plot they inspected was Andrew Nowland's—the one on the heights overlooking the Huron.

To the east of both sites, a long ravine ran down to the river.

Exactly what the members of the selection committee said about either site was never recorded. All we have are the bare parliamentary minutes. They tell us that the committee members came to the meeting the next day and recommended the University's buildings should be "located upon the farm called the Nowland farm, commencing near the fence upon the brow of the hill near the river, bounded westerly by State Street, extending easterly about seventy rods to the center of the ravine, and extending southerly about ninety-one rods . . . ."

Dr. Zina Pitcher of Detroit moved the recommendation be accepted. But then his fellow physician, Samuel Denton, member of the Ann Arbor Land Company, moved an amendment—to substitute the Rumsey property for the Nowland property. When the vote was taken, it was six to five in favor of the

Rumsey land. The three Ann Arborites split—Denton and Mundy for Rumsey, Governor Mason for Nowland.

Thus the location of the Diag was determined by the vote of one man—Samuel Denton—who stood to profit by the decision.

The site of the University's original campus in Ann Arbor took its final form a year later, in 1838, when another Regents' committee—this one comprising Dr. Denton and Judge Fletcher—arranged for a little more land trading just north and south of the Rumsey property. When that was done, the campus-to-be was a precise rectangle bounded by State Street on the west and three new avenues—North University, East University, and South University. (The signs for Fletcher Street, running north and south between Huron and North University, remind us of the judge's old title to the land north of the Diag.)

As things turned out, the decision to build on the Rumsey property never did make the principals of the Ann Arbor Land Company rich. The founding year of the University in Ann Arbor was also the year of a nationwide financial panic—fueled in part by the craze for land speculation in the West—and the start of a long and deep recession. And "in spite of all the Land Company could do," an early historian of Ann Arbor wrote, "the real estate boom failed to materialize, lots near the [Rumsey] 'forty' selling for no higher than $200 each, and many as low as $50. When the affairs of the company were finally closed up, it was found that no one had made or lost a dollar and that the five [sic] men had in reality donated the land to the State, their investments and expenditures, except for the forty acres, just striking a balance."

But no tears need be shed for Dr. Denton, leader of the faction that pushed through the decision in favor of the Rumsey property. If anyone raised an eyebrow at the doctor's apparent conflict of interest in voting on a matter bearing so directly on his own financial position, it certainly didn't hurt his standing in the community. After three years as a Regent, he served a term in the state senate, then was appointed Professor of the Theory and Practice of Medicine and Pathology in the University's young Medical Department—not bad for a small-town frontier doctor. (Still, although streets are named for three proprietors of the Land Company—Maynard, Thayer, and Fletcher—there is no Denton Street in Ann Arbor. There was, for a while, but it was renamed to honor Henry Philip Tappan, the great philosopher-educator who, as the University's first president, was in earnest about creating a school "of unparalleled munificence.")

Since there is no record of the Regents' discussion of the relative merits of the Rumsey and Nowland properties, we simply do not know why the Board overruled the committee that recommended the site overlooking the Huron. Possibly it occurred to the Regents that the Nowland site, so close to the river, might be vulnerable to flooding. Or perhaps some other sound reason cropped up that had nothing to do with the Ann Arbor Land Company.

But there is no denying that the Regents passed up a chance at beauty.

"I don't think aesthetics played a role in this," said Jonathan Marwil, author of the authoritative *A History of Ann Arbor*. "I think these were very practical men in their own professions, and practical decisions required practical thinking. And 'practical' could extend not simply to the financial benefits, though that might have been primary, but to the ease and swiftness of building. That may have been part of their calculation. But then or now, aesthetics have seldom governed the development of the University."

So the Church of St. Thomas the Apostle, with its tall stone tower, the School of Nursing, and the old St. Joseph Mercy Hospital (now the North Ingalls Building) wound up with the commanding views of the Huron—those and a few nondescript blocks of houses. The slope that might have been the University's front lawn now drops to the river unnoticed under a camouflage of weedy underbrush, and no one now remembers the one-vote decision that put the Diag six blocks back from "the brow of the hill."

In the early 1900s, some did still recall that decision, and regretted it. One of them was Wilfred B. Shaw, the long-time director of the University's Alumni Association and a historian of the University. The Regents' choice had been "the wrong one," Shaw wrote in 1920, "and we now have the present campus, undistinguished by any natural advantages . . . . We can only imagine now how much more beautiful and impressive the buildings of the University might have been, lining the brows of the hills overlooking the Huron Valley, rather than spreading over the flat rough clearing of the Rumsey farm . . . ."

Gradually, of course, the featureless Rumsey property was planted with hundreds of trees. And the pleasant landscape that emerged over the years came to look rather like the oak openings that once had beckoned to John Allen and Elisha Rumsey as they drove their sleigh along the frozen Huron.

2: Professor White's Trees

For all the luminaries who have spent their entire careers at Michigan, the University's faculty also has prepared a dismaying number of young stars for careers of distinction elsewhere. The first of these to go was Andrew Dickson White (1832–1918), a major U.S. historian who is now remembered chiefly as the co-founder and first president of Cornell University in Ithaca, New York. In a connection that must be unique in American higher education, no fewer than five Michigan scholars and scientists have followed White to Cornell's presidency—the historian Charles Kendall Adams in 1885; the economist Edmund Ezra Day in 1937; the geologist Frank H.T. Rhodes in 1977; the legal scholar Jeffrey Lehman in 2003; and the computer scientist Martha E. Pollack in 2017.

White spent the rest of his career at Cornell, except for brief diplomatic postings abroad. But he remained so fond of the University of Michigan that when plans were drawn for a new library twenty years after he left Ann Arbor, he conspired with friends to donate five great bells for the library's west tower. The bells would toll the Westminster quarters every day for nearly forty years, reverberating among the elms that had grown up on the old Rumsey farm— elms planted by Andrew Dickson White and his students.

The Ann Arbor campus was barely twenty years old when Andrew Dickson White first saw it. Just married, he arrived from Yale in October 1857 to teach history and English literature. He was only 24, the youngest member of the faculty, and he looked even younger. In fact, a student at the train station mistook him for an entering freshman and showed him all the way into town before realizing the newcomer was a professor.

It was the time of year when Michigan's leaves are aflame in yellow and red, and White's first impression as he entered the village, he wrote later, was of "a beautiful place." But he saw one glaring drawback.

"The 'campus' on which stood the four buildings then devoted to instruction, greatly disappointed me," he later wrote. "It was a flat, square inclosure [sic] of forty acres, unkempt and wretched. Throughout its whole space there were not more than a score of trees outside the building sites allotted to professors; unsightly plank walks connected the buildings, and in every direction were meandering paths, which in dry weather were dusty and in wet weather muddy. Coming, as I did, from the glorious elms of Yale, all this distressed me . . . ."

A scrubby field was no fit place for learning, and he was not going to leave it that way.

White asked around: Why so few trees?

Well, people said, it wasn't that no one had tried.

In the early '50s, Dr. Edmund Andrews, who doubled as professor of anatomy and superintendent of grounds, had rounded up some citizens and students for a program to plant a thousand trees. But most of the seedlings died. People said the ground was too hard and dry.

White didn't believe it. In the village blocks west of the campus, he saw plenty of "fine large trees, and among them elms" growing in "the little inclosures [sic] about the pretty cottages." And you only had to look at the virgin woods nearby to know the soil was perfectly well suited to trees.

White decided the problem must have been lack of proper care. So, with neither permission nor funding, he took matters into his own hands.

✢ ⁛ ✢

Professor Andrew Dickson White looked so young when he stepped off the train in Ann Arbor that the man who showed him to the campus thought he was a student. (*Rare Book and Manuscript Collection, Cornell University*)

The fashion in landscape design just then was to create outdoor corridors shrouded in green canopies. This was the effect White wanted. So he marked off several walkways—including, apparently, the basic X of the Diag—and set to work.

"Without permission from anyone," he would write in his *Autobiography*, "I began planting trees within the University enclosure; established, on my own account, several avenues; and set out elms to overshadow them. Choosing my trees with care, carefully protecting and watering them . . . and gradually adding to them a considerable number of evergreens, I preached practically the doctrine of adorning the campus. Gradually some of my students joined me; one class after another aided in securing trees and in planting them, others became interested, until, finally, the University authorities made me 'superintendent of the grounds,' and appropriated to my work the munificent sum of seventy-five dollars a year."

Not that White was neglecting the work he had been hired for.

His devotion to history had arisen as the Northern and Southern states approached a collision in their long dispute over slavery. White was an abolitionist, but he felt a particular calling apart from politics. "Though I felt deeply the importance of the questions then before the country," he wrote, "it seemed to me the only way in which I could contribute anything to their solution was in aiding to train up a new race of young men who should understand our own time and its problems in the light of history."

After graduating from Yale, he took more training in Berlin and Paris, then returned to New Haven for a master's degree. In U.S. colleges, very few courses were devoted solely to history, and most classes consisted of droning recitations out of textbooks. But in Europe, White heard professors give sparkling talks that treated history as "a living subject having relations to present questions." He thought he might do the same in the U.S. "Great as was my love for historical studies, there was something I prized far more—and that was the opportunity to promote a better training in thought regarding our great national problems then rapidly approaching solution, the greatest of all being the question between the supporters and opponents of slavery."

The question was where he would do this work—in the East, or somewhere new.

Friends who heard White's ideas about teaching urged him to stay in the East and join the faculty at Yale. But on the day of his commencement as a master's candidate, he heard an address by President Francis Wayland of Brown University, who told the graduates: "The best field of work for graduates now is in the *West*; our country is shortly to arrive at a switching-off place for good or evil. [He meant the coming clash between North and South.] Our Western states are to hold the balance of power in the Union, and to determine whether the country shall become a blessing or a curse in human history."

"I had never seen him before," White wrote. "I never saw him afterward. His speech lasted ten minutes, but it settled a great question for me. I went home [to upstate New York] and wrote to sundry friends that I was a candidate for the professorship of history in any Western college where there was a chance to get at students, and as a result received two calls—one to a Southern university, which I could not accept on account of my anti-slavery opinions; the other to the University of Michigan, which I accepted . . . ."

It was a very good match. Michigan's president, Henry Philip Tappan, spotted White as just the sort of bright young scholar who could help fulfill Tappan's vision of a citadel of higher learning dedicated to the public good. White's students liked him and he returned their respect. They were "worth teaching," he said, "hardy, vigorous, shrewd, broad, with faith in the greatness of the country and enthusiasm regarding the nation's future. It may be granted that there was, in many of them, a lack of elegance, but there was neither languor nor cynicism. One seemed, among them, to breathe a purer, stronger air . . . .

"I soon became intensely interested in my work, and looked forward to it every day with pleasure."

And when classes were over for the day, Professor White went outside to check on his trees.

For two years he nursed his seedlings. He pruned them and protected them from insects. In the heat of summer he made sure they had enough water. They survived, then thrived and grew.

Students began to join him. Young men soon to board trains for Southern battlefields went out to the woods around Ann Arbor and returned with seedlings. Two nurserymen from New York sent a gift of sixty trees that were planted in a grove near the northern edge of the central grounds. The class of 1858 placed fifty young maples in concentric circles around the great native oak. White added more maples along one side of the fence that bordered State Street on the west. The literary faculty donated 42 elms for the other side of the street.

"So began the splendid growth that now surrounds those buildings," White would write.

He tended the trees, taught his students, and began the research and writing that would make him one of the leading U.S. historians of his generation. Then, in the spring of 1861, the Civil War began, "and there came a great exodus of students into the armies," he wrote, "the vast majority taking up arms for the Union, and a few for the Confederate States. The very noblest of them thus went forth—many of them, alas, never to return, and among them not a few whom I loved as brothers and even as my own children."

✣ ✣ ✣

As the war approached its climax, White's father died, and he had to go home to manage his family's business affairs. Almost immediately he was elected to the New York state legislature. In 1865 he co-founded Cornell University and became its first president.

For a number of years he retained a lectureship at Michigan and returned periodically to teach, but after a while his duties in Ithaca made that impossible, "and so ended a connection which was to me one of the most fruitful in useful experiences and pregnant thoughts that I have ever known."

But those trees in Ann Arbor remained "to me as my own children."

White was president of Cornell until 1885, U.S. ambassador to Germany from 1879 to 1881, minister to Russia from 1892 to 1894, president of the American Historical Association, and president of the American Social Science Association. As the 20th century began, he continued to write and speak widely.

Down through the decades of his long life, he returned to Ann Arbor from time to time to see friends and give lectures. He always visited his trees "to see how they prosper, and especially how certain peculiar examples are flourishing." On one visit, he was seen out on the Diag at night, going from tree to tree with a lantern.

At Cornell in the spring of 1911, he had a sudden whim. From his papers he pulled out an old map, then boarded the train for Ann Arbor.

The next day, on the Diag, a student recognized the old man walking slowly from tree to tree, looking from his map to the trees. The student asked him what he was doing.

"Yesterday," he said, "while sitting in my library at Ithaca, I happened to think that fifty years ago today the class of 1861 planted these trees under my direction. I had among my papers a plot of the ground, the location of each tree and the name of the student who planted it."

He gestured at the trees and said: "There are more trees alive than boys."

The tall native oak that White saw on his first visit to the campus still stands just west of the Hatcher Graduate Library. Since 1858 it has been called the Tappan Oak, to honor the president who launched the modern University of Michigan and, among other foundational acts, hired Andrew Dickson White.

Nearly all of White's elms went down in the plague of Dutch elm disease that crept across Michigan in the 1960s and '70s.

Nearly all, but not quite.

On the last morning of May 2011—150 years after the Confederate attack on Fort Sumter—U-M foresters took a last look at a massive elm in the northwest corner of the Diag. Dutch elm had weakened it. The foresters had tried to keep it alive. Now it was beyond saving. It was a hazard. By nightfall they had brought it down.

They counted the rings—not an exact science with a large, multi-lobed elm—and concluded the tree was at least a century and a half old. It was almost certainly one of White's. They think a few others still survive.

A few weeks later, a few yards away, they planted a sugar maple to take the old-timer's place.

For a time, that maple was the youngest of some 14,000 trees that stand on the Ann Arbor campus. But that distinction is now claimed by an even younger tree, a bur oak given by students, faculty, and staff to commemorate the inauguration of Mark Schlissel as Michigan's fourteenth president. If all goes according to plan, it will grow tall in the northwest corner of the Diag, about where Andrew Dickson White stood when he first saw the campus.

The beauty of the Diag is improvisational. It is less elegant than a formal landscape design, but more comfortable, even homey, partly because the trees have been planted piecemeal. They were planted here and there as buildings came and went and as walkways changed, creating a particular sense of place that has changed over time, but only gradually, so that each generation has had its own Diag, slightly different from the Diag of the generation before and after.

In 1940, when the U.S. was preparing for its all but inevitable entry into World War II, an anonymous writer captured the feelings of a moment at the center of the campus:

"A warm summer day has given way to a perfect summer night, overcast but with a quarter-moon breaking through the clouds above the campus trees. It is a few minutes past nine as you swing onto the Diagonal. The darkness insulates you, the air is caressing; you move almost effortlessly under the long aisle of trees. It is quiet except for the insistent cheeping of insects among the leaves, and occasional distant voices . . . .

"This is the heart of a great university; warm, tranquil, peaceful, democratic. It is one of the things worth preserving."

3: When Heads Rolled

For a long time I heard fragments of fact and rumor about the difficult man who gave the money to build the Law Quad. When I looked into it, I learned that several writers before me had told the story of William Wilson Cook and his vision of a magnificent new home for the Law School. But one fragment had never been told in detail, and I thought it was the most interesting.

This was the story behind the stone heads that peer down at passersby who enter the Quad through its central archway—a story, as I discovered, of not just one but two difficult men. I still smile when I think about it, and I wonder if my dad, hurrying through the arch on his way to class at the Law School in the late 1940s, ever heard how the stone heads came to be.

In the 1920s, the job of secretary of the University of Michigan was held by a man of many competencies named Shirley Wheeler Smith. He was the school's chief financial officer, chief liaison between the administration and the Board of Regents, and chief troubleshooter. He was an expert on the University's history. He knew which closets held skeletons from the Medical School to the homes of Ann Arbor's finest families. In short, he probably knew as much about the University as anyone in town.

But one evening in July 1924, as Smith sat down to dinner at his home on South University, he learned an alarming fact that had entirely escaped his notice.

It was his teenage son, Donald, who clued him in.

Donald had been earning money that summer as a laborer on one of the biggest construction projects Ann Arbor had ever seen. It was the Lawyers Club, the audacious new gothic building at the corner of South University and State. University leaders devoutly hoped it was going to be the first in a series of buildings that would comprise a magnificent quadrangle for the Law School.

But that was no sure thing—not yet.

More money for more buildings depended on the good will of William Wilson Cook (LSA 1880; Law 1882), a millionaire alumnus living in New York City. Cook was brilliant, eccentric, reclusive, and cranky. As U-M officials knew, he was touchy enough to send his money elsewhere if Michigan annoyed him.

All this likely flashed through Shirley Smith's mind when his son Donald came out with his news.

That day, Donald said, he had looked up from his work to see his father's face carved in stone at the Lawyers Club, right in the central passageway.

The other Smiths were dubious.

Oh, it was Dad, all right, Donald said—a dead likeness, the head of Shirley Smith carved as a stone gargoyle.

The next morning, Smith went over to see for himself. Sure enough, there was his face, along with five others. Staring up at the archway overhead, Smith saw the likenesses of himself; then the first three presidents of the University (Henry Tappan, Erastus Haven, and James Angell); a former dean of the Law School, Jerome Knowlton; and Henry Moore Bates, the Law School's current dean.

The whimsical figure of Henry Phillip Tappan was one of six carved to look down on passers-by through the central archway of William Cook's Law Quad. But Cook had workmen take a hammer to two of the original six. (*University of Michigan Law School*)

As Smith stood there, a neighbor lady passed by and looked up at the archway. She laughed and asked: "Are you looking for your *own* statue, Mr. Smith?" She did not realize that was precisely what Smith was looking for. He just laughed along—shakily—and kept the truth to himself.

Smith was dumbfounded. Who was he to be depicted alongside such Michigan giants as Tappan and Angell?

But the worst of it was that stone head in the likeness of the sitting dean of the Law School, Henry Bates. For as Shirley Smith well knew, Dean Bates was cordially detested by the Law School's irascible new patron, William Cook.

Dean Bates's head—immortalized in stone? Who in the hell, Smith wondered, had authorized *that*?

✧ ⁝ ✧

Shirley Smith was one of the few people in Ann Arbor who knew William Cook at all. Cook professed to love his alma mater but he turned down every invitation to return. No one knew why.

It was only one of his peculiarities. Years later, Smith would describe Cook as "a strange composite of the urbane and the tyrannical, the generous and the suspicious, the dreamer and the dictator."

Born to a prominent family in Hillsdale, Michigan, in 1858, Cook had earned his bachelor's and law degrees in Ann Arbor, then hastened to New York to make his career. He helped to shape the field of corporate law just when U.S. corporations were ascending to great power. With his fees, his investments, and wealth inherited from his father, by the 1920s Cook was a millionaire many times over.

He was a workaholic and a loner. After his only marriage ended in divorce—rare for a man of his social position in that era—he divided his time between his sumptuous townhouse on Manhattan's Upper East Side (next door to the "robber baron" Henry Clay Frick), his office, his clubs, and a country estate. "His acquaintance at the bar was limited," said a contemporary, "and his intimate friendships few."

In the early 1910s, Cook agreed to pay for a fine women's dormitory at U-M. He had it named for his mother, Martha Cook. After the dormitory opened in 1915, Cook began to consider where to leave the rest of his money. Michigan's president, Harry Burns Hutchins, a former dean of the Law

School, began to woo the New Yorker for the largest gift in the University's history.

Cook liked and respected President Hutchins, and he quickly gravitated to the idea of a gift that might transform the Law School. But he had his own ideas about what the Law School should be, and his manner with U-M officials was downright impossible.

When Hutchins retired in 1920, the job of nailing down Cook's millions fell to the new president, Marion LeRoy Burton, and Dean Bates of the Law School. Those two began to regard their distant benefactor in New York like wayward schoolboys fearing the wrath of a tyrannical principal.

Cook believed he had good reason to be highly particular. To him, the stakes were enormous. He was donating his millions to save a republic in danger.

He was in the midst of writing a dense and thorny book entitled *American Institutions*. Those institutions, he said, were under siege from a sinister combination of concentrated wealth, organized labor, and the emigration of "millions of impossible people from southern and eastern Europe." (Cook's xenophobia was far from uncommon among WASP elites of his era, though not many elaborated as extensively as he did.)

To safeguard the nation, he counted on higher education and the nation's lawyers, whom he believed to be its natural leaders. His example was ancient Rome. "The American Republic will fall apart or a new Caesar will seize the power and rule by force unless the American Bar holds the Republic together . . . ."

In this mood, Cook began to sketch plans for "a great center of legal education and of jurisprudence for the common good of the people."

Unabashedly elitist, he imagined a setting so beautiful it would lure the nation's brightest students to study law in Ann Arbor. It would be a place where they could mingle with professors, senior lawyers, and jurists—in effect, a fine gentlemen's club with its own splendid clubhouse.

Cook shared Dean Bates's hopes for expanded faculty research, and he thought the first goal could nurture the second. That is, a Lawyers Club for the brightest students of the Law School and the literary college might generate an endowment; then the endowment could pay for faculty to do more research. Other buildings, including a great law library and a classroom building, would follow—or so Cook promised, vaguely—but he said the Lawyers Club must be built first. In his mind, it was the key to the whole project.

"[T]he character of the legal profession depends largely on the law schools," he wrote President Burton. "Hence in my opinion nothing is more important than those schools and anything that tends to elevate them tends to perpetuate American institutions. That is the reason I am doing all this."

For his architects, Cook chose Edward York and Philip Sawyer, leaders of a respected New York firm. Following Cook's orders, they drew breathtaking blueprints in the style known as "College Gothic," with strong echoes of medieval cathedrals and the great English universities at Oxford and Cambridge. Soon, the old houses sitting on what Cook called "the finest seven acres in Ann Arbor" were being torn down and the Lawyers Club was rising in their place.

But none of this was happening quickly enough for Dean Bates. He was watching the whole business of transforming his Law School with an uneasy mixture of ambition, irritation, and ill will toward practically everyone involved.

✛ ✚ ✛

Restlessly ambitious, Bates had been appointed dean in 1910. Ever since, he had been complaining about the cramped old Law Building that stood on the northwest corner of the Diag. He wanted a new building and a big expansion of the Law School's mission. But when he failed to get the state legislature's backing, he fell back on waiting for "some generous alumnus" to step forward.

William Cook was just that man, of course. But the two disliked each other from the first.

Bates had his strengths, but an easygoing temperament wasn't one of them. After one meeting with Bates, Regent James Murfin wrote President Burton: "Much as I deplore my own disposition, which goodness knows is bad enough, I thank heavens I do not possess his."

Everything about Bates irritated Cook. He grew tired of the dean's needling pressure to promise more funds for the Law Quadrangle. It was rumored that Cook once refused to see Bates when the latter arrived for a conference in New York. And in letters Cook began to address Bates as he might a hapless junior law partner.

Once, when the dean was slow to send Cook a promised document, Cook informed Bates that in Wall Street law firms, "instructions are obeyed or off comes his head. [The Michigan law faculty] remind me of the lawyers in my native town when I was a boy. They would hibernate most of the year and sit around and put their feet on the table and tell stories and smoke bad seegars. . . . What I am trying to do is to wake you people up."

Bates steamed. He griped about "Mr. Cook's little pleasantries . . . his digs . . . the abject humility which he seems to like in others." After the latest dressing-down, he wrote to President Burton: "All of his arguments could be easily demolished; but where a man is proposing to give 20 or more millions—and won't listen to your arguments—all you can do . . . is to lie down and be rolled over, as gracefully as possible. . . ."

But grace was not Bates's strong suit, and his behavior toward Cook began to cause serious concern.

✛ ⁘ ✛

Bates had wanted to be named president of the University. When the Regents chose instead the president of Smith College, Marion LeRoy Burton, the dean nursed a cold resentment of the Regents and Burton alike.

In a private letter to the dean of the Harvard Law School, Bates went so far as to call President Burton a "platitudinous mountebank" whose "intellectual and moral standards are disgusting," whatever that might mean.

If Bates said something like that to William Cook, administrators feared, the donor might just give his money to someone else.

So Regent Walter Sawyer, a boyhood friend of Cook's who practiced medicine in their home town of Hillsdale, made it his mission to soothe Cook whenever Dean Bates was acting out.

"Don't let Bates annoy you," Sawyer advised Cook at one point. "He is so childish about a lot of things . . . I have feared he would make a nuisance of himself. . . . It is unfortunate but so often true that men of distinguished ability have decided handicaps in disposition or character."

Then, in the spring of 1923, Bates's disposition apparently went right off the rails. At a meeting with the Lawyers Club architects in New York, he broke out in a full-scale rant, shouting: "When these buildings are done I am going to have my way. . . . I don't want to harm the University but I could do it in either of two ways: I could resign or I could write a letter to Mr. Cook which would keep him from giving the buildings." (What Bates meant by that is anyone's guess, but it's possible that Bates was tempted to uncork his venom about President Burton's allegedly "disgusting moral standards.")

When President Burton heard about this, he became genuinely concerned about Bates's mental health.

"I urged the Dean strongly to get some *real* rest," Burton wrote one of the Regents. "He admitted that his nerves were 'raw' . . . Either someone *wants* a fight or is going to pieces."

❖ ⁝ ❖

In the summer of 1924, the Lawyers Club was moving toward completion. After months of heavy construction, the noise and dust were beginning to settle down, and work was underway on the building's myriad details.

In the midst of it, stonemasons were carving small works of decorative art. The most striking of these were charming human figures that would sit atop stone supports called corbels in the open-air archways that passed through the building at three points.

They were designed by artists in the New York shop of Ulysses Ricci and Angelo Zari, whose stonework adorned Detroit's General Motors Building and Fisher Building as well as U-M's Graduate Library and Angell Hall.

Once mounted, the figures would look as if they were holding the vaulted ceilings of the archways on their shoulders, so architects called them "atlas figures." (They were also called corbels and gargoyles, though, to get technical, a true gargoyle spews rainwater from a gutter.)

The effect on visitors was surprising and winning, as if they were seeing a cartoon tucked into the stone face of a forbidding castle.

In the easternmost passageway, near Tappan Street, there were a dozen of these atlas figures. They represented the four seasons (including the seasonal sports of football, hockey, baseball, and tennis) and several professions, including law, engineering, and architecture.

In the west passageway, near State Street, four more disciplines were symbolized—astronomy, medicine, business, and military science.

And in the largest passageway, in the center, the masons hoisted and installed the six largest figures.

Three of these were the likenesses of past presidents: Henry Philip Tappan, the first president of U-M; his successor, Erastus O. Haven; and James Burrill Angell, the longest-serving president.

Then there were those three figures that Shirley Smith saw—Smith himself; Jerome Knowlton, a law professor who served as dean from 1891 to 1895; and Henry Moore Bates, the least favorite Michigan man on William Cook's list.

Cook exploded.

It's not clear who sent him the news about the sculptures. Possibly it was Shirley Smith himself, who knew a red flag when he saw one.

Cook tried to find out who had chosen the heads, but no one admitted to knowing. So he sent a blast to his architects, York and Sawyer: "I was astonished to learn . . . that without my knowledge or approval and at my expense you have placed in one of the passageways of the Lawyers Club building . . . six heads of persons connected with the University. . . .

"Who suggested this and who selected them and who furnished the photographs and on what principle were the selections made and why was not I informed?

"I cannot imagine you undertook the selection yourselves, as you were never connected with the University and know little of its history.

"If the selection had been confined to notable Presidents, that would be one thing, but to bring in the secretary [Smith] (who is not even a lawyer) and the Dean, who has had predecessors and will have successors, is another thing. Can you not see the impropriety of magnifying minor University officials in a building constructed and equipped on such a high plane as that?"

The three presidential statues were all right, he said, but the other three should have been "filled in as Time approved."

"They have no place there. I don't care how the removal may look. If new ones cannot be substituted later, let the gargoyles stand headless."

The architect Edward York ordered workmen to hack the offending figures off the building. Then he moved swiftly to mollify his unhappy client.

"There is nobody to blame for this slip except myself," York wrote Cook, "and I didn't realize as you do the incongruity of the last three [Smith, Bates and Knowlton] until I saw them when I visited the job last. I can't understand why I didn't use ordinary horse sense and consult you in the matter."

By assuming the blame, York took one for the team. But he must have been protecting somebody. For as Cook himself said, the architects knew little about the history of the University. They never would have chosen an obscure figure like Jerome Knowlton on their own. Regent Walter Sawyer, the doctor in Hillsdale who was Cook's personal friend, told Cook the selection "was done without the suggestion or influence of any one connected with the University." But it had to be *someone* connected with the University. The architects knew Dean Bates and Shirley Smith, but they didn't pull Jerome Knowlton's name and face out of a hat. So Regent Sawyer likely was telling a white lie to placate Cook.

So if not the architects, who chose the heads?

It must have been someone with some measure of authority in the building project. It also had to be someone who knew U-M well enough to know that Shirley Smith and Dean Bates were important administrators with key roles in the Lawyers Club construction project. And it had to be someone who knew the Law School's history well enough to suggest Jerome Knowlton.

President Burton might fit those criteria. But in all the records of the Law Quad's construction, there's no hint that he took a hand in minor design decisions.

Conceivably it was a University regent. Walter Sawyer, Cook's friend, was the Regent most involved in the project. But records show that Sawyer learned about the stone figures only after Cook did.

It could have been Shirley Smith, who had dealings with the architects. But Smith's expression of bewilderment at seeing his own face in stone seems wholly sincere. And Smith was well aware of the need to tread softly with Cook. He never would have thought it wise to include Dean Bates among the stone figures.

So who else?

The only obvious candidate is Dean Bates himself.

Perhaps the rattled and embattled dean, steeped in bitterness at Cook and envy of his boss, President Burton, thought it might just be a droll joke to have himself immortalized in limestone in Mr. Cook's grand edifice.

✦ ⁞ ✦

William Cook had a beloved niece, Florentine Cook Heath, who tried to tell people that her uncle was not the ogre he sometimes seemed to be.

Many years after the archway lost its heads, she said that "when the presence of the gargoyles was first reported to Mr. Cook . . . he really had a good laugh over the whole business. He was delighted that Shirley Smith was included but was considerably irritated that Dean Bates was among those represented and decided 'Off with their Heads.' He really got a great deal of amusement out of the whole affair."

"Most of the disturbing letters he wrote with a twinkle in his eye," she said, "but the twinkle didn't show in Ann Arbor."

After the offending heads were guillotined, Evans Holbrook, a popular law professor, told friends that he had combed the rubble for one of Dean Bates's stone ears, "so that he might thereafter always have the ear of the Dean."

In New York, William Cook puzzled over the episode for days. He couldn't understand the choice of Jerome Knowlton, whom he had never heard of. In a follow-up letter to Edward York, Cook made his best guess. "I presume his name and photograph were given you by Dean Bates," he wrote, "but why I can't imagine . . . If there are any other freak things about that building kindly let me know, so that I may have them cleaned out before the students move in."

In place of the smashed figures, three more were sculpted and set in their places, completing the set of all six U-M presidents down to the 1920s. To the figures of Tappan, Haven, and Angell, the sculptors added Henry Simmons Frieze, a beloved professor of the late 1800s who served two brief terms as acting president; Harry Burns Hutchins, who had urged Cook to give his millions to Michigan; and Marion LeRoy Burton, whose figure holds a stone hammer to commemorate his nickname, "Burton the Builder," since so many campus buildings were constructed during his term.

Despite all his threats and bluster, Cook stayed true to his intentions. After a long struggle with tuberculosis, he died in 1930, but not before he had provided funds for the John P. Cook Dormitory (named for Cook's father and completed in 1930); the Legal Research Building, better known as the Law Library (1931), and Hutchins Hall (1933).

In early 21st-century dollars, his gifts to Michigan would exceed $250 million.

✢ ✥ ✢

Henry Bates served as dean until 1939. His 29-year term in the office is the longest in the Law School's history.

The Law Quadrangle, now named as a whole for Cook, is arguably the most distinguished and famous edifice on Michigan's campus. Hailed for its beauty, it has provoked "a sense of protectiveness and trusteeship" among generations of alumni, said Francis Allen, dean of the Law School from 1966 to 1971. The Law School's physical setting has been "of enormous importance," Allen once told an interviewer, "and it can't be measured, of course, in any precise way.

"It was always a delightful thing to go out into the Quad on a May morning [and] see a family group walking across the Quadrangle," Allen said. "This was [a] father who had been a student here, and he is bringing his wife and his children to the Law Quadrangle, and he is pointing out where his room was and reliving his student days."

Whatever their differences, Cook and Dean Bates shared an ambition—to make Michigan's Law School one of the greatest in the world. As Cook's biographer, Margaret Leary, has written, "Cook was driven primarily by an ideal that remains pervasive at Michigan Law today: to preserve the institutions of our democracy and to raise the standards of legal education as a means to that end."

Certainly the Law Quadrangle helped to accomplish those aims.

The six presidents memorialized atop the Law Quad's corbels were all deeply serious men. But if you stand in the half-light of the Lawyers Club's central passageway and look closely at the atlas figures, you may glimpse a hint of amusement on several faces, especially those of Harry Hutchins and Marion Burton. They were the two presidents who best knew the tempestuous donor in New York and the grumbling dean in Ann Arbor.

Cook's own bust, made from his death mask, stands at the west end of the Law Library's magnificent Reading Room. Words he wrote are carved over the State Street entrance to the Lawyers Club: "The character of the legal profession depends on the character of the law schools. The character of the law schools forecasts the future of America."

4: Hangouts

Regents and presidents and millionaires may have situated the campus on its particular site and raised its enduring edifices. But saloonkeepers and store-front merchants gave Ann Arbor the places that many alumni remember more clearly than any classroom. I chose three to write about.

I often heard my parents speak with affection of "the Bell" and "the P-Bell." By my time as a student, the Pretzel Bell was starting its slow decline toward extinction. But when I wrote about it—some thirty years after the health department shut it down and the Tiffany lamps were sold—I learned just how many people still held it close in memory.

In their courting days, my parents would meet for "Coke dates" at Drake's Sandwich Shop. (I think my mother met lots of boys at Drake's. No brag, just fact—she told us those were the times when a girl might have three or four dates in a single day.) When the old sign came down in the 1990s, my wife and I asked: If we can't buy cherry-chocolate cordials at Drake's, can this still be Ann Arbor?

In graduate school, I often drudged away at my dissertation in the old base-ment of the Michigan League. It was one of the drabbest rooms on the campus, but my memory of it is fond. I got a lot of work done on those crappy old tables. Years later, soon after I joined the faculty at Miami of Ohio, I met a math pro-fessor named Zevi Miller. When I said I lived in Ann Arbor, he asked: "How's Dominick's?" When he told me what the place had meant to him, I thought the story would resonate with anyone whose true education occurred in some small, familiar spot away from everyone else.

The doors opened on the night of May 24, 1934, five months after the end of Prohibition. The site was 120 East Liberty, in the block between Main and Fourth, in the space long occupied by an old grocery. It was a healthy walk from campus, but it couldn't be much closer, since Ann Arbor remained "dry" east of Division Street. The proprietors, John and Ralph Neelands, said they opened the place "so the boys might have a place to sit down and have a glass of beer." Boys and girls alike were happy to make the walk.

The brothers left the grocery's tin ceiling in place and brought in fixtures from pre-Prohibition days. From Joe Parker's Saloon on Main they got a lovely old bar. From the Oriental Bar came stout oak tables carved with the initials of generations of U-M students. (The decorating, intentionally or not, brought back the words of an old song often sung by students of the 1930s: *I want to go back to Michigan, to dear Ann Arbor town; back to Joe's and the Orient, back to some of the money I spent . . .*).

From the ceiling the Neelands brothers hung an old bell that was said—not with rock-solid documentation—to have come from a farm southwest of town that dated at least to the Civil War. It was supposed to have come into the hands of the great Michigan football coach Fielding H. Yost, who rang it at Ferry Field before giving it to the owners of the new tavern. The name of the place was said to derive from two signals of hospitality in the beer gardens of German university towns—a basket of pretzels and a bell to call in neighbors to hear important news of the day.

The Neelands brothers got the jump on post-Prohibition competitors, and the Pretzel Bell became *the* watering hole for thirsty U-M students. In no time it became known simply as "the P-Bell" or "the Bell." It became the favorite of athletes, musicians, and the staff of *The Michigan Daily*, who helped to pass the word in print.

In fact, Tom Kleene, the *Daily*'s editor in 1936, refreshed himself so often at the Bell that he started to get his mail there—a fact that John Neelands made plain one night by delivering a stack of letters to Kleene's table just as he was sitting down for dinner with his mother.

On weekend nights the hubbub was uproarious. The bell was rung to announce: "There's a telephone call for . . ." One night the legendary conductor Leopold Stokowski, fresh from the May Festival at Hill Auditorium, took a seat among cheering students and demanded to hear some college songs. He wound up standing on his chair and conducting the crowd in "Varsity" and

Drake's possessed a drab charm that sparked many a campus romance. An alumnus who liked to drop in for a cinnamon roll after tough classes in German courted his future wife there. "I don't remember much of my Deutsch," he said, "but Drake's is still vivid in my mind." (*Bentley Historical Library*)

"The Victors." Coach Yost, dropping in for lunch, would call for eleven salt shakers and eleven pepper shakers to diagram Wolverine plays.

In 1944, new owners, Clint and Helen Castor, took over. In their time a second and larger bell was hung from the ceiling, this one a gift from the men of Alpha Delta Phi. A ritual began that would continue for decades. It was known as the "Bell Party," which reached its high point when a student, on the day of their majority, climbed onto a table and downed a prescribed quantity of lager while the bell rang overhead. By the mid-1970s, the Castor family would estimate the total number of Bell Parties at 30,000.

Signed photographs began to accumulate on the brick walls—the Heisman Trophy winner Tom Harmon; Harmon's blocker, Forest Evashevski; Bob Ufer, later the ecstatic voice of Michigan football, in track duds; Robert

Allen Wahl, captain of the 1950 football team; Gerald Smith, captain of the 1960 team. (One group photo hanging at the Bell was signed by five Michigan football coaches—Harry Kipke, Fritz Crisler, Bennie Oosterbaan, Bump Elliott, and Bo Schembechler.)

One day in the late '50s, a patron dropped in with a Tiffany-style hanging glass lamp shade. The Castors liked it so much they acquired dozens more to hang from the ceiling, giving the place the distinctive look of its modern era.

On it went into the 1960s, with beats and hippies jostling for tables among aging alums and townie business types. But in 1969, a fire started in the furniture store next door. When the flames were extinguished, the Bell's ceiling had collapsed, destroying lamps and priceless memorabilia.

But the Castors' heir, Clint Jr., remodeled and expanded to the adjacent storefronts. When the Bell's doors reopened, loyalists returned in droves. With bluegrass suddenly hip in the 1970s, the place gained a certain new-old chic by giving a regular gig to the RFD Boys, a local group that gained national renown.

In 1971, a creative type in the Law School recorded his gratitude for the Bell in a poem. It read in part:

> One dark night with red eyes blinking,
> And my head in need of shrinking,
> With my life entombed in thinking,
> My emotions all a'swell,
> On the brink of sheer disaster,
> Came a vision of Clint Castor
> And the joy and the laughter
> Of his Bell.
> Yes his Bell, Bell, Bell —
> Pretzel Bell.

But by the late 1970s, the younger Castor was laboring against heavy competition in the blocks closer to campus, and he was apparently not the business manager his parents had been. Health violations closed the place for a time. Then the IRS came calling, asking Castor for more than $100,000 in employees' withholding taxes. On a rainy day in April 1985, the tax representatives auctioned off the furnishings for a total of $208,000. "Students nowadays look on it as quaint but dull," said the presiding IRS agent. "It simply got passed by time."

Maybe so. And yet in the years since, nostalgia for the Pretzel Bell has enjoyed a peculiar longevity even as other memories faded. Jim Carty, a sports columnist for the *Ann Arbor News*, said as much in 2009. "Never has such a long-shuttered restaurant evoked such long-time mourning," Carty wrote. "To me, who moved to A2 in 2001, mourning the Pretzel Bell is part of what makes Ann Arbor, well, Ann Arbor. If you're of a certain age, you seem to mourn the Pretzel Bell. I like that."

Entrepreneurs opened a new Pretzel Bell in 2009 at the corner of Main and Liberty, a prime location just a block from the old place. It's a nice restaurant. But no one called it the Bell.

+ ⁘ +

When Herbert Hoover was president of the United States, a young fellow named Truman Tibbals took a job washing dishes for 35 cents an hour at Drake's Sandwich Shop at 709 N. University. He worked his way up to waiting tables, and after a while he bought the place from old Mr. Drake.

He made just one change. He took out the tables and installed high-walled booths. From that day until he sold the shop when Bill Clinton was president, Truman Tibbals left everything else pretty much the same, including the name over the candy-stripe awning in front. Through the Great Depression, World War II, the Baby Boom, the Beatles, Vietnam, Watergate, disco, and Reagan, Drake's sold chocolate cordials, orange marmalade sandwiches, pecan rolls, and limeade (fresh-squeezed, with the rind in the glass) to generations of University of Michigan students.

The walls were a milky, Depression-era green, like faded linoleum. Shelves held scores of glass jars filled with tea (Alfalfa Mint, Travencore, and Constant Comment among them) and even more of candy—jelly beans, candy corn, rum raisins, malted milk balls, cherry cordials, strawberry cordials, raspberry cordials, shelf above shelf. Candy went out the door in bags adorned in red and white stripes, like the awning outside.

The sandwich menu included the "American cheese," the "bacon and peanut butter," the "chopped green olive nut," the "cucumber and tomato," and the "head lettuce" sandwich. Ten specialty sandwiches (double-deckers on toast) included the "Harvard" (boiled ham, lettuce, tomato, and mayonnaise), the "Princeton" (American cheese, lettuce, tomato, and mayonnaise), and the

"Michigan" (chicken, lettuce, tomato, and mayonnaise). The mayo was real and the grilled cheese sandwiches were grilled with bona fide butter. Tea was poured from a teapot. Pecan rolls and cinnamon buns were imported from Quality Bakery on Main, but Mrs. Tibbals baked her own cakes in the basement. You wrote your own order with a tiny pencil on a green soda-shop pad.

The staff comprised Mr. Tibbals, Mrs. Tibbals, and a team of waitresses (plus the occasional waiter), many of whom appeared to be trained in the owners' distinctly taciturn style of service. For people who dispensed small pleasures for a living, the Tibbalses made a gloomy pair. They were of opposite physical types, Mrs. Tibbals being massive and ponderous in her movements, Mr. Tibbals little and quick. They often could be seen perched on counter stools, well apart from each other, glowering at the wait staff. Students found them fearsome. But Mr. Tibbals was a pal of the Ann Arbor police, who often rolled in for breaks late at night.

The Tibbalses did bring in the occasional new item. They served toasted bagels with cream cheese years before bagel franchises spread through the Midwest, and they were early providers of gummy bears. In the '40s Mr. Tibbals opened the room upstairs for records and dancing. First it was the Walnut Room, later the Martian Room, but in the shop's last decades the stairs were closed and the only thing left of the Martian Room was the sign. For a time there was dancing downstairs, too, and a burger bar in the back. But the innovations always faded, and back the Tibbalses would go to the candy, the tea, the limeade, and the sandwiches.

When the *Michigan Alumnus* solicited memories of Drake's from readers, a surprising number said they had dated their future spouses there. The privacy of the tall-walled booths fostered intimacy. The "Coke date," a perennial getting-to-know-you ritual, was often set at Drake's. One night in January 1969, Rick and Roberta London got engaged at the corner of South University and Washtenaw, then strolled across the Diag to mark the occasion at Drake's.

"I will forever associate the small wooden benches, a toasted bagel, and cup of tea at Drake's with the wonderful emotions of that day," Roberta London remembered.

Another who wrote in was Ron Marabate, who—also in the late 1960s— would soothe his mind with a cinnamon roll on North U after rigorous German classes in the Frieze Building. "Drake's was also memorable whenever I was joined there by a young lady," he wrote, "especially the one who later became my wife. I don't remember much of my Deutsch, but Drake's is still vivid in my mind."

Mr. Tibbals died in 1993. The place was sold about the same time. A franchise bagel shop moved in.

The first problem on the mind of Zevi Miller in the late 1970s ran along the following lines: If K were a pure n-dimensional simplicial complex, and if $\Gamma_0(K)$ were the automorphism group of K [and so on], then what is the minimum number of points $M_0^{(n)}$ in K such that $\Gamma_0(K) \cong A$, and the minimum number of n-cells $M_1^{(n)}(A)$ in K such that $\Gamma_n \cong A$?

The second problem was where to find a good place to think about this question for several hours at a time, day after day, month after month, while nursing a single caffeinated beverage without getting hassled to buy refills. Earning his PhD in mathematics might not depend on finding a solution to this second problem. But it would help.

So Miller would go over to 812 Monroe Street—the eccentric, rambling restaurant and bar called Casa Dominick's—pay for a single café mocha, and slip down to a booth in the basement, where he figured no one would notice him. "I spent incredible amounts of time there," Miller remembered. "It was such a lively, cheerful place, and yet you could get work done there, too."

Early in the 20th century, the address had been a neighborhood grocery. After World War I, it became a coffee and sandwich shop. By 1959 the business was failing, and Dominick DeVarti spotted an opportunity.

A Connecticut native, DeVarti had been a bombardier-navigator in World War II. He came to Michigan for an engineering degree on the G.I. Bill, then worked for Kaiser Industries in Ypsilanti, then shifted to construction. He bought and sold three pizzerias (one of them, in Ypsilanti, to Tom Monaghan; it became the first Domino's, its name inspired by the original owner), and ran unsuccessfully for mayor of Ann Arbor on the Republican ticket in 1957.

About that time, DeVarti saw that 812 Monroe Street—within a few steps of the Law School, the School of Business Administration, the College of Art and Architecture, and the School of Education—couldn't miss as a student emporium if only he could get the food right. So he bought the place in 1959,

brought in pizza and Italian submarines—exotic casual fare in those days—
and when he won a liquor license, he began to serve homemade sangria in
glass jars. Dominick's was soon the preeminent student hangout in town.
In the early 1960s, movie enthusiasts gathered there to found the Ann Arbor
Film Festival, and it became the informal point of rendezvous for the radical
Students for a Democratic Society.

In the 1970s, DeVarti bought the house next door and joined the two
together, with outdoor seating in front and back. For a while he ran a separate
white-tablecloth Italian restaurant upstairs, then shifted to Vietnamese food,
then turned the second story back over to the pizza-and-sandwich operation.
In all those long afternoons with his single café mocha, Zevi Miller often saw
Dominick make his rounds through the place. But neither Dominick nor anyone else ever so much as hinted that Miller should either purchase a second
café mocha or move along. Miller concluded that no one had even noticed
his routine. He had been just another anonymous student in the crowd. After
many, many hours, he concluded that, given certain other things:

$$M_1^{(n)}(A)=M_0^{(2)}(A)=\Sigma_p p^a p^\alpha e(p^\alpha) \text{ when } n \geq 4 \text{ [and so on]}$$

That done, Miller was awarded his PhD. His extended explication of the
problem he had solved was published in *Transactions of the American Mathe-
matical Society* in 1982. He joined the Department of Mathematics and Statistics at Miami University in Oxford, Ohio, where he went on to new research in
graph theory, graph embeddings, combinatorics, and theoretical computer
science.

One autumn ten or twelve years after Professor Miller completed his doctorate, he went back to Ann Arbor to see Miami play Michigan. Before the
game, he stopped by Dominick's. At the counter he found Dominick's son
Rich DeVarti, who had taken over management of the place. Miller told Rich
that he remembered Rich's dad well. "He's out in back," Rich said. "Go say
hello." In the garden courtyard where students and football fans filled the
benches and chairs, Miller found Dominick DeVarti at his customary table.
Dominick looked up at him. "Hey," Dominick said, "I remember you. You used
to go downstairs and sit all afternoon with one mocha."

Dominick DeVarti died in 2001.

"The funny thing," Zevi Miller said, "is that he was the only guy in the
world who knew about that part of me—that little ritual that was so important to me."

PART II: A GATHERING OF MINDS

On my last day as an undergraduate in 1978, I arrived a little early at the LSA Building and sat chatting with William Porter, a fine professor of journalism then nearing retirement. I mentioned that it was my very last class. Porter, a working writer/professor without a PhD, laughed and said he could hardly do justice to the occasion. "It should be somebody like Sidney Fine," he said.

I was graduating as a history major, but I had never taken a course from Professor Fine. I knew his reputation among students—popular, demanding, large in personality. When I came back to campus for graduate school and enrolled in Fine's "studies" course in modern U.S. history, I learned why Bill Porter had held him up as an exemplar of the faculty. Fine became the director of my doctoral program and, after my parents, the most influential older figure in my life.

He was a native of Cleveland who became a Michigan man through and through. A navy veteran of World War II, he earned his PhD at U-M in 1948, then taught in Ann Arbor for 53 years, apparently the longest span of any U-M faculty member ever. He loved the University in all its dimensions (though never with uncritical eyes), from the Bentley Historical Library on North Campus, where he was an indefatigable researcher and adviser, to Michigan Stadium, where he seldom—if ever—missed a home game. The Michigan legislature did away with its mandatory retirement rule for college professors principally to allow Fine to keep teaching beyond the age of seventy. (One of his former students ushered the bill through the state senate.) By the time he left the classroom in 2001, he had taught between 25,000 and 30,000 students, and there is little doubt that he was one of the most popular teachers in the University's history.

Fine was master of a teaching method that students considered dull and outmoded in the hands of many other professors—the lecture. He scorned the showmanship that makes some teachers popular. Instead, he earned students' attention and respect through a magnetic combination of personality, intelligence, and enthusiasm for the story he was telling day by day.

He was also a prolific and influential writer. He moved from intellectual history—his first book, *Laissez Faire and the General-Welfare State: A Study of Conflict in American Thought, 1865–1901*, remains a classic of that field—to labor history, where he made his main mark as a scholar. Many of his books told the story of 20th-century U.S. history as seen through the prism of urban, industrial society in Michigan—its labor strife in the 1930s, its racial turmoil in the 1960s, its public policy throughout the 20th century. He wrote a three-volume biography of one of Michigan's most important public servants, the Detroit mayor, governor, and U.S. Supreme Court Justice Frank Murphy.

Every week, students lined the third floor of Haven Hall to seek Fine's advice. He never behaved as the students' pal, but he did establish a sympathetic connection with them. Students saw what happens when a keen native intellect is applied to a discipline through decades of study and analysis. Talking with him could be something of a spectator sport, since his ebullience was often unstoppable. Yet it was a delight to see. His memory appeared to be limitless. He could reach into brain storage for an anecdote from his boyhood in Depression-era Cleveland, an obscure fact about Woodrow Wilson's role in the peace negotiations after World War I, an ancient baseball statistic. In the seminar rooms where he taught graduate students, he set an example that has radiated through many academic careers to touch students who never have heard his name.

I say all this not so much to praise Sidney Fine, though the praise is deserved, but because, as I thought about Fine in later years, I would reflect on what it took to establish the University as a place where someone of his caliber would choose to spend his career. Though I decided not to follow him into academic history—a decision that led to the only difficult moment between us—he set an example of industry, passion, and commitment to vocation that has been a beacon to me ever since.

He was there in my life in the 1980s because long before, men of profound purpose (yes, all men at first) constructed an institution devoted entirely to the creation and propagation of knowledge—the twin paths of research and teaching that professors at a school like Michigan follow.

One of Fine's contemporaries, the Michigan law professor Hart Wright, was so knowledgeable about U.S. tax law that the Internal Revenue Service would consult him about its own tax codes. Wright was once asked why he had chosen to be a professor of law when he could have made millions as a corporate tax attorney in Washington, DC, or New York. He is reputed to have shrugged and said, "I like to profess."

The word *profess* does not mean simply "to teach." It includes the connotation of devotion to a discipline, even of personifying that discipline. To be a professor is to have an extraordinary job. If you polled the public and asked: "Do you authorize the state to take some of your money to pay people whose work will be to profess?" the answer, if applied to state budgets, might put many faculty out of work. Yet that is the remarkable thing that came to pass when the founders of Michigan and universities like it got the whole enterprise going in the mid-1800s. It has had literally incalculable benefits for the society.

It seemed to me that students and even many faculty took all this for granted. So I tried to write about how it happened at Michigan—how a place was built where extraordinary minds could come together for the society's good. I wrote about professors who, like Sidney Fine, exemplified the professorial ideal. And I wrote once or twice about how the meeting of minds resulted in spectacular results that no one could have predicted.

5: Tappan's End

If we cut out the tangled knot that is the story of the University's founding in Detroit in 1817, we can agree that the institution we know in the 21st century is the handiwork of Henry Philip Tappan. His dream for the place came true. But he paid dearly for it. As I read about Tappan's extraordinary ambitions and achievements, I thought his ultimate defeat at the hands of his governing board symbolized the University's whole long struggle to justify itself to a skeptical public.

Henry Philip Tappan's imposing intellect and commanding presence inspired devotion and resentment in roughly equal measure. Students revered him. But one foe on the faculty spoke of "the crushing hauteur and arrogance with which he causes me to feel his power." (*Bentley Historical Library*)

M rs. Tappan had tried to make the best of things, after all.

Did these uncouth Westerners realize what she and her husband had given up?

And now they meant to depose him? When his accomplishments in Michigan had only begun?

Did they have the remotest appreciation of the sacrifice she and her husband had made by abandoning their lives in New York and Europe in order to plant the seeds of higher education in this remote village at the edge of civilization?

They had made the journey to the Michigan frontier in 1852. In the decade since, her husband, the University's first true president, had brought about something akin to a miracle. Because of him, a ragtag little college now aimed to become a university like the great academies of Europe. Because of him, the first astronomical observatory in the West stood at the edge of the campus with telescopes trained on the heavens. Because of him, the institution was bringing honor to its young state.

Yet almost since the beginning, her husband had been mocked and pilloried by jumped-up farmers and press hacks educated in one-room schoolhouses—he, a philosopher honored in European seats of learning, and a doctor of divinity, no less! And the locals were still hooting and howling over that perfectly innocent remark she had made to some ladies to the effect that she and her husband saw themselves as "missionaries to the West."

And why *not* put it that way? After all, she was a Livingston. Her family tree included Hudson Valley landholders of immense wealth, a signer of the Declaration of Independence, and a member of George Washington's cabinet.

In fact, it had been rather beneath her station to marry a mere clergyman, even one as distinguished as Henry Philip Tappan. But they had made a happy life together, and raised four children, and when he decided he must accept an invitation to become president of this fledgling school in the Western woods, she had gone along and done her best.

And now, it seemed, a rabble wanted to take it away.

✦ ✦✦ ✦

The president's chief antagonist in his early years in Ann Arbor was Wilbur Storey, owner and editor of the *Detroit Free Press*, a fierce Democrat of the Andrew Jackson stripe in the days when U.S. newspapers were warring organs of the political parties.

Storey set up Tappan as a target for the Democrats' antipathy toward all things that smacked of exalted manners, European tastes, and rule by fancy-pants aristocrats. He attacked Tappan for referring to himself as the University's "chancellor." The word was in the state's constitution, but Storey said it sounded European, "ridiculous, and contemptible."

Then he slammed the president for hiring an actual German, Franz Brunnow, as professor of astronomy—even suggested the two men enjoyed illicit relations.

The state's other Democratic papers picked up the scent and joined the chase.

"Of all the imitations of English aristocracy, German mysticism, Prussian imperiousness, and Parisian nonsensities, he is altogether the most un-Americanized—the most completely foreignized specimen of an abnormal Yankee, we have ever seen," said the editors of the *Lansing Journal.*

But Tappan's defenders fired back. Students loved the president. A number of the faculty regarded him as an inspirational leader. One letter-writer put the *Free Press* on notice: "The Prussian system thus far has worked most admirably, and the course of our institution is onward and upward."

After a while, Storey lost interest and went off in search of other prey. Tappan's new antagonists would be closer to home.

How he was doing as president depended on whom was asked. Some professors believed he was just the right man for the job. Tappan made a deep impression on Andrew Dickson White, the young historian who would become the founding president of Cornell University. "His influence, both upon faculty and students, was, in the main, excellent," White would write. "He sympathized heartily with the work of every professor, allowed to each great liberty, yet conducted the whole toward the one great end of developing a university more and more worthy of our country."

Others took a very different view. Alexander Winchell was at the root of the trouble.

Winchell was appointed to the faculty on the recommendation of a good friend on the Michigan faculty, Erastus O. Haven, a professor of Latin and English. Both men were fervent Methodists. From the first, they were ill at ease with Tappan's intention to favor the truths of secular science over biblical truth.

Winchell started as professor of physics and civil engineering. Tappan thought his work in those fields was sub-par, so he was fired. Then he was rehired as professor of zoology, geology, and botany. (This was before strict faculty specialties took hold.)

Next, Winchell began to feud with Silas Douglas, a founder of the Medical Department. When Tappan sided with Douglas, Winchell took it personally.

Skirmishes between Winchell and the president broke out again and again, and other professors were drawn in. Most were trivial, but they brought out an imperious streak in Tappan. "We must have a University and nothing less," he wrote a friend back East, "and then this earth will be firm beneath us, and the skies above will fight for us." A man who saw God on his side in every minor argument was sure to irritate people after a while. Even those who respected him got tired of it.

Winchell, too, was something of a dramatist. Complaining about Tappan to a friend, he wrote: "I cannot . . . enumerate nor even recall a tithe [tenth] of what I have suffered; and still less can I depict the crushing hauteur and arrogance with which he causes me to feel his power."

Writing under pseudonyms, Winchell began to criticize Tappan in the newspapers, especially Storey's *Free Press*. When the Methodist Conference of the state passed resolutions criticizing the "moral condition" of the University, it was whispered that Winchell was behind it.

Fights about who taught which class and who ran the University's telescope were insider stuff. Not many beyond the campus cared. But when religion became the issue, they certainly cared. You have to remember that before the Civil War, almost every U.S. college was an auxiliary of a religious denomination. The main purpose of most was to train men for the ministry. That was only beginning to change. U-M had been set up as a secular institution. But the churches still held a good deal of sway over how it was run. So until Tappan, faculty slots had been doled out by an unspoken rule among the main Protestant denominations—Methodist, Baptist, Presbyterian, Congregational, Episcopalian.

Tappan opposed this kind of power-sharing. He wasn't anti-religion; far from it. He was an ordained member of the Presbyterian clergy. But he didn't want the churches in charge. He hired faculty for their brains alone, with no questions about where they went on Sundays.

This caused trouble. Leaders of the church-based colleges—Baptists at Kalamazoo and Hillsdale, Methodists at Albion, Congregationalists at Olivet—raised a perennial stink about public support. Weren't *their* colleges good for the state, too? So why favor the upstart in Ann Arbor with land and special breaks?

Tappan tried to explain. But to certain ears, anything he said about pursuing the truth regardless of religious affiliation sounded downright atheistic.

He tried to make everyone happy by attending services at all the churches in town. But this struck his fellow Presbyterians as a little odd, and it apparently struck others the same way.

He got into a spat with his fellow Presbyterians over the parish's money. Then there was the matter of wine and beer. Anti-saloon sentiment was running strong, especially in the new states. The territories might have been settled by people who grew apples for hard cider and made moonshine out back.

But more respectable types had followed them, and they were cracking down. Since statehood, Michigan had enacted tight restrictions on hard liquor. Beer and wine were still allowed, but they were in foul odor among a great many people.

The Tappans had spent years in Europe. At their table, according to the European custom, they served wine with dinner. When this got around, eyebrows rose. When a student died in a drunken fraternity initiation in 1857, temperance advocates pointed at the president's poor example.

In the eyes of many, this fellow with his rich Eastern wife and his New England accent and his pompous turns of phrase, who praised European professors and pooh-poohed the dangers of drink, was surely some species of a snob—and if not downright godless, he was hardly the sort of plainspoken, good-hearted fellow who ought to be shepherding youngsters into Christian manhood.

In 1858, the Regents who had appointed Tappan and supported his initiatives were turned out of office. The president was now on his own.

✛ ⁝ ✛

Of the ten Regents elected in 1858, eight had never been to college. One had sat on the board of the Albion Female Collegiate Institute. The rest had never played any part in managing a college.

Their informal leader was a Detroiter named Levi Bishop. He had gone to work in a tannery at the age of fifteen and risen to the management of a shoe factory. On the Fourth of July in 1839, Bishop lost his right hand when a cannon discharged at the wrong moment. So he became a lawyer.

In public life Bishop cherished two causes—public education and capital punishment. "Bitter and venemous" by nature, according to one student, he "possessed many peculiarities of character, and was often inclined to take the opposition of any question rather than concur with the majority."

Bishop apparently had read every word the *Free Press* published about Tappan and sided entirely with Wilbur Storey's view of the president. Once he joined the board, his expectations were confirmed. At one commencement, he sat on the stage with the other Regents, barely containing himself as Tappan unloaded multi-syllable words and grand ideas. Finally, Bishop stood up in the middle of the speech, stormed off the stage and then outside, where he stamped around and "declared, in the profanest form of swearing, that he could endure such stuff no longer."

He had not been a Regent long when he told people in Detroit that before his term was up, he would have Tappan's head on a platter.

According to one commentator, "Bishop came in assuming the air of one who had been sent by the people to reform corrupt and negligent practices."

He sent his own pseudonymous critiques of Tappan to the *Free Press*.

He slammed Tappan for appointing his son as University librarian and for retaining his son-in-law, Franz Brunnow, as director of the Detroit Observatory even after Brunnow had married Tappan's daughter.

By 1859, Bishop was leading a sort of revolt from above. He challenged Tappan's power on constitutional grounds, saying the Regents, not the president, were supposed to run the University. Bishop rammed through a plan by which the Regents, for all intents and purposes, would run the University themselves through an unwieldy set of committees. Tappan's executive freedom would be limited; in fact, his remaining duties would be little more than ceremonial.

Tappan challenged the scheme, appealing to the faculty, the legislature, the attorney-general of Michigan. And the Regents fought back. Behind the scenes, Professor Winchell acted as an agent in the anti-Tappan cause, spreading ill will for the president among his colleagues. "He has long striven for absolute power," Winchell wrote. "Whatever power he has been permitted to exercise has been wielded generally for the purposes of personal or family aggrandizement."

For two years, then three, then four, this bureaucratic battle raged even as the nation plunged into civil war.

Tappan nourished his resentments. He couldn't overlook a slight or put an argument behind him. And woe unto any professor whom he had helped and now dared to disagree with him.

He tallied up his grievances:

About Professor Boise: "I [was] with him in sickness. I . . . performed the funeral rites over his sainted wife . . . .[but] that he has long been hostile to the President . . . every one knows."

About Professor Fasquelle: "Although often invited to my house, together with his family, [he] never invited me or my family to break bread with him."

About Professor Winchell: "attempted to form a cabal . . . for the removal of the President . . . "

About Professor Watson: "None of the cabal were more openly hostile or active than himself."

But worst of all was the man Tappan saw as the mastermind of the conspiracy, the puppet-master of all his enemies, "the Regent from Detroit," Levi Bishop, whose "presence seemed to be ever hanging over the University like an incubus," spreading "anonymous reports and letters, reviling the President of the University, fostering intrigue in and about the institution."

Regent Donald McIntyre of Ann Arbor, who began calling himself "the resident regent," took on day-to-day powers over the University, "holding grounds and buildings, museum, library, laboratory and observatory within his grasp, directing everything, governing everywhere."

McIntyre's son, the University's steward, bragged around town that the president and professors were simply the "employees" of the Regents.

Tappan stewed. He thought about resigning.

But friends urged him to sit tight. The Regents would face the voters early in 1863, they pointed out. Many of the state's men of influence sided with Tappan. So did most alumni. If he just outlasted the current board, all would come out right. So he waited for the election.

Tappan and his supporters got their wish. Eight members of the board were turned out of office. New members were expected to back Tappan. But the existing board would remain in office for several more months. And the two who had generally backed Tappan were now far away in the Union Army. As Tappan put it later, "disappointed regents were now ready to carry out the long cherished purpose which the Regent from Detroit had years previously announced with an oath. They took, at the last moment, the revenge which remained to them."

June 25, 1863, was commencement day. Tappan presided as usual. After the proceedings, the Regents assembled for their regular meeting.

They asked President Tappan to step out of the room.

They didn't take long.

A bill of grievances was presented: The president had taken on too much power; he was too often absent from Ann Arbor; there had been excessive rancor between Tappan and the faculty; when he disagreed with professors, he attacked their character and motives; "habits of wine and beer drinking to excess, and other improper habits, were not sufficiently discountenanced."

It was moved, seconded, and decided "that Dr. Henry P. Tappan be and he is hereby removed from the offices of President of the University of Michigan and Professor of Philosophy therein."

Then they fired Tappan's son, too.

And they voted to offer the presidency to Erastus Haven.

Tappan was called back in and given the news.

According to one account, Tappan stood, went to the door, then turned back and said: "The time will come, gentlemen, when my boys will take your places. *Then* something will be done for the University."

The news spread quickly. Students were shocked. They converged on the President's House and sang songs to honor the Tappans. Night fell and they moved in a mob toward Regent McIntyre's house uptown. They pelted the windows with rocks and burned McIntyre in effigy.

For several days the party of Tappan held out hope. Angry Ann Arborites gathered to denounce the Regents as "jackasses" and urged Erastus Haven to turn down the presidency. Letters flooded the regents demanding Tappan's reinstatement. Word came by telegraph that U-M alumni in the Union Army massing at the Confederate stronghold at Vicksburg had held a meeting to protest Tappan's firing. There were cries of outrage in the national press, too; the editor of the *Journal of Education* called the firing an "act of savage, unmitigated barbarism."

But then, in the first few days of July, dispatches from Vicksburg in the South and Gettysburg in the East brought news of great battles with enormous loss of life, and suddenly it seemed petty to make such a fuss about a college president.

If the faculty had united behind Tappan, he might have had a chance. Instead, a number of them sent a pledge of cooperation to the new man, Erastus Haven.

Even professors who might have preferred Tappan were in no mood to fight for him.

One of these was Thomas McIntyre Cooley, leader of the law faculty. He wrote to fill in his friend, Andrew Dickson White, who had recently left the faculty.

"You will have heard . . . that Dr. Tappan has been removed," Cooley wrote White, "& that some people would pull the institution down about our ears for very spite. . . . It has certainly not been especially pleasant here."

Despite the "great danger" of losing Tappan, Cooley said, "when the thing was done, there was no other . . . than to stand by it & make the best of it."

And Cooley thought the president had hardly helped his own cause.

"It was a great mortification to Dr. Tappan to be removed just as he had got everything fixed here to suit him," Cooley remarked. "His imperious manners were more noticeable than ever, & for a brief period he was monarch of all he surveyed. Then came the blow. For a short time he was doubtful that it had hit him, & expected the public voice to compel a reverse of the action. But . . . by this time he must have lost hope."

For some time Tappan apparently held out hope of being recalled, at least until the new Regents took office. But no reprieve came. Eventually he and his wife sailed for Europe and settled in Switzerland, near their daughter and her family, taking frequent trips to European capitals.

Tappan continued to correspond with friends in Ann Arbor and elsewhere at home. In 1869 he was offered the presidency of the University of Minnesota. If he had been ten years younger, he said, he might have taken it, but not now, in his sixties, and with his family replanted in Europe.

In Michigan, the weight of opinion slowly began to swing back in his favor. James Burrill Angell, who succeeded Erastus Haven as president in 1871, could not quite believe that an educator of Tappan's vision had been so shabbily treated. "Tappan was the largest figure of a man that ever appeared on the Michigan campus," he would write, "and he was stung to death by gnats!"

Of course, Angell was overlooking the traits in Tappan that had contributed to his own undoing—his intellectual and moral arrogance, his hamhanded ways of dealing with faculty, legislators, and Regents. Angell's own presidency was far longer and arguably more successful than Tappan's for the very reason that Angell was far more astute than Tappan as an academic politician.

The tale was not quite done.

❖ ⁛ ❖

For some time, Tappan's loyalists in Michigan, perhaps with a helping hand from Angell, had been nudging the Regents to make a conciliatory gesture to the proud and aging philosopher abroad.

In 1875 their efforts were rewarded when the board formally invited Tappan to attend the University's commencement exercises that spring. When he declined, citing temporary poor health, the Regents agreed on an extraordinary expression of regret for what their predecessors had done a dozen years earlier.

In their official proceedings, they said they hoped Tappan might be able to come to Ann Arbor for the next year's commencement.

Then they recorded their "full recognition of the great work done by him in organizing and constructing this institution of learning upon the basis from which its present prosperity has grown," and their "regret that any such action should ever have been taken as would indicate a want of gratitude for his eminent services . . . ."

Finally, they approved "a repeal and withdrawal of any censure, express or implied, contained in the resolution which severed his connection with the University."

Tappan was touched, though not quite surprised. "These resolutions are full and handsomely expressed," he wrote to a friend. "They appear to me to cover the whole ground. This act of justice has been long delayed, but 'my boys' have been laboring for it until they have accomplished it. Their fidelity & devotion to me affects me deeply. Next year, now that the way is prepared, I hope to visit them . . . God knows I labored with a single eye to the good of the University. It was with me a labor of love."

Tappan never returned to the United States. He died of a heart attack in 1881 at the age of 76.

6: The Making of Michigan

In the prologue I mentioned Francis Blouin, who was for many years the director of the Bentley Historical Library. Fran's deep study of the University's development persuaded him that in the late 1800s, four extraordinary members of the faculty, connected by ties of intellectual kinship and friendship, set the mold for what U-M would become. When I read Fran's original version of these findings, I suggested that we collaborate on an article that would flesh out the personal stories of these four great scholars. He agreed, and the story below is the result. He developed his ideas in depth in "The Components of Reputation: Pragmatism, Science, and the Transformation of the University of Michigan, 1852–1900," *Michigan Historical Review*, 43:1, 57–84 (Spring 2017).

In 1855, several years before his battle with the Regents began, President Tappan sent an invitation to an acquaintance back East, a promising young painter of landscapes named Jasper Cropsey. Tappan told Cropsey he was trying to build a true university, a new American center of science and culture, and he wanted the scene captured on canvas. So Cropsey came West and spent a few days in Ann Arbor. From his sketches, the first painting of the campus emerged.

The scene is decidedly rural. A rolling pasture dotted with cows and sheep leads the eye to a modest spread of stark white buildings in the distance. A solitary figure drives a horse-drawn wagon along a dirt road. It's a picture of a frontier settlement carved out of a forest.

The contrast with another painting, showing the same plot of ground just fifty years later, could hardly be more striking. In this view the year is 1907. The artist is Richard Rummell, a specialist in bird's-eye landscapes. He looks from the southwest, as if he were floating in a balloon above the corner of State Street and South University. Multi-story buildings crowd the scene. Academic towers point skyward. It's a place of purpose and activity, heavily settled and flourishing.

The two images—Cropsey's and Rummell's—symbolize an extraordinary transformation. But the change was deeper than bricks and mortar.

In those fifty years, Michigan's campus became not just a bigger place but a new kind of enterprise entirely, embracing a new conception of the world.

In 1850, U.S. college professors were teaching students to understand their place in a universe fixed by the unchanging mind of God.

By 1900, Charles Darwin and his interpreters had turned the God-centered universe on its head.

If, as Darwin argued, living things were always changing in response to their physical environment, then the same must be true of human society, even of individual human beings. Nothing in the human landscape was fixed and immutable—not humans themselves, not social classes, not economies, not the law, not government. Everything was up for grabs.

So, between 1850 and 1900, big questions about the world multiplied. The pursuit of knowledge became a far more ambitious enterprise, since knowledge might transform the world. A handful of U.S. universities were among the first to grasp this new role. Michigan was one of them, and as a result it grew from Jasper Cropsey's modest outpost to Rummell's colossus.

How did this come about in that short span of half a century? What brought the University of Michigan, set in what had been a remote corner of American provinces, into the company of Harvard, Chicago, and Johns Hopkins as a leader of American learning?

A comprehensive answer would include too many threads for a short account like this. But we can catch a glimpse of the pattern in the stories of four Michigan professors of the late 19th and early 20th centuries. They crossed paths on the Diag, knew each other's families, talked things through together. They were John Dewey, who blazed a path from philosophy to psychology; George Herbert Mead, who established the intellectual foundations of social reform; Henry Carter Adams, who envisioned the science of economics as a vehicle for social change; and Charles Horton Cooley, who seldom strayed more than a few blocks from the Diag, yet unearthed "enduring structures" beneath everyday life.

These four helped to shape a new way of understanding society—a *science* of society. And the pursuit of that science became the central mission of the new American university. All four might never have come to Michigan had it not been for one leader who opened the door to the new ways of thinking.

❖ ⋮ ❖

James Angell was Michigan's president from 1871 to 1909. He was not the visionary Henry Tappan had been, and he made no mark as a scholar. His achievement was to make Michigan a congenial home for minds greater than his own. He recruited talent and rewarded it. And though he saw the world through the eyes of a conventional Protestant, he welcomed the ideas that swept intellectual life in the U.S. after the Civil War.

Born in Rhode Island in 1829, Angell had divided his early career between academe and journalism. At the end of the Civil War, he moved from the editor's chair at the *Providence Journal* to the presidency of the University of Vermont. His growing reputation attracted the attention of Michigan's Regents, who spent two years wooing him. When they finally met his salary demands—and promised to install a flush toilet in the President's House—he accepted the job.

John Dewey during his decade at Michigan, where he developed ideas that would leave major imprints in philosophy, psychology and education. (*Bentley Historical Library*)

When Cornell fired Henry Carter Adams for his admiring remarks about a railroad strike, Michigan became the beneficiary. His challenge to the doctrine of laissez-faire economics helped to lay the ideological foundation of the progressive movement. (*Bentley Historical Library*)

Encouraged by John Dewey, George Herbert Mead (pictured here with his son) conceived ideas about the self and society that would shape the emerging disciplines of sociology and social psychology. (*Special Collections Research Center, University of Chicago Library*)

Charles Horton Cooley, son of a great dean of the Law School, grew up at the corner of State and South University. He developed the concept of socialization in part by closely observing his own children. (*Bentley Historical Library*)

Angell understood his mission to be the fulfillment of Henry Tappan's urge—to create a great research university—and he set out to hire professors who would expand the boundaries of knowledge all across the spectrum of human inquiry.

Once he landed them, he made them feel welcome. He had "an ability . . . to let the right men alone," one admirer wrote, "never harrying them in their work."

When Angell was president of the University of Vermont, he became friendly with a Burlington couple named Archibald and Lucina Dewey. Mr. Dewey's business was the family grocery. Mrs. Dewey's business was to steer her four sons toward college. She never thought that advanced study might turn one of them against her strict Congregationalist faith.

Shy, "seclusive and bookish" as a youngster, John Dewey showed such exceptional promise at the University of Vermont that James Angell would remember him fifteen years later, when he was looking for a philosophy instructor.

As an undergraduate, Dewey was deeply influenced by scientific methodologies derived from Charles Darwin's *On the Origin of Species*. He taught high school for one year; read the masters of Western philosophy for another; then pursued a PhD at Johns Hopkins, the first U.S. university to model itself on the German academies where research was the coin of the realm.

Dewey earned his doctorate with one foot in traditional philosophy, the training ground of Christian clergy of an intellectual bent, the other in a new branch of the field—psychology. Here, the object of study was not God's mind but the human mind. Dewey would become one of the new field's pioneers. Angell hired him on the recommendation of George Sylvester Morris, head of Michigan's Department of Philosophy, who had taught Dewey at Hopkins.

Dewey's ten years in Ann Arbor were furiously busy. His undergraduate courses included Empirical Psychology, Special Topics in Psychology, and Psychology and Philosophy. He taught Bible classes at the Students' Christian Association on State Street. ("He evidently claimed to be a Christian," one of his students wrote, "but he was certainly the most liberal one I had ever met.") He also published the earliest in a cascade of articles and books that would continue into the 1940s: "The New Psychology" (1884); "The Psychological Standpoint" (1885); *Psychology* (1887).

With a handful of other scholars, Dewey was setting out on a perilous bridge. At the near end lay the familiar realm of a God-centered universe in which humans are the handiwork of an all-powerful Creator. At the far end lay a new realm of thought, where God's role, if any, was obscure. In this new conception, humans were of their own creation. They might or might not stand upon God as the origin of being, but they were surely the product of their relationships with their physical and human environments.

Child to parent, student to teacher, spouse to spouse, worker to supervisor—in all these relations, Dewey saw the origins of the human self, never fixed but always in flux. This was a Darwinian world of constant change. Like other organisms, humans were evolving in an unfolding relationship with their surroundings and each other.

The implications for the study of the human situation were profound.

To Dewey's way of thinking, American scholars should shift their point of focus. Their object of study should not be a remote and unknowable God. Instead, they should study here-and-now humans and the societies they made. Ideas did not float in the mind of God, waiting to be grasped by mortals. They were tools made by humans for the purpose of solving human problems.

That idea lay at the foundation of the distinctly American school of philosophy that would become known as pragmatism. Dewey became one of its chief theorists.

Implications for higher education were equally great.

If humans and societies were adaptable, like plants and animals, then universities might find a broader mission—to discover what made the human species and its communities tick, and to devise ways to fix what ailed them.

And in the late 19th century, everyone agreed they were ailing.

With the decades-old split over slavery settled, the railroads were pushing West. Corporations were spawning phalanxes of factories. Cities were sprawling past old boundaries. Problems of a new urban-industrial age were crying out for solutions. As Dewey leaned over his books in Ann Arbor, he kept one eye on the newspapers. Soon he was convinced that philosophers and other academics must apply their brains to society's ills.

"My forenoons now are spent in the library reading up on machinery and wages," he wrote his fiancé. "It has opened up a new field to me. I almost wish sometimes I was in political science, it is so thoroughly human."

The challenge of reforming a society in disarray led Dewey to the field in which he would make his deepest imprint—education.

If the human brain was a product of its environment, he argued, then scientific studies of how the brain best developed should be used to shape the schools. In time, Dewey would use this basic idea to create a comprehensive theory of education. He imagined the American school as a microcosm of society where children would learn by doing, not by the rote memorization of facts and skills.

This led Dewey to conceive a plan for an experimental school, and that, in turn, led to his departure from Michigan. The University of Chicago was looking for a new chair in philosophy, and its leaders promised Dewey a lab school where he could try out his ideas.

He spent ten years in Chicago, then moved to Columbia University in New York, where he remained one of the central thinkers of his era. He died in 1952.

He always remembered Michigan fondly. As one biographer put it, "Among the happiest times in the Dewey family history were those early years in Ann Arbor."

✛ ✛ ✛

In the summer of 1891, after years of spiritual uncertainty and intellectual doubt, George Herbert Mead was finally feeling pretty good. He was 28 years old. He had found his feet as a promising scholar in philosophy and psychology. He was pursuing a PhD at the University of Berlin, one of the world's great universities.

Then a letter arrived in his mailbox. It was from John Dewey, who asked Mead to join him in the Department of Philosophy at Michigan in the fall.

It was an extraordinary chance. But Mead had not finished his graduate work.

He wrote to President Angell, asking if he might accept the job but postpone his arrival. He wanted to complete his doctoral thesis, a study of how the mind contemplates physical space.

No doubt Angell asked Dewey if Mead was worth waiting for. The answer, it seems, was a definitive "yes," since Angell gave Mead permission for a late start.

Like Dewey, Mead had rebelled against a strict Christian upbringing. Born in the middle of the Civil War, he was raised in Oberlin, Ohio, where both of his Christian-intellectual parents taught at Oberlin College, then a bastion of conservative New England theology. (His mother later became president of Mount Holyoke College.)

As he grew toward adulthood, the serious youngster began to doubt the strict tenets of his parents' faith. He was tied to it by his urge to help others, but the writings of Immanuel Kant, the leader of German idealist philosophy, pulled him toward an unhappy agnosticism. "I have been praying and reading the Bible," he confided to a friend, "[but] to be sure I do not know that there is a God." He dreamed of teaching philosophy but believed he could never be more than "a poor weak writer, a literary hack."

For a time he scraped by on fees he earned for tutoring high school boys in Minneapolis. Then he steeled himself and went east to Harvard, where he finally found success. He earned a master's degree in philosophy, magna cum laude, and gained enough confidence to further his studies in Germany. The University of Leipzig and the University of Berlin were centers for the study of new ways of thinking. There Mead read deeply in philosophy, grasped the principles of experimental psychology, and explored evolutionary theory. His restless mind abounded in materials for theorizing about human nature and society.

Then Dewey's invitation to teach at Michigan arrived. He would teach one course in the history of philosophy, a half course on Kant, and a course on evolution. "Doesn't it make your mouth water[?]" Mead wrote a friend.

According to Mead's biographer, Gary A. Cook, it was only after reaching Ann Arbor that the young scholar began to reconcile his three intellectual preoccupations—philosophy, psychology, and social reform. Cook attributes this largely to Mead's growing friendship with Dewey.

Mead arrived at Michigan just as Dewey was working out the terms of his own transition from Christian philosopher to social scientist. Both men were struggling to imagine how they might help to reform American society in the absence of traditional theology. In Ann Arbor, they became colleagues and friends, and in their conversations, Mead began the train of thought that would lead him to a new conception of the human self.

In Mead's view, the self at the core of a human life is not a soul created by an omniscient, supernatural God. Rather, the self emerges through interactions between the mind and its social environment. The self has two halves—a "me" and an "I." The "me" is the sum of all the standards and expectations of the individual's social group, and of how the members of that group perceive the individual. The "I" is the individual's response to those expectations. "Me" is object, the recipient of society's messages, while "I" is subject, the individualist who decides how to act in response to the messages received by "me."

His conception of the self led Mead to embrace a theory of social reform. The self was not at the mercy of its environment, he said; it was a force in its own right, capable of pursuing the goal of a society "in which the golden rule is to be the rule of conduct, that is, a society in which everyone is to make the interests of others his own interest"—a resounding echo of his early schooling in the church.

Mead had been prophetic about his shortcomings as a writer. It wasn't a matter of laziness. He wrote all the time, producing plans for courses, letters, reviews, essays, and snippets of theory. The problem was an inability to develop his ideas in the extended form of a book. He never wrote one. "I am vastly depressed by my inability to write what I want to," he once confided to a relative. "The distance between what I want and what I can is so unbridgeable."

But he conveyed enough to his fellow scholars to make a deep impression. His ideas helped to establish not one but two new disciplines—social psychology and sociology, both of which deal in the interactions between individuals and the societies in which they live.

The most important of Mead's admirers was John Dewey himself. When the University of Chicago asked Dewey to chair its new Department of Philosophy, he agreed on one condition—that his friend Mead be offered a position, too.

After just three years in Ann Arbor, Mead followed Dewey. He remained at Chicago for the rest of his career. Eventually, several of his students would combine their notes of Mead's lectures with various other writings to create a series of four books, including *The Philosophy of the Present* (1932) and *Mind, Self and Society* (1934). They still echo in 21st-century discussions of who we are, why we act as we do, and how we might construct a better future.

✢ ⁙ ✢

Andrew Dickson White gave Michigan its elms and the bells in its library tower. He also repaid Michigan for his early departure through a case of mistaken identity.

In the summer of 1878, White was on the lookout for a young historian to fill a vacant professorship at Cornell. Traveling in Germany, he heard that just such a man was in the neighborhood, Adams by name, a recent graduate of Johns Hopkins. Believing this to be Herbert Baxter Adams, a brilliant Hopkins man of whom he had heard great things, White asked for a meeting. The two men talked and White was much impressed—until he learned that he was speaking with one *Henry Carter* Adams, a Hopkins PhD, yes, but in economics, not history.

The meeting appeared to be over. Then White thought for a moment. He asked: *What sort of course would you offer at Cornell?* Adams stayed up all night to write a syllabus. White read it, then offered Adams a semester-long trial.

Adams proved a success in the classroom, but economics was not in high enough demand to warrant a full-time professor. So White put Adams in touch with his old contacts at Michigan, who agreed to hire Adams for the second semester.

Like John Dewey and George Mead, Adams had suffered a crisis of faith in college. Though a powerful moral purpose survived, he turned from theology to studies of history, philosophy, and social problems. He won a fellowship at Johns Hopkins, where his dissertation may have been the first scholarly study of taxation and public debt.

Unable to find a full-time post, he pieced together one semester after another at Cornell, Michigan, and Johns Hopkins. He longed for a permanent post in Ann Arbor.

"A man who has any thing to say on social questions can exert a wider influence there [at Michigan] than here [at Hopkins]," he told Angell. "The chief thing [is] you have the men to talk to."

But in 1886, Adams's ideas got him into trouble. At a conference on Cornell's campus, he was asked to comment on the day's major news—a massive railroad strike in the Southwest. Adams favored the workers. In his remarks, he sketched the economic doctrine taking shape in his mind. He was an individualist in the "American tradition," he said, but freedom was under fire in the harsh new industrial economy. Workers must have the right by law to control their destiny; it was folly to believe "the liberties of men should be judged by the wording of the law, rather than by the actual condition in which men find themselves . . . ."

The newspapers quoted Adams and conservatives saw red. Henry Williams Sage, a lumber baron on Cornell's board, demanded Adams's head. President White caved to the pressure and let Adams go.

But news of Adams's sacking barely got out before James Angell wrote from Ann Arbor. He asked a question or two about Adams's remarks on the rail strike. Then, having satisfied himself that Adams had not become a bomb-throwing revolutionary, Angell promptly offered the economist a full-time professorship at Michigan.

But there was to be no letup in Adams's migratory life. In Washington, DC, President Grover Cleveland had just established the Interstate Commerce Commission (ICC)—a response to the same anti-railroad sentiment that Adams had endorsed. The ICC might seem tame by latter-day standards, but it was the federal government's first attempt to regulate the nation's economy—a breach in the wall of laissez-faire doctrine.

For the chair of the new commission, Cleveland chose Thomas McIntyre Cooley, dean of Michigan's Law School and chief justice of the Michigan Supreme Court. Though the railroads had benefited from massive public largesse, they did their business in secret. If they were to be regulated, Judge Cooley realized, the government must know precisely what they were up to. Someone was going to have to collect statistics on the nation's most important industry. That task, thanks to U-M connections, now fell to Henry Carter Adams.

Once again, Adams divided his time. In Ann Arbor he chaired the new Economics Department. In Washington, DC, he developed statistical and accounting systems to keep track of the railroads, first as a staff of one, then as head of a growing bureau. In time, his systems would spread to other industries.

Meanwhile, he made war on laissez-faire economics in a series of seminal essays. Competition might be good or bad, he contended; it was the duty of the state to harness its power for the public welfare. "It should be the purpose of all laws touching matters of business," he wrote, "to maintain the beneficent results of competitive action while guarding society from the evil consequences of unrestrained competition." The same notion should apply to monopoly. If a monopoly hurt people, it should be outlawed. If it helped—as it did, say, in the field of utilities—it should be fostered by the state.

In many quarters, this was heresy. Like the notion of God as the foundation of all human purposes, the principles of free-market economics were regarded as sacrosanct. Adams was questioning them in the spirit of pragmatic philosophers like John Dewey. In economics as in philosophy, ideas were to serve people; it was not the other way around.

Despite his reputation as a radical reformer, it was Adams who brought about Michigan's first courses in business administration, including Principles of Industry, The Theory and Practice of Manufacturing Costs, Investment, as well as courses in accounting, finance, and marketing. So many students enrolled in these courses that Michigan's economists backed the idea of an autonomous program in business. Indeed, Adams is credited as the faculty forerunner of the Ross School of Business.

He split his time between Michigan and the ICC for nearly 25 years. Turning down many offers from other prestigious universities, he remained chair of U-M's Economics Department until his death in 1921. He was mourned as a giant of his field, "an amiable and lovable personality," and a moralist who wielded the tools of science. In decades to come, historians would depict him as one of the intellectual fathers of the Progressive movement and the New Deal.

Thomas McIntyre Cooley, who led the Law School as professor and dean from 1859 to 1884, built one of the most conspicuous houses in Ann Arbor at the corner of State and South University. In that stone manse, his timid son, Charles Horton Cooley, grew up with stomach trouble that often kept him home after school. "I did a little," he recalled, "read a great deal, and fancied infinitely."

He imagined he might become a great statesman, an ambition he conceived at least in part to measure up to his father's example and expectations. Thomas Cooley had been a frontier striver who climbed to prominence through herculean work. But his son soon realized he was too shy and contemplative for that kind of career. As he grew to adulthood, he watched his father suffer from "a lifelong habit to care only for action and applause," leaving him dissatisfied and bitter. So Charles resolved to take the opposite tack, seeking "things that are good in themselves, like beauty, truth, sympathy . . . ."

His ragged health prolonged his undergraduate years at Michigan. After graduating in 1887, he struggled to find a career. He picked up training in mechanical engineering, tried it for a time, then quit. He earned a master's degree in economics at U-M, then took a post at the ICC, where he spent two years studying railroad accidents. At the ICC, Henry Carter Adams recognized the young man's promise. With President Angell's blessing, Adams hired Cooley as an instructor in Michigan's Economics Department.

It was Cooley's final career move. In the shadow of a father who seemed always in transit between Ann Arbor, Lansing, and Washington, DC, the son would seldom be seen more than a few blocks from Michigan's Diag.

After his first book, an economic analysis of transportation in the U.S., he shifted his gaze to the organization of society at large. A close observer said Cooley was beginning to search "below the noisy and confusing currents on the surface to the enduring structures and processes that lay beneath."

Cooley came by his theories in quiet contemplation. "A patient grower of ideas," he called himself. He would have shaken his head in wonder at latter-day sociologists who march into the field with questionnaires and surveys, gathering masses of digital data to analyze by computer. Instead, he did his work on the quiet blocks of Ann Arbor, contemplating the micro-societies around him. He paid particular attention to his own children as they grew and changed in the family's home at 703 S. Forest Avenue.

Like Dewey and Mead, who were leaving Michigan's faculty just as Cooley joined it, he was trying to fill the vacuum left when Christian theology no longer seemed sufficient to explain man's place in the world. His thinking was a mixture of philosophy and science. His fascination was the organic relationship between the individual and society. Year by year, he assembled a body of ideas that came to undergird much of 20th-century sociology.

For example, the now-commonplace notion of socialization—the idea that individuals, though born with inherited traits, are fundamentally shaped by the people around them—owes more to Cooley than anyone else. He developed the concept of the "primary group" as the guiding force in the formation of an individual's character—parents, siblings, play groups, elders.

Most famously, Cooley developed the notion, still powerful today, of the "looking-glass self."

From earliest childhood, he argued, individuals develop the sense of who they are by watching the reactions of the people around them—first the "primary group," but also the people they meet in everyday life. Through these interactions, they learn not only how to behave but what to think of themselves. We gain a sense of who we are, Cooley thought, by observing our own actions, yes, but we also pay close attention to what others think of us—or, to put it more exactly, what we *think* others think of us. From these impressions, human beings define who they are.

It's a fluid process, like evolution itself, capable of change as the person proceeds through life. So some saw the looking-glass self as an antidote to the theories of Sigmund Freud, who believed the experiences of the child forever determined the fortunes of the adult.

One of Cooley's best students was his nephew, Robert Cooley Angell, a major sociologist in his own right with genes from U-M's two most prominent clans. (His parents were Alexis Angell, son of the U-M president, and Fanny Cooley, Dean Cooley's daughter.) In an essay on his uncle's work, Angell noted that Charles Cooley and George Mead had mapped the same social terrain but reached different theories about what happened there.

According to Angell, Cooley "thought that the actual interactions of daily life are dominated by the interactions between *ideas* of persons [emphasis added] that go on within their minds. His view is much like saying that the rehearsal of a play determines the performance. Mead, on the other hand, thinks of the ultimate interaction as the important thing and the mental process that precedes it as ancillary. To him the performance is what counts."

Cooley was deeply serious and self-contained. Yet his students came to revere him.

"The quiet, sincere manner of one who was obviously an intellectual master evoked deference spontaneously," his nephew recalled. "His ideas seemed simple and yet they illuminated many corners of life hitherto obscure . . . In his hands sociology became a door to wider cultural vistas and deeper cultural treasures. He seemed above and beyond his age, so that learning from him was like participating in the broad sweep of human history."

✢ ✠ ✢

In 1900, as James Angell was entering his last decade as president of U-M, he traveled to Chicago to see the presidents of thirteen other universities. After two days of meetings, the group announced the formation of the Association of American Universities (AAU).

The purpose was to make common cause on behalf of the best in U.S. higher education. They were raising the banner for three shared endeavors—original research, advanced training for post-undergraduate students, and innovative courses for undergraduates.

The AAU included five older private schools—Harvard, Yale, Columbia, Princeton, and Pennsylvania. There were five younger private schools—Johns Hopkins, Cornell, Chicago, Clark, and Stanford. And there were three public universities—Wisconsin, Berkeley, and Michigan.

Michigan's place on the list affirmed its transformation. It had gone far toward the university that Henry Tappan had envisioned, due in no small part to Professors Dewey, Mead, Adams, and Cooley.

They led and exemplified three fundamental changes:

1. Based on their exposure to new ideas and methods in psychology, philosophy, and biology, they helped to redefine how we understand ourselves and our social environment. They found a common focus in exploring the complexities of industrial societies. They sought to make things better by understanding, then shaping, the underlying dynamics of social change. Instead of preparing individuals for an eternal reward after life, they focused on the practicalities and possibilities of economic and social reform in the here and now.

2. They defined new sources for understanding self and society. Before, sources for human understanding had lain in sacred texts. Now, sources would be accumulated through observation of how individuals and societies function over time. That society was constantly changing meant that each day would offer possibilities of new knowledge—so knowledge was inexhaustible, requiring constant study and research.

3. Their new emphasis on social science and its divisions—sociology, social psychology, political science, and economics—helped to shift the center of human exploration from the church, synagogue, and temple to university campuses.

With these ideas, they laid the foundation for Michigan's enduring reputation.

7: A War over Words

For many years the words "Middle English Dictionary" aroused my curiosity.

As students, we heard rumors that spectral creatures in an attic of Angell Hall were painstakingly writing a dictionary for a form of English that no one had spoken for centuries.

Years later, an old reporter I knew at the *Detroit News* tore open a press release from the University, signaled for silence, and declared: "They've finished 'O'!"—then roared with laughter. I didn't think it was very funny. I thought it sounded fascinating, though with little idea of what it was all about.

When I looked into it, I stumbled on the story of Sanford Brown Meech— that prize of a scholarly name—and Hope Emily Allen. It was hard to see into their world. But in time I did, at least a bit, and what I saw struck me as a noble work of civilization and a prime example of what a university is for.

Closed out of tenured
professorships, Hope
Emily Allen, shown
here at her typewriter,
became a celebrat-
ed medieval scholar
essentially on her own.
*(Wikimedia Creative
Commons)*

Michigan, like every university, has seen plots, rebellions, and ugly turf
wars. Professors have schemed against chairs, chairs against deans, and
deans against presidents. But there was never a bomb-throwing plot quite
as violent—rhetorically speaking—as the one that Sanford Brown Meech,
a lowly assistant editor of Michigan's renowned *Middle English Dictionary*,
waged against the dictionary's chief editor, Thomas Knott, a distinguished
professor of English.

It happened in 1938—Depression times. U-M was eight years into the pro-
duction of an enormous dictionary of English as it was spoken in the late
Middle Ages, the era of Chaucer's rollicking *Canterbury Tales*. But now money
was so tight that the project was close to strangling. To keep it alive, Professor
Knott, the editor in chief, was applying for a grant from the American Council
of Learned Societies. But Sanford Meech believed Knott, his boss, was such a
disaster that he coolly tried to sabotage the older man's bid for funding.

The following is only a spoonful of the muck that Meech hurled at Knott—
while Meech was working for Knott.

Meech sent his attack on Knott to a major figure in medieval studies whose support was needed for Knott to win his grant. Meech said he had "reached the conclusion that Mr. Knott was incompetent." Knott's definitions of Middle English words were "often laughable." Knott's failures as a manager "come partly from his ignorance of linguistics and partly from his lack of common sense." The only thing worse than Knott's incompetence, Meech said, was "his lack of scholarly conscience. He cares nothing for scholarly accuracy or depth."

No surprise here: Sanford Meech was soon packing his bags and leaving Ann Arbor. But that is hardly the whole story.

✢ ⁝ ✢

Some readers are now undoubtedly thinking of this old saw: "Academic politics are so vicious precisely because the stakes are so low."

After all, what stakes could be lower than defining some word that nobody has used in six or seven centuries—a word like "a," to take the first word of Volume One of the *Middle English Dictionary*, which in the early 1400s meant "river" or "stream"?

How could Sanford Meech get so worked up about something that trivial? Especially in the middle of a depression?

But only someone outside the academic battleground, with no knowledge of what such a fight is really about, would ask a question like that. On the inside—that is, from the point of view of someone like Meech—the stakes seemed very high indeed. To him and others—not many, perhaps, but their zeal was mighty—the *Middle English Dictionary* could be a portal to a lost civilization. And for that, wouldn't it be wrong *not* to make a heroic sacrifice?

To see why Meech did what he did, and to learn why he is now seen as the unsung hero of one of Michigan's greatest scholarly achievements, requires the telling of this tale.

The *Middle English Dictionary* was the offspring of a "literary Everest"— the *Oxford English Dictionary (OED)*, which was built by three generations of expert lexicographers and two thousand volunteers who contributed five million quotations showing the proper use of more than a quarter-million English words plus their variations—414,825 words in all.

It was 15,490 pages long, in ten volumes.

The work had begun in England before the American Civil War. It ended the year after Babe Ruth hit sixty home runs—seventy years later.

All those years and pages and words—yet the *OED* was not really complete.

Its subject was modern English roughly since Shakespeare. But English was much older than that. The *OED* pointed out antecedents of modern English words but not in the detail needed to understand earlier versions of the language in full.

It explained each word's development over generations, but not all the way back to the word's origins. Sir William Craigie, the first edition's final editor, said the *OED*'s purpose would not really be fulfilled until every age of English had its own comprehensive dictionary. There should be dictionaries of Old English (pre-1100), Middle English (1175–1500); and Early Modern English (1500–1675), not to mention Older Scottish, Newer Scottish, and American English.

So as the *OED* neared completion in the 1920s, lexicographers on both sides of the Atlantic took a deep breath and said: *All right, let's get going.*

❖ ⁝ ❖

In the United States, Ann Arbor became the epicenter of English lexicography. First, in 1928, the University landed the *Early Modern English Dictionary* (*EMED*) project, thanks to Charles Fries, a Michigan lexicographer who enjoyed the high regard of *OED*'s chieftains. Then in 1930 came the *Middle English Dictionary* (*MED*) project. It had begun at Cornell but funds there ran out. In Ann Arbor, sponsors figured, the two projects could share resources. So separate offices were set up on Angell Hall's fifth floor, three stories above freshmen struggling through Chaucer and Shakespeare.

Countless boxes began to arrive in the mail from England. Each held a thick stack of plain paper slips. On each slip, one of the *OED*'s army of volunteer readers had copied a quotation—an example of how a single Middle English word had been used in some medieval book or poem or document.

This was the start of the *MED*'s raw material. The staff would sort the slips word by word, A through Z, then check the slips for accuracy against the original sources—a job that by itself would take years. Then more slips would be solicited from a new battalion of volunteer readers using more works in Middle English. Then, for each word, the staff would pore over the slips and make judgments about the word's definition, spelling, pronunciation, variations, and most important, its history.

The man put in charge was Samuel Moore, a professor of English who looked like a lexicographer from a folktale. He was small and bespectacled with an intent, peering gaze. He could be hard on students who didn't share his love of words, a friend conceded, but "no genuine student of language ever failed to find in him a sympathetic, enthusiastic, inspiring master and staunch, devoted friend."

Moore's vision was not "radically ambitious," according to Michael Adams of Indiana University, an expert in lexicography and its history who was trained in Michigan's English Department. Rather, Moore saw the *MED* as a straightforward supplement, following *OED* methods and organization.

But he faced one terrible complication that *OED* editors hadn't. Modern English, the language of the *OED*, has its variations, of course, depending on where and by whom it's spoken. But it's still a single, unitary language. Middle English was different. It was a dense stew of related dialects. In the 1300s, two friars—one from the South of England, one from the North—could probably hold a chat, but it wouldn't be easy. And no one knew which Middle English dialect had been spoken where. Nor did they know how a dictionary should handle the differences.

Moore, needing expert help to solve these problems, hired only the best talent, and the best of all the candidates was apparently Sanford Brown Meech. So Meech was named one of Moore's three assistant editors at just 27, his doctoral diploma from Yale barely dry.

Meech was the only child of New England bluebloods. His mother was descended from *Mayflower* Pilgrims. His doctoral supervisor had recommended him to Michigan as "an uncommonly learned young man. I do not recall any other graduate student in English here who has reached out more widely for information, and has shown a sounder scholarly equipment in interpreting it."

His new colleagues in Angell Hall noticed a certain Ivy League attitude about Meech, and yes, he wore his Phi Beta Kappa key to work. But a little arrogance could be overlooked in a man so clearly competent and hard working.

Professor Moore sent Meech searching for words in especially important and difficult Middle English writings. (One of these was "Hali Meidhad"—"Holy Maidenhood"—a sermon on virginity aimed at the religious recluses called anchoresses, whom Meech would encounter again.)

And Moore sent Meech to England to study the vexing problem of Middle English dialects. He motored and trudged through cities and rural shires all one summer.

The work piled up. By 1934, the staff amassed 280,000 new quotations from 66,000 pages of Middle English text.

Then, at the age of 56, Professor Moore suddenly died.

U-M's Advisory Committee on Dictionaries replaced Moore quickly. They simply returned to the man who had been their first choice to lead the *MED* in 1930—Thomas Knott of the University of Iowa, who held a PhD from the elite University of Chicago.

Knott had co-written (with Moore) a standard work on Old English, and he was co-editor of *Webster's New International Dictionary, Second Edition,* the largest general dictionary of its day. He had said no to Michigan's earlier offer only because he'd been in the middle of the *Webster's* project.

Now he said yes. His credentials seemed impeccable.

But "Webster's Second," as Knott's dictionary was known, was a commercial book for general readers. It sold well. But it was not a book such as the *MED* was meant to be—a deep, dense dictionary for scholarly specialists.

In fact, the two dictionaries were about as similar as a great physicist's magnum opus on quantum mechanics and the "Physics" entry in the *World Book* encyclopedia.

Sanford Meech said Knott's appointment was "welcome news."

Then the *MED* staff got a letter from Knott that was nothing if not honest.

"I shall tell you a vast secret," Knott told them. "I don't yet know much about the editing of the *Middle English Dictionary . . . ."

Meech would soon think even that modest admission overstated Knott's ability, and others at Michigan would be forced to agree.

But first, Meech's reputation was in for its own radical change—for better and worse—thanks to his collision with a remarkable woman.

✤ ⁝ ✤

When Hope Emily Allen met Sanford Meech in 1931, she was 48. Before she was born, her parents had belonged to a utopian Christian commune in Oneida, New York, whose unorthodox rules about matrimony and sex were enforced by a community council, with strong roles for women approved. Their radicalism steered Hope toward an unorthodox life of her own.

She grew up bookish and so sickly that for a time she was expected to die. She recovered and became a brilliant student at Bryn Mawr, Radcliffe, and Cambridge University. But tenure-track careers at major universities were closed to women in her era.

Undaunted, she made herself an independent medieval historian. By the 1920s, she was a recognized expert. Thanks to a modest private income, she could steer her own course.

She scorned the conventional path toward marriage, choosing to live in close association with like-minded women who admired the advice of Bryn Mawr's feminist president, Carey Thomas: "Only our failures marry." (Some report that Thomas actually said: "Our failures only marry," but either way, her take on matrimony was a bracing departure from Seven Sisters' norms.)

When the Depression pinched her income, Allen accepted a post as assistant editor of the *Early Modern English Dictionary* at Michigan. She worked down the hall from Sanford Meech, whom she came to know and respect.

"Miss Allen came to our 4:30 tea breaks from time to time," recalled Frederic Cassidy, a lexicographer who worked for the *MED* as a graduate student and went on to edit the massive *Dictionary of American Regional English*. "I remember her as a vivacious person altogether given to the scholarship in hand, pleasant with our staff and with students generally ... but always seeming to soar above us, as she had every right to do.

"She came and went her intense, birdlike way, moving quickly, lightly, with piping voice and eager questions."

Early in her career, Allen had begun to study the anchoresses whom Meech had encountered in the essay "Holy Maidenhood." They lived celibate lives of devotion governed by a guidebook called the *Ancrene Wisse*. In some ways, Allen's life mirrored theirs, and she became an expert on their guidebook.

In 1934, that expertise of hers led to the most important moment in her career.

It happened when Allen was called to London to inspect a mysterious volume owned by a wealthy landowner, Col. William Butler-Bowdon. It had been in his family "since time immemorial," he said, but lately it had turned up in a Ping-Pong cupboard.

Turning the pages carefully, scrutinizing Middle English words that few people in the world could decipher, Allen realized she was holding the memoir of a Christian mystic of the 1400s, a proto-feminist brewer's wife and anti-clerical evangelist named Margery Kempe.

Margery was illiterate. She dictated her words to others, recounting her mystical visions, her pilgrimages to mainland Europe and the Holy Land, her fights with priests and archbishops, and her trial for heresy. Surviving from a time when books of any kind were exceedingly rare, *The Book of Margery Kempe* threw open a window into the England of the 1400s. In time it was recognized as the first autobiography written in English and one of the more important literary finds of the 20th century.

"I am informed evil of thee," the Archbishop of York tells Margery at one point. "I heard it said that thou art a right wicked woman."

"I also heard it said that thou art a right wicked man," she retorts. "And if ye be as wicked as men say, ye shall never come to heaven."

As one scholar would later say, Margery "charms any reader who likes a rebel."

When the news spread, Hope Allen's star soared in the small cosmos of medieval studies. And it was obvious that Margery Kempe's tale must be published.

Nearly all Middle English writings were handwritten. So Allen took her treasure to the Early English Text Society, which printed the works so any scholar, student, or library could buy them.

Allen's own field was history, so she planned a historical supplement to explain Kempe's mysticism. To transcribe the memoir and explain what it showed about Middle English as a language, Allen needed a Middle English linguist as a collaborator.

For that she settled on Sanford Meech, whose training and experience fit the bill. He delightedly accepted.

But Allen was in England and Meech was in Michigan, and they never quite nailed down who would do what. Soon, through increasingly chilly letters, they were at odds.

Allen had understood that she and Meech would be recognized as co-editors and equals—a generous gesture to Meech, her junior in years and experience. But Meech wasn't so sure of that, and Col. Butler-Bowdon, who still owned the *Book*, took Meech's side. Soon a major mess was afoot.

Before long Allen cordially detested Meech, calling him "supercilious and languid." When she accused him of bad faith, he exploded.

"A friend says I am a good judge of character," she wrote to him at one point, "but that I have been mistaken in you. I was mistaken in not realizing how touchy you were."

To Meech, the problem was hers, not his.

"Miss Allen is not an easy person for the ordinary man to get on with," he wrote to a colleague. "As I have experienced it, Miss Allen's ideal of cooperation is that she should decide, and I should obey."

In the end, the Margery Kempe affair turned out sourly for both of them, even as it made their names in medieval studies.

The title page of *The Book of Margery Kempe* wound up crediting "Professor Sanford Brown Meech" as editor while "Hope Emily Allen" is mentioned only as author of a "prefatory note."

But Allen had already taken her revenge.

Unafraid to fight with a man, she sent Meech-damning reports of the affair to the editors of both U-M dictionaries and other authorities in the field. Meech's superiors quickly sided with Hope Allen. They now viewed Meech as an arrogant, disloyal opportunist.

❖ ⁝ ❖

The scramble for primacy between Allen and Meech may look petty, especially to anyone outside their rarefied realm of scholarship. But to the principals, their standing in that realm mattered so much because they cared so deeply about their work. Both had given their lives to what one of Allen's biographers has called "speaking with the dead"—the dead of many centuries past, who lived in a mysterious time impossibly remote from the mid-20th century, yet also connected to it by a single fragile strand.

That strand was the language of English, twisted and transmuted over the centuries yet still inscribed with a code that might be broken by those who gave their lives to understanding it.

Frederic Cassidy remembered Hope Allen's fascination with the humble Middle English word *bug* and "all its folkloric ramifications." Harry Potter fans would applaud to see her skipping from one creepy variant of *bug* to the next—*bogey* and *bugbear* to *bogle* and *boggart*, all spirit-allies of the Devil, yet playful, too.

"She tracked down the phrase 'to put a bug in one's ear' . . . meaning to give a secret hint for one's good," Cassidy wrote, "which led in turn to the word *fly*, another familiar spirit, and the senses of *bug* and *fly* as spies."

Meech had trekked all over England to find differences in ancient dialects from one shire's old documents to the next. When the photostats of Margery Kempe's handwritten pages reached his mailbox in Ann Arbor, he and his wife stayed up late night after night, Meech puzzling out the arcane symbols on each page, his wife transcribing the words on a typewriter.

Meech and Allen labored under the same spell.

In the eyes of a man like Meech—perhaps especially a young man, still starstruck by his own ambition—the *MED* was a sacred trust. It must be protected against all enemies.

Only a passion like that can explain his meltdown over the idiocies he came to perceive in his new superior, the editor in chief, Professor Thomas Knott.

✢ ⁘ ✢

Knott had barely been installed as editor of the *MED* when Meech's grievances started to mount.

The work on every major dictionary is slow. But Knott's procedures would have inspired a snail. He once directed Meech and another editor to document the history of one variation of a single word—the verb to *lie*, in the sense of reclining—with Knott to decide which man's work was better. He dragged out the process for an entire semester.

One variation of one word.

Yet, bizarrely, he also urged his aides to save time by skimping on essential details, including proofreading, no less. The staff was appalled.

Then Knott sent outside experts the first thirteen-page sample of the *MED*—covering words between *L* and *laik*—with a request for advice. He asked the experts: "Should we try to do anything about dialects? In our judgment, this would demand too much time and space and the solution of very difficult, if not insuperable problems of presentation."

The experts were bewildered. Dialects? *Of course* the *MED* had to deal with dialects!

"This is too vast a question to be answered," replied Howard Mumford Jones, who had just left Michigan's English Department for Harvard's. "What is meant?"

When Michael Adams, the historian of dictionaries, studied the *MED* archives many years later, he concluded Knott just was not the man for the job.

"There's no way to describe Middle English accurately if you *don't* deal with that problem," he said. "What kind of a dictionary will you have?"

In other words, Knott's question—"Should we try to do anything about dialects?"—suggested that he did not fully understand what Middle English was.

"Anything that was tough, Knott tried to sidestep," Adams said. "I don't mean to be ruthlessly mean about Knott, but I think that's the way you have to look at it—that he just lacked the imagination to deal with the things a Middle English dictionary would necessarily confront, were it to be a dictionary that people decades later, even a century, could use to great effect."

To be sure, Knott was in a vise. *MED*'s funding was being siphoned off by bigger needs. A later editor of the *MED*, Sherman Kuhn, told Michael Adams no one could have done better than Knott, given U-M's terrible financial constraints in the late 1930s. Knott had no choice but to slash the *MED*'s original scope and publish a stripped-down dictionary for students picking through Chaucer.

Maybe so—but no such rationale could soften Meech's rage.

So, early in 1938, Meech proceeded with his professional suicide mission.

His wife had just had a baby, so he had more reason than ever to fear for his job security. But he knew the *MED*'s budget was being slashed, and he suspected the project was on its last legs. So at least he could bring justice down on his tormentor's head—and maybe, in the long run, save a larger vision of the *MED*.

He listed Knott's sins in a long letter to Kemp Malone of Johns Hopkins, the dean of U.S. etymologists, who was supporting Knott's bid for funding. Meech told Professor Malone that Professor Knott:

- had "only the most meagre [sic] equipment in comparative linguistics, and in medieval history and archaeology"
- had "no gift for linguistic analysis"
- had "little administrative capacity"

- had "never attempted any etymological work for the Dictionary himself" and was "unable to criticize such work by others"
- had wasted money by collecting reams of useless new word slips
- had approved "sample pages which teem with inconsistencies, and inaccuracies, and . . . misspellings," and when these errors had been pointed out, had pronounced them "good enough"
- was preparing the dictionary "only for popular appeal and superficial show."

With that, Meech destroyed his own standing at Michigan.

Professor Malone, shocked, told colleagues about Meech's sabotage, and the news quickly got back to Ann Arbor.

"Meech is very definitely out to knife you," a friend wrote to Thomas Knott, "and the Dict. project with you unless he can become editor."

Meech's superiors—Knott and Michigan's Committee on Dictionaries—were shocked as well. In short order, Meech was fired.

But that was not the end of it. To get a favorable reference from Michigan, the Committee on Dictionaries demanded that Meech withdraw his charges against Knott in writing. When he did so, committee members said his letter was insufficiently contrite and demanded a second letter.

So Meech had to grovel.

"It was unwise on my part to criticize the scholarly capacities of an older man like Professor Knott," he wrote.

He conceded that he should have expressed himself differently.

But he never said he had been wrong.

He landed in the English Department at Syracuse University, where he enjoyed a productive career.

"Meech seems to have fit perfectly the stereotype of the self-assured, even smug, Ivy League graduate," Michael Adams writes, "one with every advantage, once the perfect student and now self-consciously an expert."

But here's the more important fact, by Adams's reckoning: "The events of 1938 were crucial to the MED's eventual success, and Meech played an extraordinarily important role in them, because he dared to criticize the dictionary and its editor publicly."

Thomas Knott remained as editor until he died in 1945. But Meech's attack on Knott staggered his reputation. Even those who defended Knott on personal grounds privately endorsed Meech's critique of his work.

At the end of World War II, U-M determined to remain in the dictionary business. But it was clear that Knott's tenure had been a dead end. A new start was needed. So in 1946, Hans Kurath, a scholar of German at Brown University, was appointed as Knott's successor. When Kurath examined *MED*'s records, he determined that Sanford Meech had been quite right about Knott's ineptitude.

Kurath then set the dictionary on a rigorous new course, aiming for an even more comprehensive dictionary than Samuel Moore and Meech had hoped for.

Under Kurath (editor until 1961) and two more editors—Sherman Kuhn (1961–1983) and Robert E. Lewis (1983–2001)—Michigan lexicographers marched through the alphabet and the decades. The Early Modern English project had to be abandoned. But in the 1980s, when the Mellon Foundation and the National Endowment for the Humanities stepped in with major funding, the *MED*'s staff grew and momentum accelerated.

In 2001, the final volume was published. In all, the *MED* consisted of 55,000 entries in 15,000 pages. It had taken 71 years, one more year than the *OED*. The entire work went online in 2007, vastly extending its influence and helpfulness. It was called "the greatest achievement in Middle English scholarship in America."

⁺ ⁺⁺ ⁺

Does any of it matter?

It does to anyone who takes a moment to ponder where the common currency of every English speaker's thoughts and feelings came from. "The language we've got today is still largely an extension of the language of the Middle Ages," said Michael Adams. "So understanding the language of today demands, in part, understanding the past stages of the language."

Then there is that matter of speaking with the dead. *The Middle English Dictionary* is the comprehensive record of a teeming, talking people who lived and died seven centuries ago. The pages of the *MED*, in print or online, "amplify all these particular voices of the past into the present," Adams said. "You would not otherwise hear any of those voices."

8: The Fourth Name on the List

When Sidney Fine spoke about the University's past, he tended to dwell on the 1950s, when he had been a young professor. He told me about a time when the administration came under severe pressure to scrutinize faculty members suspected of ties to the Communist Party. That was when I heard the three names that conservatives and liberals alike had recited like a tribal chant in 1953 and 1954—Davis, Markert, and Nickerson.

Many years later, I thought I would write a story about those three. But I soon learned about a fourth name that never reached the headlines. In the 21st century, he was revered as a giant in his field. But hardly anyone remembered what had happened to him in Ann Arbor in the 1950s. I found the evidence in scattered boxes of old papers in the Bentley Library. I thought they revealed the fragility of the freedom of thought, even on the campus of a great university, where thought is supposed to be prized above all else. Instead, fear and even hatred carried the day. It was one of the University's worst moments. It should be remembered as a cautionary tale.

In the days of Senator Joseph McCarthy, when Americans feared a Communist conspiracy to subvert the West, three junior members of Michigan's faculty were tarred by the brush of suspicion. Investigations ensued—one by the House Un-American Activities Committee (HUAC), two by committees of the faculty. For months these events made headlines. In the end, President Harlan Hatcher fired two of the men and censured the third.

For many years, the controversy was all but forgotten. But in the 1980s, as academe reconsidered its record in the McCarthy years, faculty members began to campaign for a gesture of reconciliation to the three scholars, all still living. When the Regents declined to approve the idea, faculty acted on their own. In 1991, they established an annual lecture on academic freedom to honor the three—Chandler Davis, Clement Markert, and Mark Nickerson.

But there was another thread to this story, one far less well known than the public ordeals of the three men who, for a time, magnetized the attention of the campus.

Behind closed doors, a fourth member of the faculty went through a parallel ordeal. He escaped the spotlight of scandal that fell on Davis, Markert, and Nickerson. But he was also denied a public acknowledgment that the University might have done him a grave wrong.

And this was not just any young scholar. This was Lawrence Robert Klein. In 1980, as a professor at the University of Pennsylvania, he won the Nobel Prize in economics.

When Klein died in 2013 at 93, he was memorialized as one of the great economists of the 20th century. But no one wrote about the ugly and secret fight that had pushed him away from Michigan so long ago.

Lawrence Klein was born in 1920. He grew up in Omaha, Nebraska. His father was an office clerk. He dreamed of a career in baseball, but at the age of ten he was disabled when struck by a car. During World War II, his childhood injury kept him out of the service. He spent the war years mostly in school, first at Los Angeles City College, then at the University of California at Berkeley, then at MIT, where he earned one of that school's first doctoral degrees in economics in 1944.

Lawrence Klein brought a reputation to Michigan as an "enfant terrible," but his colleagues found him congenial and conscientious, not to mention brilliant. All but one or two got past the fact that he'd once been a Communist. (*University Archives and Record Center, University of Pennsylvania*)

His early brilliance earned him a job straight out of graduate school at the prestigious Cowles Commission at the University of Chicago. There, a few pioneering scholars were infusing traditional economic theory with statistics. This was a new specialty called econometrics.

The Chicago group was trying to predict what would happen to the U.S. economy when the war ended. Many Americans, including most economists, feared another depression. Klein was fascinated by the use of statistical modeling to predict the economic future. Like a meteorologist using radar to study the weather, he fed streams of data into his models. Results in hand, he said no, the U.S. wasn't heading for another depression. In fact, there was going to be a boom after the war.

The war ended. Servicemen flooded home. The economy shifted from war to peace, and soon the U.S. was heading into a great economic expansion.

The doomsayers had been wrong and Klein had been right. Not yet thirty years old, he was one of the most promising young economists in the world.

In quick succession, Klein designed economic models for the government of Canada; studied with major economists in Europe; and worked in Washington, DC, under Arthur Burns, future chair of the U.S. Federal Reserve.

In 1949, Michigan snapped him up and made him a research fellow in the Survey Research Center. In 1950, he accepted a joint appointment as lecturer in the Economics Department, where he was promised swift promotion.

His output was prodigious. He wrote a definitive study of Keynesian economics, a history of economic fluctuations between the world wars, and the leading textbook on econometrics. With his students in a graduate seminar, Klein designed a statistical model of the U.S. economy that became a standard tool in the field.

Members of the Economics Department realized they had an academic superstar on their hands. Early in 1953, Professor Leo Sharfman, the longtime chair, told Klein that in one more year, the Department would propel him upward from the low rank of lecturer to full professor with tenure, a rare and prestigious sign of confidence.

Then U-M's leaders were told by investigators from the U.S. House Un-American Activities Committee (HUAC) that Klein's name was on a list of some fifteen professors and students suspected of being secret members of the Communist Party.

✦ ⁝ ✦

A decade earlier, when Klein was in his early twenties, he had been attracted to left-wing politics. This was hardly unusual among idealistic intellectuals of the 1930s and early '40s, many of whom were troubled by the shortcomings of Franklin Roosevelt's New Deal and appalled by the rise of Nazi Germany.

But in 1944 or '45, Klein went farther than most by doing work for the Communist Party. In practical terms, this meant, by his own account, that he went to some Party meetings and taught some adult classes on Keynesian economics offered at Party-run schools in Boston and Chicago.

He dropped the connection after he married in 1947 and began to raise a family. He remained a leftist. He defined himself as a democratic socialist in favor of national economic planning on the Scandinavian model. But his time and attention were now consumed by his work in economic forecasting.

✢ ⁝ ✢

Joe McCarthy was only the most famous of the politicians who cast themselves as red hunters. His special targets were the State Department and the U.S. Army. Others scrutinized Hollywood, the theater, the labor movement, the civil rights movement—any institution that might be purveying Communist propaganda.

U.S. Rep. Harold Velde, an Illinois Republican and former FBI agent who became chair of HUAC after the congressional elections of 1952, took aim at the nation's schools and colleges. He deputized U.S. Rep. Kit Clardy, a Lansing Republican just elected to the House, to find Communists on Michigan's campuses.

In January 1953, Detroit newspapers reported that HUAC had compiled a list of some fifteen Communists, past or present, on U-M's faculty. President Hatcher immediately cabled Velde: "We wish to inform you of our willingness to cooperate with you to the fullest extent," and he directed any faculty member who received a HUAC subpoena to do the same.

Hatcher sent his chief lieutenant, Marvin Niehuss, a law professor and vice president for academic affairs, to find out who was on HUAC's list. Niehuss got HUAC to cut the names to a handful—a couple of graduate students and five faculty members, including Chandler Davis, Clement Markert, Mark Nickerson, and Lawrence Klein.

Klein did exactly what the University asked of him. With the HUAC hearing looming, he went to his chair, Professor Sharfman, and Vice President Niehuss. He told them frankly about his earlier association with the Communist Party—why he had joined and why he had quit.

Next he met with HUAC investigators and did the same. HUAC gave him a clean bill of health and said he would not be called to testify in public. A few friends and colleagues knew what had happened, but Klein's name never surfaced in press reports.

Congressional red hunters normally demanded a price for the absolution that HUAC had given Klein—the person under suspicion must "name names." That is, he must inform on other Communists to prove he had renounced the Party. Whether Klein did so in his private meetings with HUAC is not known.

He quietly went on with his work.

Then, in public hearings in Lansing in June 1954, Davis, Markert, and Nickerson refused to answer HUAC's questions about any ties with Communism. (Another professor, who was gravely ill, was excused from testifying.)

Davis invoked his First Amendment right to political freedom and the Fifth Amendment protection against self-incrimination. Markert and Nickerson invoked only the Fifth Amendment.

President Hatcher promptly suspended the three men and directed the faculty to investigate. Their jobs, not to mention their reputations, hung in the balance.

The three met various fates.

Chandler Davis told faculty committees that his politics were none of their business. Hatcher then fired him. After years in court, he served several months in prison for contempt of Congress.

Clement Markert and Mark Nickerson acknowledged that their faculty colleagues, unlike members of Congress, had a right to ask where they stood on Communism. Each spoke frankly with the committees about past Communist ties and said they were no longer members.

Markert's penalty was only to be censured by the administration for refusing to cooperate with HUAC. Strong support from colleagues apparently helped save his job. But he soon left Michigan for a position at Johns Hopkins. He wound up as chair of biology at Yale.

Nickerson appeared to be in the same position as Markert. He had told all to the faculty committees, and he was regarded as one of the most important pharmacologists of his generation. But he was a difficult man, and he had bitter enemies in the Medical School. When his superiors said they could no longer tolerate him, Hatcher fired him, too.

With the matter resolved, Hatcher gave a long summing-up to the faculty.

Any professor, he said, "owes his colleagues in the University complete candor and perfect integrity, precluding any kind of clandestine or conspiratorial activities. He owes equal candor to the public. If he is called upon to answer for his convictions it is his duty as a citizen to speak out. It is even more definitely his duty as a professor.

"Of one thing I am sure. Nobody's freedom has been invaded or abridged at the University of Michigan, and the proper way to keep it sturdy and productive is to exercise it responsibly in keeping with our high and honorable tradition."

The scandal over reds at Michigan appeared to be over. But the matter of Lawrence Klein had only begun.

The laborious process of promoting Klein to a full professorship in Economics had been put off at least once already. Professor Sharfman, the chair, was buying time until the HUAC storm had passed, though he had "to suppress a modest staff rebellion" by those who wanted Klein to be promoted with no further delay, according to one professor.

Now Klein himself asked for a postponement. In the fall of 1954, as the faculty conducted its hearings with Davis, Markert, and Nickerson, he took a leave without pay and went off to England, where he worked as a senior researcher at Oxford University's Institute of Statistics.

In Ann Arbor, Sharfman was just stepping down as chair of the Economics Department. He was replaced by Gardner Ackley, a macroeconomist who was a star in his own right. Ackley wasted no time in proposing that Klein be lured back to Ann Arbor with a promotion from lecturer to full professor with tenure.

To win that promotion—nearly unheard of without intermediate promotions to assistant and associate professor—Klein would have to pass muster at four levels in ascending order: the Economics Department; LSA; the vice president for academic affairs and the president; and finally, the University Regents. To propel Klein's name up and over these obstacles, Chairman Ackley prepared an exhaustive dossier.

When U-M had first hired Klein in 1949, Ackley told LSA's leaders, rumors had reached Ann Arbor that he was an *enfant terrible*, a "genius intolerant of mere mortals." But "either this report was untrue," Ackley said, "or something had happened to him before he arrived; for we have observed a modest, cooperative, and tactful individual . . . always friendly [and] conscientious in performance of his responsibilities."

Ackley and his colleagues—most of them—were satisfied that any questions about Klein's judgment or character could now be safely forgotten.

"We have observed him closely for four years . . . . He is as objective, experimental, and open-minded as any among us . . . " and he had shown "no evidence of any Marxist dogma, no indication of rigid positions, no blindness to facts or arguments on any side."

As for his stature in economics, there was no controversy at all.

Very few scholars, even after decades of work, ever win the kind of endorsements that now came in for Klein. His promotion had the backing of no fewer than six future winners of the Nobel Prize in economics, not to mention Arthur Burns, then chair of President Dwight D. Eisenhower's Council of Economic Advisers.

Summing up his case, Ackley said: "We have no fear of his views. Nor need any member of the University community. There is every reason to suppose that Klein's scholarship and teaching will continue to add luster to the reputation of the Department and the University."

Eighteen senior members of the Economics faculty endorsed Ackley's plea for Klein's promotion to full professor. Two dissented. Both held joint positions in the School of Business Administration, which had a rocky history with the Economics Department.

One was Robert Spivey Ford, an associate dean.

The other was William Paton, the star of U-M's Business School, a professor at Michigan since World War I, widely regarded as one of the founders of modern business accounting, and a man so conservative he thought Social Security "was a curse on our society," as an admirer once put it.

✢ ⁞ ✢

William Paton was born in 1889 and raised in Michigan's Copper Country. He was the son of a small-town school superintendent. His mother oversaw the town of Calumet's rotating collection of fifty books lent by the state library for six months at a time, and her son always read all fifty.

With money he earned from odd jobs, he raced to three degrees at Michigan—BA in 1915 (after which he started teaching economics), MA in 1916, PhD in 1917. His dissertation was published as *Accounting Theory with Special Reference to the Corporate Enterprise*, a foundational document in the new field of public accounting.

By 1921 he was a full professor with appointments in the Economics Department and the new School of Business Administration. Even in his thirties, he was certainly the Business School's best-known figure and arguably its most brilliant.

During the Great Depression he helped to restore faith in accounting with key innovations in standards and practices. He authored leading textbooks, won all the major awards in his field, and earned one of Michigan's first named professorships.

In the classroom he was a powerful and exacting presence. One student recalled "his incisive mind, his impatience with sloppy reasoning, his endless stock of homely anecdotes and Biblical references, his interest in his students' careers, and his amazing ability to remember names and faces." He was charming, earthy, charismatic, funny, stubborn, and intolerant of mediocrity.

In national politics, he revered free enterprise, hated Franklin Roosevelt, and assaulted the safety-net thinking of New Deal economists.

In campus politics, he was a gadfly on the right who often fought with liberal colleagues in the Economics Department. Even his admirers said Paton was "a poor compromiser" who was seldom, if ever, troubled by self-doubt. He once published an article on the virtues of living in underground dwellings. "If this aberrant idea be taken by some of his critics as proof that his notions of economics and politics are those of a caveman," one of his students wrote, "he would be totally unconcerned."

When Gardner Ackley took up the cause of Lawrence Klein's promotion in the fall of 1954, Paton declared war.

In the fall of 1954, Klein's supporters and foes in the Economics Department argued about his promotion in two long, contentious meetings.

Paton charged that Klein's "conversion" from Communist ideology was "only skin-deep" and that he was "aggressively socialist in his entire outlook." Besides, Paton said, there were already enough leftists in the Department.

Ackley retorted that Klein now believed in nothing more radical than the sort of welfare state favored by left-leaning New Dealers and the democratic socialists of Scandinavia. "Obviously," he said, "such views can be compatible with (1) complete loyalty to the American way of life, and (2) scientific objectivity in his professional work. . . . We are convinced that Klein feels no mission to convert anyone to his own social and political views."

As for the admixture of "left" and "right" in the Department, Ackley said: "Professor Paton stands at the edge of such a spectrum. For him, such institutions as Social Security are not only 'humbug' but dangerous to the social fabric. I am glad that we have such views represented. They may even be the 'truth.' I am only unhappy that Professor Paton sometimes finds it necessary to lump together all views not his own as 'leftist,' which also can mean 'pink,' or 'Socialist,' or worse."

Colleagues detected an ugly subtext in Paton's accusations against Klein.

As William Haber, a senior member of the Economics Department and later dean of LSA, would recall it, Paton's remarks had "an anti-Semitic overtone. He [Paton] referred to the voice of Larry Klein, that it had . . . a sound that's associated with Jewish speakers or Jewish people. And he didn't spell it out; he didn't have to. It was too crystal-clear to me, and it was clear to others who were less sensitive about it."

Haber made a retort that sent Paton storming out of one meeting. He was brought back, but he said the Department might as well pay dues to the Communist Party if members insisted on promoting Klein—and if they did, he would personally lobby members of the Board of Regents to block the appointment.

The Department voted 18-2 for the promotion.

Paton went in search of more ammunition. Acting on his own, he solicited opinions of Klein from ten more economists. None was an expert in Klein's field of econometrics.

Three returned letters highly unfavorable toward Klein, while three were only mildly unfavorable. The rest were favorable, and even Paton concluded that one of the "highly unfavorables" should be discounted.

"This is not a very good percentage" against Klein, Ackley remarked in a letter.

The 18-2 majority in Klein's favor was good enough for Ackley, who forwarded the recommendation to LSA Dean Charles Odegaard. Ackley proposed that Klein's appointment should consist of a three-quarter-time post in the Economics Department and a one-quarter commitment to the Survey Research Center—with tenure, meaning lifetime job security.

Members of the Economics Department waited in suspense. So did Klein.

Across the Atlantic, officials at Oxford University offered him a permanent position with tenure. Klein put them off, waiting to see whether Michigan's chief administrators would approve Ackley's proposal.

Twice, LSA Dean Odegaard and the College Executive Committee came back to Ackley to ask for more information about Klein's fitness. Both times, Ackley patiently stuck to his guns. "Klein," he repeated, "is a scholar of remarkable technical competence, achievement and promise."

Finally, the dean endorsed Ackley's recommendation—promotion to full professor with tenure—and passed it up to Vice President Niehuss. The decision now lay with him and President Hatcher. They held an informal discussion about the matter with members of the Board of Regents.

On June 8, 1955, Niehuss sent the administration's decision back to Dean Odegaard. It was a compromise. The president would recommend to the Regents that Klein be appointed full professor, but without tenure. At a later date, he could be considered for tenure again.

Now the decision fell to Klein—Michigan or Oxford. Ackley cabled the young economist to urge him to accept U-M's offer, then followed up with an impassioned letter.

Klein replied by telegram: "BADLY WANT TENURE." Ackley tried again, but on the matter of tenure the administration would not budge.

When he had left Ann Arbor the previous year, Klein promised himself he would return to the United States only to accept a tenured position. Now, "in recognition of the sincere efforts made on my behalf by friends and colleagues" at U-M, he decided on a compromise of his own. He would accept Michigan's offer, despite the lack of tenure.

That seemed to be the end of it.

But the battle between Ackley and Paton was not over, and in the fall of 1955 it came to a climax.

✦ ❖ ✦

Professor Paton now interceded again. First he followed through on his threat to lobby Regents to reject Klein's promotion.

His letter to them has not survived, but he likely repeated what he wrote to Vice President Niehuss: "This appointment has no justification. [Klein] was a postwar member of the Communist Party, and remains a 'dedicated' supporter of the Norwegian type of socialism, generally conceded to be the nearest thing to the totalitarian brand to be found outside the Iron Curtain. Some of us here regard him as an arrogant and generally disagreeable person. . . ."

Next, Klein received an anonymous letter in England. He recalled years later that it was "a very nasty letter . . . telling me not to come [to U-M] and all the dire things that would happen if I did come." Authorship of the letter was never verified, but members of the Department told Klein later that Paton had written it.

In some distress, Klein wrote Ackley: "A few weeks ago, I received an anonymous letter outlining Paton's recent moves against my appointment. I am not certain whether the tip was sent as a warning by a friend of what to expect on my return or as a threat by a foe against my returning at all.

"Should I take seriously Paton's activities? He now approaches the regents and administration directly to let my appointment expire at the end of the current year and makes the veiled threat of carrying the case to the public if he gets no satisfaction from University authorities.

"I had planned to come back full of enthusiasm for various research and teaching projects, but I don't look forward to the bother of carrying on this fight over again."

A deeply bitter exchange of letters between Ackley and Paton followed.

Ackley wrote, in part: "I will not dwell on the fact that your new actions have again cruelly exposed a man and his family—who had already suffered a great deal—to renewed uncertainty, insecurity, and doubt. . . . I can imagine circumstances in which any of us might feel compelled to dissent from the actions and judgments of all of our colleagues, just as you have done. But I cannot imagine doing it behind their backs. . . . We had to learn of your actions through a rumor which reached us from England.

"Please do not pretend that this was a mere oversight . . . Your action . . . appears to me to have deliberately flouted the rules of behavior which are necessary for any kind of responsible group life and action."

Paton replied: "This is wild and grossly insulting talk and I deny your accusations and insinuations point blank . . . [Y]our effort to castigate me and put me in a bad light with my departmental colleagues and with College and University officials is an almost incredible performance, without justification . . . ."

But whether Paton had written the anonymous letter or not, he had already won his war.

Klein wrote to Vice President Niehuss to ask for his frank assessment of his future at Michigan.

Niehuss's reply was guarded, even tepid. At the end of the academic year, he said, he would recommend that Klein's appointment—still without tenure—be extended for another year, but "I cannot predict the action of the Board of Regents on this recommendation."

That sealed Klein's decision.

In a handwritten note back to Niehuss shortly before Christmas 1955, Klein resigned his posts at Michigan and said he had accepted Oxford's "magnificent offer, with long tenure. . . . This and other British universities have given me such a strong sense of freedom of thought that I feel I cannot refuse this offer at Oxford."

When Gardner Ackley begged Klein to change his mind, Klein replied: "Your letter is very kind and certainly makes me hesitate, yet I can't banish the feeling from my mind that there is a serious deficiency of academic freedom in the summation made by Niehuss. It isn't the risk or uncertainty of the situation that bothers me so much. . . . And it isn't any fear of Paton's actions. It is simply a feeling that it is wrong for the regents to pay heed to Paton. I don't put much value in tenure as such; I simply don't like the reasons for which it is withheld. . . .

"I shall miss Ann Arbor a lot . . . I am sorry to have proved to be such a nuisance and only hope that the fight for some basic principles was justified because of the nature of the issues at stake."

✢ ⁜ ✢

Many years later, in 1979, Gardner Ackley was interviewed for a history of the Economics Department. The interviewer was Marjorie Cahn Brazer, wife of the economist Harvey Brazer, who joined the Department in 1957.

Brazer already had interviewed William Paton, including questions about the Klein affair. In her conversation with Ackley, she said: "[Paton's] position is that it was not because [Klein] was a former Communist that he objected to the appointment, but rather the elevation to a high professorial rank with tenure of someone who had been only a lecturer . . . ."

"Well, that may be what he says," Ackley replied. "I don't believe it.

"There were two reasons he opposed it. One was the former Communism. The other was—I'm sorry to have to say this but I think it might as well get into this record . . . —was pure anti-Semitism. . . .

"One day . . . [Paton] came over to explain to me that this was all a plot by Sharfman and Haber and [Richard] Musgrave and [Wolfgang] Stolper . . . all the Jews he could think of in the Department . . . to solidify the Jewish control of the Department. And I ought to understand that and to recognize it for what it was, and that the Klein appointment was just part of that."

Ackley said he had all but thrown Paton out of his office and never had spoken to him again.

✛ ✚ ✛

Gardner Ackley spent several years as chair of the Economics Department, then joined President John F. Kennedy's Council of Economic Advisers. He served as chair of the council under President Lyndon Johnson from 1964 to 1968. He spent another year as U.S. ambassador to Italy before returning to the U-M faculty. He retired in 1984 and died in 1998.

After the Klein affair, William Paton had nothing more to do with the Economics Department. He retired from the faculty in 1959 after more than forty years of teaching and research. He remained active in academic accounting circles for many years, corresponding with hundreds of former students.

In 1976, the Business School named its new accounting building for him, acknowledging him as both a superb teacher and a founding member of his profession. He died in 1991 at the age of 101.

In 2004, over the objections of some alumni and Paton's descendants, the Paton Building was torn down to make way for the new Ross School of Business building. But to continue the recognition, the Ross School's new Center for Research in Accounting was named for Paton.

In the late 1980s, Marvin Niehuss, long retired, was interviewed by a student, Adam Kulakow, who made a documentary about the Red Scare at Michigan. Kulakow asked if Lawrence Klein had been forced out of Michigan on political grounds.

"I don't know," Niehuss replied. "I'm afraid so." Then he qualified his answer, saying Klein had chosen to leave "on grounds that he had been mistreated here. I don't think he did it on grounds that we didn't accept his politics. I don't think the department [of Economics] was a happy place for him to be. Of course he made a great name for himself, and he was making it here, if we could have kept him."

William Paton had once been Niehuss's teacher in the Business School. Later the two became faculty colleagues and friends. "He was one of our great teachers and a great person," Niehuss said, "but he was very inflexible on things of this sort. . . . He was a strong-minded conservative who said what he thought, and what he said about [Klein] was not correct."

Harlan Hatcher also was interviewed by Adam Kulakow. He wasn't asked about Klein, specifically, but his responses about Davis, Markert, and Nickerson reveal much about his view of the entire episode. "It's very difficult—I must emphasize that—to recreate the tensions which were produced in the society as a result of the confrontations with Russia following the war," he said. "Here you have a unique situation, in a period of cold war and of deep tensions, a period critical to the University's welfare—we were starved for money. . . . How were you going to build this institution unless you have the support and the confidence [of the public]?

"The McCarthy hysteria and the extremes to which they were going had become entirely apparent. They were very destructive, and the question was how to preserve the integrity of our institutions in the face of that threat . . . . The president . . . has got to be terribly aware at all points of a hundred different points of concern that affect the welfare of the institution . . . . You have a vision for the institution. You want it to serve. You want it to be preserved. It's a precious thing that you've created. You can't destroy it, and you can't allow it to be destroyed. You build it up over a hundred years; you're not going to kill it by some wayward act . . . .

"The issue is the rights of the individual versus the good of the institution. . . .

"I must say it was a most painful and difficult period."

Lawrence Klein's brush with McCarthyism made no headlines in Michigan, nor did it taint the rest of his career. After several more years at Oxford University, he moved back to the United States in 1958 to accept a full professorship with tenure at the Wharton School of the University of Pennsylvania. By common consensus, his life's work established a new paradigm in economics. He did more than anyone else to show how a statistical model could represent a nation's entire economy, and to use that model to predict the future.

In 1976, he was Governor Jimmy Carter's chief economic adviser during Carter's run for the presidency. After Carter was elected, Klein turned down Carter's invitation to chair the Council of Economic Advisers. He returned to his work at Penn.

In 1977, U-M awarded Klein an honorary degree, though with no public acknowledgment of how he had left the faculty in the 1950s.

Harold Shapiro, later president of U-M, then of Princeton University, was chair of the Economics Department when the degree was awarded. The honor to Klein, he recalled in an interview many years later, "to my knowledge was never thought of as a token for anything but his outstanding work . . . Nevertheless in the back of my mind I felt some satisfaction that here was one more piece of evidence that the University had put the earlier set of issues behind them."

In 1980, Klein was awarded the Nobel Prize in economics. The Nobel committee said: "Few, if any, research workers in the empirical field of economic science have had so many successors and such a large impact."

He retired in 1991 and died in 2013.

Ellen Schrecker, the Princeton historian whose book, *No Ivory Tower: McCarthyism and the Universities*, remains the definitive treatment of the subject, said Klein's departure from Michigan, unheralded as it may be, was "perhaps the most egregiously political denial of tenure" that occurred in the 1950s on any American campus.

9: The Warrior Scholar

One day when I was looking for something else at the Bentley Library, I came across the transcript of an oral-history interview with the law professor Yale Kamisar. At the start, he was asked about his life as a boy in the Bronx. I began to read and could not stop. Then I looked him up and learned that he was a transformative figure in his specialty. He had done more than any other legal scholar to change the laws that govern police procedure and the treatment of criminal suspects and defendants. (He made other major impacts on the law, but this was his best known.)

It occurred to me that Kamisar's career could be recounted as a case study in the effect that a single mind can have on a society. Many people—most people—have no idea what those called "scholars" actually do, nor why scholars at public universities have any claim on the largesse of taxpayers. I wanted readers to see what can happen when a mind like Kamisar's is given free rein for fifty years to think, write, and teach. I thought that even those who disapproved of his ideas would gain something by reading about a single truly devoted scholar.

It was years ago, late one Saturday night outside the Law Quad. A well-oiled crew of law students was sloshing home from the Pretzel Bell. By Hutchins Hall, they looked up at the dark facade. One office window showed a light. They knew whose it was.

They started to yell.

"Kamisar! *Kamisa-a-a-r!*"

They knew he wasn't up there. The guy just left his light on to make them think he worked harder than they did. Middle of the night on a weekend? No way. He was home in bed.

"*Hey, Kamisar, you_____, we know you're not up there!*"

They heard a noise overhead. The silhouette of a balding head appeared, round as a dinner plate. Then that voice, a mixture of the Bronx and the Army, high-pitched and hoarse.

"*Will you knock it off! Trying to get some work done here!*"

Yale Kamisar's ferocious defense of the underdog extended from law-review articles that influenced the Supreme Court to explosions at law students in Hutchins Hall classrooms: "We cannot trust the prosecutors or the police or anyone else!" he would roar. "That is why we have the Bill of Rights!" (*Bentley Historical Library*)

✛ ✛ ✛

The middle of another night in a ranch house on the east side of Ann Arbor. A boy, ten or eleven, out of bed.

"Dad . . . what are you doing? It's three o'clock in the morning."

"Working on an article."

"How much are you getting paid for it?"

"I'm not getting paid anything for it."

"Well, then, why are you doing it?"

He tried to explain it. If he wrote a good article, he said, maybe the Law School would give him a pay raise. And then maybe another law school would offer him a job. And then he could ask the Law School for a bigger raise.

But he knew that wasn't it. Put in a couple hundred hours on some law review article and wind up with maybe a thousand more a year? Compared to how much an hour if he were consulting? Not to mention if he were practicing law in Washington, DC, or New York?

"I don't know," he told his son finally. "You do something, you want to do it right. And once you get into something, it always involves more work. Far more work than you ever thought."

✛ ✛ ✛

What exactly is the public supposed to get when a state university hires young professors and, after a few years, gives them something close to lifetime job security and pays them a nice living to teach fewer classes than any high school teacher handles? What benefit, exactly, do "learned scholars" give back to the public for thirty or forty years on the payroll? And what does that mean, anyway—"learned"? How does that help anybody?

People have been asking the question since universities started, especially public universities like Michigan, with their claim on society's till. Along with the fond image of the absent-minded professor goes an image of the pointy-headed dreamer who doesn't have to work very hard. Where is the payoff to the public, the value added?

The answer is that the public is supposed to get a lifetime of work from somebody like Yale Kamisar.

✢ ✤ ✢

During World War II, the schools in the Bronx would have essay contests—topics like "Fire Prevention Week" or "What It Means to Me to Be an American." Kamisar would write four or five answers, put his name on the best one and turn it in, then give the others to his twin sister and her friends. He'd win the prize. They'd be runners-up.

His parents were Eastern European immigrants. His father finished the eighth grade and got a job selling supplies to bakeries. His mother finished high school but couldn't afford college.

One time her only son came home with a report card with three As and one C. She hit him—for the C.

Wait a minute, he said. The kid down the street got three Bs and a C, and he wasn't getting a beating.

His mother thought about it. She asked if he could honestly say the C was the best he could do. If he could say that, she said, she'd never lay a hand on him again.

No, he said. No, he couldn't say that. But he said he'd make sure he could say it from then on. And she never hit him again.

She was a difficult woman, he would say later. She liked to claim credit for his achievements. "He practiced law on me," she would tell friends. And in a way it was true, he said. "She was my first contact with injustice."

He disappeared into books. There was a book about a guy who talked so well he turned back a mob, and he remembered that. He was a talker himself. "Jeez, that kid can talk," people said. "He ought to be a lawyer." But he wanted to be a sportswriter.

He and his buddies would take a broomstick and a ball into the street and play stickball. A window would break and a neighbor would call the cops. When the cops came, they would chase the boys and shove them down on the pavement and act irritated, like it was beneath their dignity to have to police kids in the street.

At the High School of Music & Art on West 135th Street, as far as he was concerned, there were only two people in every classroom—the teacher and him. Every question the teacher asked, Yale Kamisar's hand would go up.

"Doesn't anybody else's parents pay taxes?" the teacher would say. "Only Kamisar's?"

Along with wanting to be a sportswriter, he thought he'd like to be an architect. But Pratt Institute in the city was only accepting World War II vets, so he went to New York University (NYU) on scholarship and took the subway from home every day. He joined ROTC to make spending money. He wrote a sports column for the student newspaper. But in those days New York dailies were merging and folding, so there was a surplus of experienced sportswriters.

He was too squeamish for medicine, didn't want to be a dentist or an engineer. So he decided to be a lawyer after all, like everybody in the family said he should.

He made Phi Beta Kappa in his junior year. He won the prize for being the best undergraduate in economics.

Then, in his senior year, NYU nominated him to compete for the Rhodes scholarships.

Final interviews for all the Rhodes nominees from New York City were held at a big Wall Street law firm where several lawyers were Rhodes alumni—men who had gone to Princeton and Harvard and Yale. Ivy League kids from Manhattan families came home from Princeton and Harvard and Yale to be interviewed. So there was Kamisar, the NYU kid with the kids from Princeton and Harvard and Yale. No attorney at that firm had gone to NYU, not in the 1930s and '40s, when NYU was still thought of as just a subway school. Kamisar didn't get picked as a Rhodes scholar. And he vowed he would go to an Ivy League law school if it killed him.

He was admitted to the law school at Yale, the hardest one of all to get into. A well-to-do aunt said she would help with the tuition. He made plans to room in a dormitory with the other guy from NYU who got into Yale.

One day his father took him aside. They didn't talk much. His mother was the talker. But on this day his father said, look, we're poor, and if you go to Yale, you're going to see how rich those kids are and you're going to be miserable. All the lawyers he knew were smooth, his father said, and he just didn't think his son could be smooth.

Well, he knew he wasn't smooth. But he thought maybe he was smart enough and that he could work hard enough to make up for not being smooth.

Then the law school at Columbia, the only Ivy League law school in his hometown of New York, offered him a scholarship.

Yale was eighty miles away in Connecticut. If he went to Columbia, he could live at home and save the room and board at Yale. And he wouldn't have to use his aunt's money, because the scholarship from Columbia would cover his tuition.

He wanted to go to Yale. He wanted to leave home, wanted to live in a dormitory like a regular college man.

Then one day the well-to-do aunt called his mother on the phone. Hold on a minute, his mother said, I'm putting chicken in the oven.

You can't afford chicken, the aunt said. Your son's about to go to law school.

His mother thought about that a second, then told his aunt she could keep the money for Yale.

So he stayed home and went to Columbia.

He spent one semester in law school. Then he had to go into the Army—his ROTC obligation. It was the time of the Korean War. He had graduated from Columbia as a second lieutenant. But before he got to Korea, when he was still stationed in the U.S., there was an incident. Not a big deal, really, but later he realized it was one of those things that nudges your life in a certain direction.

One of his jobs was to supervise the sergeants and corporals who gave bayonet training. One day there was a bayonet class, and a colonel came around and asked who was in charge.

Well, nobody was in charge. Kamisar wasn't there. He thought his superior officer, a career Army captain, was supposed to be there, and the captain thought Kamisar was supposed to be there. So neither of them was there.

It didn't matter. Neither he nor the captain did the actual training anyway. But this colonel was a stickler for the rules, and he wanted to know who had screwed up.

Kamisar and his captain talked about it. The captain asked Kamisar to take the blame, as a favor. Kamisar was just an ROTC guy, whereas the captain was career Army, and a black mark on the record of a career Army man could really hurt. So Kamisar said okay, sure, he'd take the blame.

But when the colonel wrote up Kamisar, the charge was going AWOL, "absent without leave," a far more serious offense than he had actually committed. So Kamisar wrote a pretty strong letter explaining precisely why the AWOL charge was wrong.

A day or two later, at the officers' mess, a new guy, a major, stopped by Kamisar's table. He said, let me tell you something as a friend. That letter you wrote made the colonel look bad and he's a little upset. You should have just confessed to the AWOL charge.

Then the major asked Kamisar how old he was. Kamisar said he was 21. Well, hell, the major said, when he was 21, he'd accidentally wrecked a tank in

France and had to pay the Army back—it took years. This was nothing compared to that—a small fine and a slap on the wrist. Why didn't Kamisar just write a new letter saying he was sorry and the whole thing would blow over?

So he said okay, he'd write the apology.

Then, as expected, he got a memo from the commanding general of the base, saying Kamisar was being fined for going AWOL. It was routine. But something at the bottom of the memo caught Kamisar's eye.

It was the name of that major, the one who had dropped by his table to give him the friendly advice, except here he was listed as the "investigating officer." And the memo said the "investigating officer" had advised Lieutenant Kamisar of his rights under the Uniform Code of Military Justice.

Kamisar went and found the major, said he was a little confused here, showed him the memo, said the major had never said anything about an investigation and certainly hadn't advised Kamisar of his rights under the Uniform Code of Military Justice.

Well, said, the major, he'd heard Lieutenant Kamisar was pretty smart, but evidently he wasn't. Didn't he realize a lieutenant's word was nothing against the word of a major?

Kamisar looked at him and said yes, indeed, he was just beginning to realize it right then.

Long afterward he said: "It was a trivial thing. What the hell did I care? I had no interest in the Army. But it's just the principle of the thing. I mean, it was just a flat-out lie."

He went to Korea, earned a Purple Heart in combat, then went back to Columbia to finish law school. Ten years would go by before he thought much about the incident with the major. By then he was making a name for himself as an expert on the law of criminal procedure—the rules about what police and prosecutors can and can't do when they arrest and interview suspects.

He was reading through the instruction manuals that tell police how to interrogate suspects, and one of the techniques they recommend is to act sympathetic to the suspect, to act like you're giving the suspect friendly advice. And then Kamisar remembered the major.

"I said, 'My God, that must have had an enormous impact on me.' It's so obvious."

Back in law school he looked for a summer research job. The only professor who needed help that summer—it was 1953—was a man named Herbert Wechsler. He was working on a big project in criminal law.

Now, in the major law schools, criminal law was considered second class. At Harvard the professors would even apologize for making the students learn it.

But Wechsler was no second-class figure. He'd been the chief adviser to the U.S. judges at the Nuremberg trials of Nazi war criminals. He had co-authored a massive casebook on criminal law at the age of 31. He would later argue and win one of the most important free-speech cases in Supreme Court history, *New York Times v. Sullivan.* And he had high standards for the work he wanted done. He once fired a research aide who went on to become director of the American Law Institute. Another one he fired became dean of law at Georgetown and head of the Federal Trade Commission.

Wechsler offered Kamisar the going wage, 75 cents an hour. Kamisar took it.

His research assignment was part of a ten-year project to write an entire penal code for the American Law Institute, which creates model statutes that are used throughout the U.S. and the world. Wechsler told Kamisar to research cases that shed light on the question of when it was permissible for police to use deadly force to prevent the escape of a felon.

He turned in his pay slips at the end of each week and, after a couple weeks, Wechsler called him in. Look, he said, you're asking to be paid for eighty hours a week. I can only pay you for the hours when you're actually working here at the law school.

Kamisar told Wechsler he was putting in fifteen hours a day six days a week—at the law school. Yeah, he went out for coffee or a cigarette now and then, but the work still came to at least eighty hours a week. Wechsler looked at him a minute and said okay. Kamisar went back to the stacks.

Finally, Kamisar turned in his research. It was thirty pages of text and sixty pages of footnotes.

Four hours later, Wechsler called him back into the office.

"I like it," he said.

That was it—"I like it." But the next summer, an old classmate of Wechsler's offered Kamisar a summer clerkship at Covington and Burling in Washington, DC, one of the most important law firms in the U.S. Again, he took it.

At the end of his last year in law school, Covington and Burling offered him a position as an associate in the firm, the first step toward a partnership. But, of course, they said, he'd want to take it easy for a few weeks after graduation. Come down later in the summer, they said. We'll see you then.

He had eight dollars. Total. He said if they didn't mind, he'd start right away.

He liked it at Covington and Burling. He worked mostly on corporate antitrust cases. It was complicated, interesting work that taught him a lot. But he worried about job security. Making partner had a lot to do with who your boss was. You're an associate for eight years, ten years, and what if your boss is out of favor the year you come up for partner? And he was working in obscurity. He might bust his hump on a case and his name wouldn't even be on the brief. How would anyone know how much he had done, how much he knew?

And there was never enough time to research a problem thoroughly and think it all the way through. Like the time he argued an appeal for a convicted drug user.

Big law firms often donate their lawyers' services to needy clients pro bono—"for the public good," free of charge. That's how Kamisar got this case.

Here's what happened. The junkie got arrested because the cops thought he was selling heroin, though they hadn't found any drugs on him. After the arrest, in the police station, the junkie pulled a cigarette pack out of his pocket and tossed it aside on the floor. A cop saw him do it, picked up the pack, and found heroin packets inside. *Hey, what's this*? So the junkie said, in effect: *That's it, you got me*—in other words, he confessed.

Kamisar got all these details and said hey, at the time of the arrest, the cops hadn't found the evidence yet. That meant the arrest was illegal, because you can't arrest somebody without sufficient evidence of a crime. And any evidence the cops found *after* an illegal arrest was "tainted"—inadmissible in court.

But what about the guy saying: *You got me*? That's an incriminating statement.

So Kamisar had to find out what the law said about that: Could the prosecutor use a self-incriminating statement that was made *after* an illegal arrest? He scrambled in the law library for a few hours and found out the precedents were against him. It turned out that confessions made after illegal arrests *had* been admitted before.

But the whole thing seemed so unfair to him. His client could barely read. The written confession the cops had taken from him looked like it had been scrawled by a second-grader. It made Kamisar so mad he got choked up.

So he made his argument anyway. If physical evidence gathered after an illegal arrest was tainted, he asked, why should an incriminating statement made after an illegal arrest be any different?

And sure enough, the prosecutors missed the precedents Kamisar had found, the junkie was let off, and that was that. Ring one bell for the Fourth Amendment's guarantee against unreasonable searches and seizures. Maybe the junkie had meant to sell the heroin, maybe not. But the Constitution protects everybody against a government that ignores the due process of law. So if you like your own right to due process, you stand up for a drug user's right to due process, too. At least that's how civil libertarians see it, and that was how Kamisar saw it.

Still, Kamisar knew that as a matter of law, the inconsistency between the tainted evidence and the tainted confession still stood. It didn't make sense. But what could he do about it? It would take months of research to argue his case as a general principle, and no working lawyer has time for that. He'd done his little pro bono stint and now he had to get back to work on regular cases.

But it bothered him. He'd sure love to have the time to run a thing like that to the ground.

Then one day he got a letter from a law school friend, Michael Sovern. Straight out of law school, Sovern had taken a job teaching law at the University of Minnesota. And just a couple years later, here was Sovern sending Kamisar a copy of his first article in a law review. Sovern was getting to be an expert in something and credited accordingly. Kamisar liked that idea—to know more about something important than anybody else.

Sovern said Kamisar should think about coming out to Minnesota. There was an opening on the law faculty. He applied for the job and got it.

❖ ⁜ ❖

Teaching and writing, that was the job now. He went to Minnesota hoping to teach antitrust. But no, that was taken. Criminal law? Okay, he'd worked for Wechsler, he could teach criminal law.

Writing .... what should he write about? An editor of the *Minnesota Law Review* said, hey, you're teaching criminal law, here's a book on criminal law to review. You just need to write a few pages; it's a good way to break into pub-lishing. He started to work on it and pretty soon it wasn't a book review—it was a seventy-page article, his first.

Then the dean asked him to help with a casebook on constitutional law. He wrote the chapters on criminal procedure—all about due process and the rights of the accused. It was police station law, nothing like corporate anti-trust issues or the First Amendment. Nobody even taught a whole course in criminal procedure back then, not at the big law schools.

But it was interesting.

He remembered the junkie in Washington, DC, and the tainted con-fession. Now he had the time to look into the thing. That was what he was supposed to be doing—taking a problem apart, reading everything about it, thinking it all the way through, and then telling people what it added up to.

After seven months of work he had an article: "Illegal Searches or Seizures and Contemporaneous Incriminating Statements: A Dialogue on a Neglected Area of Criminal Procedure." He argued that it made no sense to exclude tainted physical evidence but to allow a self-incriminating statement that was similarly tainted.

The article was published in 1961. Two years later, the U.S. Supreme Court handed down its decision in a case called *Wong Sun v. United States*. It dealt with a confession made after an illegal arrest. The Court said a tainted con-fession had to be tossed out. The opinion was written by Justice William Bren-nan, who noted that "verbal evidence which derives . . . from . . . an unautho-rized arrest . . . is no less the 'fruit' of official illegality than the more common tangible fruits of [an] unwarranted intrusion."

That was complicated language for the exact point Kamisar had grasped when he made his case for the drug user in Washington, DC.

Justice Brennan's passage had a footnote. It read: "See Kamisar, 'Illegal Searches or Seizures and Contemporaneous Incriminating Statements' . . . ."

That meant that with one article in a law review, Kamisar had helped to change constitutional law.

The same thing happened with another article on the so-called exclusion-ary rule, the rule that says prosecutors can't use evidence gathered in an ille-gal search.

Then another, this one having to do with whether a defendant with no money had a right to a court-appointed lawyer. Kamisar was doing research on this just as the Supreme Court was about to hear a case on the matter—a very big case.

The defendant in this case was one Clarence Earl Gideon, a penniless drifter in his early forties with a long record of petty crime. In 1961, in Panama City, Florida, a pool hall had been burglarized. A witness said he'd seen Clarence Gideon walk out of the pool hall just after the burglary had supposedly happened. The police arrested Gideon.

In front of a judge, Gideon said he was innocent. He also said he couldn't afford a lawyer and he wanted the court to appoint one—the Constitution said he was entitled to it. The judge said no, not according to the Supreme Court, which had ruled in 1942 that a state had to appoint an attorney for an indigent defendant only in "special circumstances," like if the defendant was mentally handicapped.

So, using prison stationery, Gideon hand-wrote a petition to the U.S. Supreme Court. And the justices agreed to consider it.

While Gideon's case was pending, Kamisar was putting together a bulldozer-like piece of research—77 pages with 368 footnotes, to be published in the *University of Chicago Law Review*. He had amassed evidence to show a sweeping movement among the states to appoint lawyers for poor defendants. And he demolished the notion that defendants who argued their own cases—many of them not just ill-prepared but illiterate—could get a fair trial.

The article was still in typescript when Kamisar air-mailed it to Gideon's newly appointed attorney in the Supreme Court, the Washington, DC, superstar Abe Fortas, soon to be named to the Supreme Court himself. Kamisar was cited by name in the oral arguments, and when the Court handed down its decision—9-0 in Gideon's favor—Kamisar's article was cited on the first page of the opinion. Gideon, in a second trial, was acquitted, and *Gideon v. Wainright* spawned the whole modern system of public defenders. (When Henry Fonda later played Gideon in the movie *Gideon's Trumpet*, "Professor Kamisar" even got a mention in the dialogue.)

Somebody told Kamisar the chief justice of Minnesota was saying they'd better pay attention to this young guy at the law school. It looked like he had a private line to the U.S. Supreme Court.

Other law schools came sniffing around—University of Chicago, University of Pennsylvania, Stanford. They asked him to come and teach for a semester or two. He said he wasn't interested.

Then Harvard called. Would he like to teach there next year as a visiting professor?

Kamisar knew it was their way of looking him over for a permanent offer. But again he said no, sorry, he couldn't do it—too many obligations at Minnesota.

A friend said: "Well, you can forget about Harvard now. They don't call a second time."

He did accept an invitation to teach summer school at the University of Michigan Law School. Then Harvard called a second time, after all. How about the year after next, they asked—would he be free then? He said he would.

But in Ann Arbor, Allan Smith, dean of the Law School, acted fast. He offered Kamisar a job—not as a visiting professor, as Harvard had, but as a permanent professor with tenure.

Smith played it tough. If Kamisar didn't want the job, Smith said he had to offer it to someone else, and he couldn't wait long. He gave Kamisar two weeks to think about it. Smith knew Harvard was flirting with Kamisar, he said, but he wasn't in the business of accommodating other law schools.

Dean Smith said later he had known exactly the game he was playing. Kamisar would see it as a case of Michigan in the hand versus Harvard in the bush. Smith bet he would take the bird in the hand, and he won the bet. Kamisar kept his promise to teach as a visitor at Harvard from 1964–1965. Then he moved his family to Ann Arbor. Nearly fifty years later, he would still be there.

In criminal procedure, every part of the process touches every other, and in 1963 and 1964, Kamisar was moving from search and seizure and the right to counsel to the law of confessions. He did some research and published a couple of articles. Then, during his year as a visiting professor at Harvard, a professor at Virginia called and said they were planning a conference to celebrate the 750th anniversary of the Magna Carta. Would Kamisar like to give a paper on confessions?

He decided to write a summary of his ideas, but with a harder edge than he had used in his scholarly articles.

What bothered him was the big difference between what happened in a courtroom, where there were lots of rules to protect a defendant's rights, and what happened to arrestees in the average police station, where detectives routinely manipulated confessions out of unwitting, lawyer-less prisoners. The Constitution was supposed to apply in both places. But in terms of justice, he thought to himself, they were as different as a penthouse and an outhouse. Not a bad title, he thought.

He showed a draft to one of the old professors at Harvard and asked him what he thought. Good work, the scholar said, but the analogy about penthouses and outhouses wasn't quite right. Call it: "Equal Justice in the Gatehouses and Mansions of American Criminal Procedure."

Kamisar didn't even know what a gatehouse was. He looked it up and realized the professor was right. It was a better analogy, and he used it.

The words of the article smoldered with the indignation of a kid who had been pushed around by bullies in uniform. He had always hated the ponderous prose of the law reviews. He wrote now like a tough, sarcastic sportswriter.

> The courtroom is a splendid place where defense attorneys bellow and strut and prosecuting attorneys are hemmed in at many turns. But what happens before an accused reaches the safety and enjoys the comfort of this veritable mansion? Ah, there's the rub. Typically, he must pass through a much less pretentious edifice, a police station with bare back rooms and locked doors. In this 'gatehouse' of American criminal procedure . . . the enemy of the state is . . . 'game' to be stalked and cornered. Here ideals are checked at the door, 'realities' faced, and the prestige of law enforcement is vindicated. Once he leaves the 'gatehouse' and enters the 'mansion'—if he ever gets there—the enemy of the state is repersonalized, even dignified, the public invited, and a stirring ceremony in honor of individual freedom from law enforcement celebrated.

If anyone doubted this account of the difference between a suspect's treatment in the police station and his treatment in court, Kamisar had proof. Remember, he had dug up those old manuals for police detectives, the ones that spelled out how to soften up, cajole, and trick suspects in custody into incriminating themselves—with no one to tell them they had the right to a lawyer or the right to keep their mouths entirely shut. The flouting of the right to due process was right there in those manuals, he argued. And most prosecutors and local judges were too close to the police, he said, too preoccupied with crime and guilt to remember the Bill of Rights and why it existed.

Somebody outside that tight circle had to make some new rules, and only the Supreme Court could do it.

In 1966, the Supreme Court handed down its decision in *Miranda v. Arizona*, the case of an accused rapist who had confessed to police without being told of his rights to counsel and against self-incrimination. The Court said that from now on, no suspect could be taken into custody and interrogated until the police had told them they had the right to a lawyer and that they had no legal obligation to tell the police anything at all. In other words, the Court said cops have to tell suspects they're protected by the Fifth Amendment's guarantee against self-incrimination and the Sixth Amendment's guarantee of the right to counsel.

In the majority opinion, Chief Justice Earl Warren cited Kamisar's "Equal Justice in the Gatehouses and Mansions" and wrote at length about the interrogation techniques prescribed in the police manuals.

The "Miranda warnings" became law. It was the crowning act in the Warren Court's revolution in criminal justice. When legal scholars spotted four footnotes to "Gatehouses" in the Court's majority opinion, said *Time* magazine, "they could well infer the impact of a zesty, gabby, witty Michigan law professor named Yale Kamisar. At 37, Kamisar has already produced a torrent of speech and endless writings that easily make him the most overpowering criminal-law scholar in the U.S."

In the law schools he was soon called the "Father of Miranda." Half a century later, he was still known by that name, and legal scholars still debate the arguments he first made in "Gatehouses and Mansions." Rereading the article long after its publication, former U-M Dean Francis Allen remarked: "The power of Yale's irony and outrage can be felt even after forty years."

Miranda became one of the most vilified decisions in Supreme Court history. It would handcuff the police, critics said. Criminals would run wild.

Kamisar set his feet on a long road. He would defend the Court's ruling on *Miranda* for forty years.

Article followed article: "A Dissent from the Miranda Dissents: Some Comments on the 'New' Fifth Amendment and the Old 'Voluntariness' Test" . . . "The Citizen On Trial: The New Confession Rules" . . . "Brewer v. Williams, Massiah and Miranda: What Is 'Interrogation'? When Does It Matter?"

Just as *Miranda* was upending the world of the police "gatehouse," it was wreaking change in the law schools as well, and Kamisar was at the center of it.

A couple years earlier, he had published a paperback casebook in criminal procedure—a set of materials for law students. Its sales were modest, since the law schools generally didn't teach stand-alone courses in that field. Once *Miranda* was handed down, the field went nuts. Every law school started offering courses in criminal procedure, and the casebook sold by the thousand, then more than ten thousand per year for many years.

Articles in law review were important. They might influence judges or even the Supreme Court. But the casebook, in a way, became even bigger, because with that, Kamisar and his co-authors, Jerold Israel of Michigan and Wayne LaFave of the Univerity of Illinois College of Law, were shaping a whole generation's understanding of the field. In the end, they (and new co-authors) would publish thirteen editions. Later, they figured out that in 45 years, something like 400,000 students used the casebook in its various editions.

Kamisar would co-author another casebook, too—*Constitutional Law: Cases, Comments and Questions*. Only eleven editions for that one.

❖ ⁝ ❖

To get anything done, Kamisar needed four or five hours at a stretch. Hard to do at the office with the phone ringing, students knocking, colleagues asking you to look over a draft. He'd go home, get dinner, and go back to work. He'd look up at the clock and it would be four or five in the morning and he'd be surprised. That was when he knew he was rolling. And he could still get in twenty hours on the weekend. Sometimes more.

One morning Kamisar came into the classroom and said he was sorry, he just didn't feel prepared to teach. He had been working on an article the night before. He thought he could finish it by two in the morning, then switch to preparing for class. But he didn't finish the article until four. Then he was too tired to prepare for class. He would reschedule the session, he said. Sorry, see you next time.

One of the students in the crowd was Jeffrey Lehman. He later became dean of the Michigan Law School, then president of Cornell University. He always remembered Kamisar refusing to teach that day because he wasn't ready. He could have faked it for an hour, Lehman said. Yale Kamisar? Are you kidding? He could get through an hour of class without being completely prepared. But he wouldn't do it.

Kamisar said once he never found writing to be fun. But some irritant would be at work inside his mind, and he had to respond. *Had* to. Later he ran across a line by George Orwell—"Writing a book is a horrible, exhausting struggle, like a long bout of some painful illness. One would never undertake such a thing if one were not driven on by some demon whom one can neither resist nor understand." Orwell said he would start to write "because there is some lie that I want to expose" or "some fact to which I want to draw attention." That was how it felt to Kamisar.

I n class he would start like a preacher, quiet. For a few minutes he'd stay behind his lectern. Then, as the meat of the day's material came to the fore, the pitch of his voice would start to rise and he'd be out in the aisle, advancing toward the front line of students opposing him.

A student named Eve Brensike (who later joined the U-M law faculty herself) remembered a day when Kamisar put a question about *Miranda* to an unlucky soul, one "Smith." When Smith struggled to get an answer out, Kamisar charged down the aisle, demanding to know what the legal scholar Fred E. Inbau of Northwestern University, Kamisar's great adversary in the national debate over police interrogation, had meant by the term "unhurried interview."

"By the time he had finished the question," Brensike remembered, "Kamisar was leaning in so close that Smith must have felt Kamisar's breath on his face. . . . Kamisar burst out the answer to his own question.

"'I'll tell you what he means! He wants to give the police free rein to interrogate! An interview suggests a certain amount of freedom. This isn't an interview! It's not a chat! These cops are out for blood!'

"Kamisar's face was fiery red at this point. His hand gesticulated wildly next to his head as he continued to rant, getting louder by the minute: 'We cannot trust the prosecutors or the police or anyone else! That is why we have the Bill of Rights!'

"He paused only long enough for the blood to start circulating to his face again. Then he leaned forward as though perched and ready for round two.

"'Okay,' he said. 'Back to you.'"

✛ ⁑ ✛

Prosecutors and their friends on law faculties wanted his scalp. In op-eds, law reviews, and conference speeches, they skewered him. But they respected him. Once, in the '70s, there was a big conference on criminal law at Duke University, and one of the speakers said the Warren Court's rules to protect the accused were hurting everybody, even the crooks themselves, because of a backlash against coddling criminals.

He said: "Yale Kamisar is the enemy."

The moderator of the panel stood up and said: "First of all, Yale Kamisar is not the enemy of anything except injustice."

His attacks on adversaries' arguments were "more than occasionally devastating," Justice Ruth Bader Ginsburg once wrote, but "his commentary never extends beyond the realm of the fair."

In the core of Kamisar's mind, there was some deep harmony between the Bill of Rights and his own experience of the world. He liked a line in a book called *The Price of Liberty* by a writer named Alan Barth, who said due process in criminal procedure had "two great values or objectives: the attainment of justice and the containment of power." The special job he had taken on—or that seemed to have been assigned to him by a long pattern of circumstance—was the containment of power.

One time he was working on a criminal justice project with a legal scholar named James Vorenberg, a Harvard professor who later became dean of Harvard Law. Vorenberg was not a conservative, but when they argued, it was often Vorenberg on the side of prosecutors and police, Kamisar on the side of the accused and the criminals. Over dinner one night, Vorenberg got talking. He said his family had owned a big department store in Boston, and his parents worried about kidnapping, so the police would come around to check on suspicious characters in the neighborhood and make sure the family was all right. Kamisar's memories were different. He thought about stickball and running when you saw a cop. And the difference was so obvious, he realized. Vorenberg saw the police as his friends, the good guys, the protectors. And Kamisar didn't. The ordinary individual in all his weakness and folly was not to be abandoned to the arbitrary exercise of power. The state wasn't supposed to hold all the cards.

"He believes it is self-evident," his colleague Francis Allen wrote, "that any nation aspiring to be a free society must provide limitations, clearly stated and conscientiously applied, to guide and limit the government's penal powers."

His very first article had dealt with euthanasia—"mercy killing." In the 1990s, with Jack Kevorkian, a renegade practitioner of assisted suicide, all over the news, Kamisar came back to the issue, and he startled all his old liberal allies.

He came out against assisted suicide—said it was a classic slippery slope.

And he plunged into a vast new scholarly enterprise far afield from his work on criminal procedure. Now he was no longer the avenging liberal, the favorite villain of the right. On the hot issue of assisted suicide, he became a powerful ally of conservatives.

"Physician Assisted Suicide: The Last Bridge to Active Voluntary Euthanasia" ... "The Reasons So Many People Support Physician-Assisted Suicide—and Why These Reasons Are Not Convincing" ... "On the Meaning and Impact of the Physician-Assisted Suicide Cases."

At the same time, *Miranda* and the exclusionary rule were under siege, and he fought for them, year after year.

"On the 'Fruits' of Miranda Violations, Coerced Confessions, and Compelled Testimony" ... "The Three Threats to Miranda" ... "Confessions, Search and Seizure and the Rehnquist Court."

In the late 1990s, the Supreme Court considered overturning *Miranda*. It was preparing to rule on the constitutionality of an old federal statute, enacted in 1968. The statute had been the work of conservative Southern senators striking back at the liberal Warren Court. Part of the statute supposedly "overruled" *Miranda*. It said confessions could be admitted into evidence even if defendants hadn't been "Mirandized." That part of the statute was reversed. But now, in a case called *Dickerson v. United States*, in which a defendant had appealed his conviction because police had not recited his rights under *Miranda*, the conservative Rehnquist Court was reconsidering it.

Kamisar went back to the *Congressional Record* to unearth examples of the scorn heaped on the Supreme Court by Southern reactionaries like Sen. Sam Ervin and Sen. John McClellan. His article wasn't cited, but the conservative Rehnquist court, ruling on Dickerson in 2000, upheld *Miranda*.

It was another victory, if an unsung one, possibly his most important. Quoting his old friend, Dean Francis Allen, he noted that there could be "no final victory" in the effort to safeguard due process and individual liberty. "Without further struggle, it withers and dies."

✣ ⁝ ✣

He would think about his mother. She outlived her husband by twenty years. Not an easy woman. But he owed her. He knew that. Most people couldn't say they'd always done their best. Not him. Not since that day with the report card.

"I learned that the hard way," he said once. "People don't do the best they can, and I think that's important. I can honestly say that I look at something I did and I can say, 'That's the best I could do.' Sometimes I say it's better than the best I can do. I reread something I wrote 20 years ago and say, 'Gee, how did I do that?' That's the amazing thing. You work on something so long that if you're doing it right, it looks like you just wrote it in one afternoon instead of seven months . . . You forget how painful it was."

His official retirement was in 2004. His colleagues wrote tributes. His foes wrote tributes. Students who had become public defenders, professors, deans, and university presidents wrote tributes. Francis Allen, the professor who had written Kamisar a fan letter for his first article on criminal procedure, dean at Michigan in the late '60s, pronounced Kamisar the "warrior scholar" of his generation.

At the retirement dinner, his colleague and old friend Ted St. Antoine, dean of the Law School from 1971 to 1978, stood up. There was no point in envying Kamisar for the work he had done and the impact he had made on the country, St. Antoine said. It would be like envying a hurricane for its power.

You might think Kamisar had been wrong his whole career, that he'd protected the criminals at the expense of the law-abiding, or that he'd hurt the cause of assisted suicide. But you couldn't say he'd done something less than his best. You couldn't say he had done less than a learned scholar could do in the service of what he believed.

He once quoted another scholar who said the law schools must steer toward an "indefinable fundamental"—the necessity of "confront[ing] the most explosive problems with which law may deal, facing all the facts and plumbing all the issues to their full depth without fear or prejudice." Each teacher of law, he said, "should joyfully accept with [Oliver Wendell] Holmes the challenge that in his work he may 'wreak himself upon life, may drink the bitter cup of heroism, may wear his heart out after the unattainable.'"

That was what the public was supposed to get for its money.

For several years after retiring from the Law School, he split his time between Michigan and California, where he took a post at the University of San Diego School of Law. In 2011, he retired from San Diego and came back to live in Ann Arbor year-round.

Every day he went to a new office high up in the stacks of the Legal Research Building. He worked on new articles and speeches and the annual supplements to *Modern Criminal Procedure.* The desk where his papers were spread was not far from his first office, the one where he opened the window in the middle of the night to shoo along a few rowdy law students. But now he generally went home in time for dinner, and he got to bed by ten or eleven.

III. A WOMAN'S PROPER SPHERE

When I was learning to read and write, I liked to pick out words on my mom's typewriter. It was a glossy-black Remington portable with a double ribbon, half-black, half-red. I liked the *chunk* of the keys and the *sizz-ding* of the carriage return. She wrote nothing more than an occasional letter to the editor. But I knew the typewriter to be the object of her particular admiration. I learned why only years later. She told me her beloved father had given it to her in the fall of 1937, when she left home for her freshman year at the University of Michigan.

She majored in French. She joined Kappa Kappa Gamma. She took courses that shaped and sharpened her reverence for literature, language, and the visual arts. She met my father, graduated, married. She waited for him to come home from World War II. She waited for him to finish law school. Then she raised three children. "I believe it's a woman's world," she would say, but she never worked outside our home. She detested the words *homemaker* and *housewife*, but no one ever coined a proper term for the hard work she did.

Now, years after her death, I think of her chiefly as a reader. She adored books and the act of reading, and she made voracious readers out of her children. One of my earliest memories is the feeling I would get—a comfortable glow spawned by soft bedtime light and emotional absorption—as I listened to her read from Frances Hodgson Burnett's *The Secret Garden* and *Racketty-Packetty House*. Her literary idol was the *New Yorker* essayist and children's author E.B. White—a devotion she passed on to me. In retirement, she and my dad once went up to Maine and tried to find White's saltwater farm. She thought she saw him out for a walk and later wrote him to ask if she had, indeed, spotted her man. White replied crisply: "You said he was 'a nice-looking gentleman' and that 'he smiled and waved.' Doesn't sound like me. Thanks for the inquiry, anyway." That sheet of stationery is framed on my wall.

Did she ever think to use the typewriter to try stories of her own? She never said so, and I don't think so. She wrote well. But she would have thought the act of creation beyond her powers. The typewriter's meaning was only symbolic. It represented the power of the word, but she never thought to take up that power and wield it herself.

As I think about it now, I see a possibility. Maybe my own aspiration to write for a living, born at the keyboard of the glossy-black Remington, came about because I adopted my mom's own sense of the finest thing a person could be—a writer. She had developed that sense at Michigan. But Michigan never encouraged her to grasp it as her own ambition. She could only convey it to a son.

10: "Our Brilliant Miss Sheldon"

When I began to write about the University's history, I looked to the beginnings of women's education in the 1870s as an obvious topic. Then I stumbled on Mary Downing Sheldon—"our brilliant Miss Sheldon," a friend called her. At Smith College I found Mary's voluminous personal papers, and I could soon see that she was a perfect representative of the first wave of American feminism and of the earliest women collegians. Few Michigan students of any era or either gender have left such a rich record of their time as a student. She offered the chance to step into another age.

On her 21st birthday, September 15, 1871, a drizzly day in upstate New York, Mary Downing Sheldon boarded the train in her hometown of Oswego, secured her luggage, and settled into her seat. The locomotive hitched forward, then gathered speed, and soon the view from her window shifted from the swamp maple and sumac of Lake Ontario's shoreline to the long salt sheds outside Syracuse. After weeks of preparation, she was on her way.

"I Start For the New Life—the long wished-for university," she wrote in her diary. "University! What visions has that word not always brought to mind, of learned professors, of new and charming knowledges, of antique buildings crowned with historic associations . . . .

"I watched the gray flying landscape through the dark night; and 'college' sounded clear through all, even when we crossed the suspension bridge [at Niagara] over the far, deep chasm."

"The day was rainy and dark," she recalled later, "but could not quench in its gray mists the joys of that great adventure." When the night came, she opened the window to let the wind blow in her face.

By her own description she was short and "well-knit" (131 pounds, she told her mother), with large blue eyes and thick, dark-brown hair. The oldest of four children, she was an idealist with a practical streak, a shrewd judge of character who nonetheless could be swept away by people she admired. Her mother was a learned woman who had raised her on books and explorations of the woods and fields. Her father was a progressive educator who was urging Mary toward a writer's life.

Classical studies and the realm of nature and science fascinated her equally. One of her earliest memories was of her mother holding her at the window at night, pointing to the dark sky and saying: "The stars are all worlds, are all suns, like our world, our sun." Mary recalled an instantaneous and "infinite longing to know the bright worlds, every one," and an awakening to "the energy and joy" of an engaged mind. To devote her time wholly to reading, thought, and discussion with learned scholars was no less than her idea of bliss.

After high school, she had taught for two years at her father's teacher-training academy, the State Normal and Preparatory School (forerunner of the State University of New York–Oswego). She yearned for further study and made plans to take a degree in Germany. But after an exchange of letters across the Atlantic, she was told that "Germany, like Yale and Harvard, was not yet ready for a woman."

At home in Oswego, New York, in 1871, Mary Sheldon caught sight of a magazine advertisement inviting women to apply to the University of Michigan. "I remember the very look of the page," she wrote later. "I knew in a moment that my hour had come." (*Bentley Historical Library*)

Then one day she opened a copy of *The Independent*, a popular magazine, to find a headline: "College Career for Women."

"I remember the very look of the page," she wrote later, "the very place and length of the article. It gave an account of Michigan University, which had just been opened to women, and which was fast-approaching its present high rank. I knew in a moment that my hour had come."

✢ ⸭ ✢

Pressure to open the University of Michigan to women had begun to build twenty years earlier, in the decade before the Civil War. But the vision of Henry Philip Tappan, U-M's first president and in most ways its founding figure, had emphatically not included co-education. Like many men on elite college faculties, he believed women possessed neither the intellect nor the physical stamina required for advanced study. The natural order predestined girls for motherhood and housekeeping, so what would be the point? Women seeking equal rights would "fail to become men," Tappan wrote to a friend. "They will be something mongrel, hermaphroditic," while men would be "demasculated. ... When we attempt to disturb God's order we produce monstrosities."

But the imperious Tappan, never broadly popular in the state, was pressured to resign in 1863, and some in the faculty began to rethink the case for women. "The present age is ... narrowing female privileges to a more fearful extent than any other since medieval times," wrote Alexander Winchell, an influential professor. "I have long been growing into the conviction that we are consenting to a wrong."

The Michigan legislature declared that "the high objects for which the University of Michigan was organized will never be fully attained until women are admitted to all its rights and privileges." Still the University resisted. Then, in early 1870, a new crop of Regents and a new president, James Burrill Angell, agreed it was time to try what some called "the dangerous experiment" of co-education.

That February, the daughter of a college professor, Madelon Stockwell, became the first woman officially enrolled, and the University published notices inviting more young women to apply. Thirty-four of them, Mary Sheldon among them, enrolled in the fall of 1871—34 women in a student body of 1,021.

Mary's dream of a classic academic grove in the West deflated as soon as her carriage left the Ann Arbor depot and climbed the steep slope of North State Street. She saw a pleasant but commonplace town—"hack drivers, ordinary people ... here a livery stable, there a mill. As we drive along, it seems strange that all things look so common on such a very uncommon morning." But she liked her first glimpse of the University itself, then thirty years old, the "quiet-colored, plain, large buildings in the wide and level campus, their square outlines softened or concealed by tall and richly-growing trees." On State Street she could see construction under way at the site of University Hall, the great domed classroom building that soon would dominate the campus.

At the corner of Division and Jefferson she found her boarding house—a roomy place with a yard for croquet—and met her landlady, Mrs. Dennis, and her new housemates, four men and three women, all students. In her "two neat little rooms . . . with sky-ey views" she quickly felt "a wonderful sense of house-holding." To keep her little library, she bought three black walnut bookshelves for $1.50 and hung them from the ceiling with scarlet cord. On the walls, she tacked favorite old drawings of Mother Goose rhymes from home. "I am very happy," she wrote her parents, with "only a little touch of homesickness."

She took quickly to her roommate, Isabel Perry. She found Mrs. Dennis's cooking "perfect." "Everyone seems to like me, and I am sure I like everyone and everything . . . I believe I was born happy."

But Mary's frothy good nature was to be tested in Ann Arbor. In her early schooling she had been a star. And she wanted more than anything else to prove her prowess as a scholar and writer in a renowned university. But for all her ambition, she harbored a nagging, silent doubt: Could women really compete with men in the pursuit of higher learning?

"I never said it," she admitted to her mother several years later, but "when I came [to Ann Arbor] I had but little faith in women's power intellectually," and she disapproved of "radical" women who "had none of that respectful belief in masculine superiority which I thought every woman should have."

Now she was a specimen in the experiment of co-education.

✤ ⁂ ✤

The campus was a domain of males, from the faculty's gray patriarchs to the condescending young professors fresh from the Ivy League to the braying freshmen barely out of adolescence. Male ritual and male decorum, or lack thereof, predominated. On the first day of class, Mary and the other newcomers opened the doors of the chapel hall to be greeted by a prolonged roar of throaty noise. It was the "Yell" that greeted entering students every fall—no gentlemanly exception for the ladies—with apple cores flying back and forth above the crowd, breaking windows and a framed portrait of Washington. When the professors filed in, "the wild confusion grew still wilder," Mary wrote, "and they stamped and clapped and yelled and hissed and transformed themselves into a whole wild menagerie."

The women were under close scrutiny. People literally stared—Ann Arborites on the street, professors at their lecterns, male students in the corridors. In class one day, Mary glanced to her side and was astonished to see two young men in the yard outside, their faces pressed to the window, apparently just to catch a glimpse of women actually sitting in a university classroom.

The women students were eyeing each other, too, on the lookout for any-one who might undermine co-education by a show of low standards, aca-demic or otherwise.

"Their standard is high and they are very watchful," Mary told her parents, "not only of their own actions and standing, but also that of others. If any girl comes below that standard, she is talked to and pleaded with . . . until she does better or leaves." One "co-ed" who had become engaged was frowned upon, and even one who became ill caused consternation, "because people will say, you know, that we break down under hard study—and on and on . . . ."

Gradually, she became accustomed to the rowdies around her. One day she would half-enjoy "their wild savagery"; the next she would feel "perfectly sick" of living among "so many masculines."

Boys would be boys, she knew. More important was the question of how the faculty would deal with women students, especially those professors who had fought the admission of women.

One of these was Edward Olney, Mary's professor in mathematics, her least favorite subject. In one of the first meetings of the class, she misplaced a decimal point on the blackboard, and Olney cracked a joke about it that made all the men in the room laugh.

Distinction was the best revenge. Mary's early performance raised pro-fessors' eyebrows. When placement exams were given, she scored extremely well in every subject but Greek. Even Olney took notice. When she handed in her placement exam in mathematics, he skimmed it and gave an approving grunt. As she left the room, she heard him mumble, "Humph . . . pretty good habits of thought."

President Angell himself told her the news: "I guess there is no doubt, Miss Sheldon, from all that I hear, but that you will go into Sophomore." She had placed out of an entire year.

"That made me happy and touched me too," she told her sister, "so that I went away with tears in my eyes. Not brought there by Prof. Olney and the staring young college boys, you 'bet.'"

Within weeks, she made an outright fan of Olney, who proved a better gentleman than he had seemed at first. One day he conceded she must have "had splendid training somewhere" and even that he "wished they had a thousand such."

It was the students who clung to all-male dogma.

One morning at chapel, all students were invited to attend meetings of the literary clubs that met every Friday evening. But when several women, including Mary, appeared at the inaugural meeting of the Adelphi Society, the most prestigious of the groups, they were treated to a mournful address by the Adelphi's student president. He voiced deep doubts about the propriety of women attending meetings and sniffed that there were few enough men, let alone women, who spoke and wrote well enough to take part. Mary claimed to find his remarks "very funny," and as a group, the women decided the Adelphi held no further attraction for them.

Mary's father, Edward Austin Sheldon, was deeply interested in questions of educational policy. When he asked Mary her opinion of co-education, she replied that there were simply too few women on campus to give any settled judgment. Michigan remained essentially a men's college with a mere sprinkling of women, she said. A kind of embarrassment seemed to have come over the men. Many kept their distance from the college women. The women simply went about their business. Those brave enough to enroll in that first year of co-education were hardly there to have fun.

"The students are very gentlemanly, but let us severely alone," Mary wrote her father. "It is a matter of great surprise to me if I see a lady and gentleman student talking together. There are no rules whatever in regard to the matter, of course, but the utmost coolness, consistent with the fact that we attend the same classes, exists. And yet there is no ill-feeling between ladies and gentlemen . . . The young ladies, especially, seem to think that they are here to learn . . .

"The [male] students seem ashamed of being seen in ladies' company at all and generally go off by themselves . . . College is the very last place where a young lady would go to receive attention from gentlemen.

"My theoretical opinion is the same now as ever, that ladies and gentlemen should be educated together."

✢ ✢ ✢

" I wish there were not so many boys here," she told her sister Lizzie. "I feel very much out of place. . . . But do not think that I am a victim and a martyr. For I am not. I have precisely what I want. I am in a University and have a chance to see it all from the inside."

She fell into a comfortable routine. On a typical day of classes she would rise early, bathe, breakfast, and study for an hour before the quick walk to campus for morning chapel in South Hall (about where the south wing of Angell Hall stands now). Here President Angell led a prayer, made announcements, and led the students in a hymn ("splendid with so many male voices"). She hurried home to study for the rest of the morning, then read Greek with her stern and serious housemate Sarah Hamlin. Classes were in the afternoon—Greek, Horace, mathematics, geography, and history, depending on the day. Then more study until tea, followed by an errand or two, and in the evening, more study, calls on professors and their wives at home, or a church "sociable," or a meeting of the little Shakespeare society that she and some new friends had formed. ("I am secretary as usual.") They would read aloud for an hour, then play "Proverbs" or "Twenty Questions" until time for bed.

"You do not know how happy I am," she rejoiced in one of her weekly letters to her close friend at home, Mary Alling. "I spend my days in a perpetual comparison of the adjective 'happy.'" All through her early months at Michigan, she was astonished and enchanted to find herself in a setting that seemed so perfectly suited to her gifts and ambitions. Ann Arbor, she wrote, was "Home of the Blest."

At first Mary was not much impressed by the teaching she encountered at Michigan. At her father's academy in Oswego, she had been raised on the progressive educational ideas of Johann Heinrich Pestalozzi, a Swiss reformer who urged the teaching of "children, not subjects." She had been taught to dig for the roots of academic problems and arrive at answers on her own. Now, too often, she ran into the old-fashioned reliance on memorization and drill—"slave work," she called it. She nearly laughed out loud one day when her young tutor in Greek presented the grammar lesson and urged his charges to "learn it just as though you were parrots"—precisely the jibe she had often heard Pestalozzians level at rote learning. "I almost feel as though I were losing the power to think the way I used to . . . For the first time in my life I hate study."

But that passed. If her Greek professor was a dry bore, Mary soon discovered wonderfully alive minds on the faculty, too. For a time she was fascinated by Professor Benjamin Franklin Cocker, a Christian philosopher whom she called, only half-laughingly, her "high priest and interpreter of the Universe." But the professor who made the deepest impression was Moses Coit Tyler.

During his dozen years at Michigan, Tyler was a professor of English who blazed trails in the study of literature in its historical and political contexts.

Later, he would join the history faculty at Cornell and help to found the American Historical Association. Mary attended his lectures and soon pronounced him "a Pestalozzian in spirit"—high praise—and began to ask his advice. Evidently she made an impression on him, too. "He advises me to read Shaw's *Manual of English Literature*" she wrote her father. "You have it at home, I am quite sure, and I would like to have it sent to me. Prof. Tyler is very kind and told me to talk to him freely and ask advice at any time."

Before long, it was a case of hero worship: "Prof. Tyler is a perfect inspiration. I never can be too thankful that I have had the privilege of learning from such a man. The happiest hour of all the day is when four o'clock comes and I climb the four flights of stairs to the room where the western sun shines in over dingy walls, and when the master, with his fine face and sympathetic heart, teaches us the grace, the power, the fine artistic use of words in language which is unrhymed and unmeasured poetry. He is . . . an ideal *gentleman* as well as a noble *man* . . . His ready wit, his fine art of speaking, his clear but poetical language, his original thought and independence of authority save that of his own ideas and researches, render his lectures almost too good to be appreciated by sophomores. He treats us as equals."

But in the spring of 1872, she was beginning to think that, despite her father's hopes, she did not want to follow Professor Tyler into the study of literature. She was hatching a new scheme.

✛ ⸭ ✛

Mary loved to take long walks into the countryside, often with her friend Ruth Hull, a medical student. They would wander "in among pumpkin-piles and apple-orchards and cornstalks and working men and rail fences and nut trees . . . I am continually coming upon some new and beautiful place around this charming Ann Arbor."

On one such hike near the end of her first year, she sat alone on a hill above the Huron River, thinking. Signs of spring surrounded her—the air softening; the river shed of its winter ice; birds and insects stirring in the green canopies overhead—so much more enchanting than the tedious discipline of studying subjects she did not care about.

"Bah! What a juggernaut do people make of discipline," she wrote Mary Alling that night. "How many of us, for instance, here at this university, are maiming or numbing our best faculties and slaying the art or science that we love with the deepest love of our mental natures for the sake of discipline? That is all wrong. Every one of us has some special work to do, and the preparation for that work and the work itself bring all needful discipline . . . Don't misunderstand me. In mental exercise I do believe, but not in mental torture."

The "deepest love" of her own "mental nature," she had begun to think, was the natural world, and she was forming an image of herself as a kind of teaching naturalist. "I am thinking," she told her friend, "of a sun-browned, well-knit red-cheeked woman studying, through the microscope, with clear eye and brain, the life and structure of sea animals which she herself has just obtained from the brine. She's better-looking and stronger-looking than I, but isn't very different in other ways. She has devoted herself, body brain and soul to the interpretation of nature." In this role, she might "open a new path for women," drawing on "my equal talent for scientific study, for writing, for teaching, for artist's work." It would be a happy, healthy life, she thought, and the more people she could encourage toward a love of nature, "the more healthy, happy, natural people will there be in the world."

It was tantalizing to think about doing such work as a woman. "I feel within me such strength to battle people's prejudices and be free as my thoughts." Were it not for a sense of obligation to her friends and her parents, she said, "I should long ago, almost penniless though I might be, have started to explore the wide world in manly disguise or committed some other wild deed, to which my aboriginal, first nature prompts me."

It was "not a fleeting plan." For weeks, she couldn't "get it off my mind that I was made for it." In the evenings, she was plunging into debates over Darwin's theory of evolution with her housemates, and "believ[ing] it just enough to defend it." Soon she informed her parents that she meant to study zoology. Earlier generations had done "the world's work in Philosophy and Art," she said. "Science is reserved for us. The spirit of the age has seized me." The world was filled with mediocre books, and there were plenty of teachers. But in science she might break new ground.

This new ambition was her parents' own doing, she told them fondly. "You have brought me up in a republic of beasts and birds and creeping things. And I love them—love them with a love so intense that I am capable of giving up my whole life to them devotedly. . . . Whatever power I have of writing, whatever appreciation I have for the beautiful, whatever artistic skill I may possess, whatever of the teacher's influence I may acquire, would all be worthily and usefully bestowed upon this."

But her shift from arts and letters to science was not to be as simple as an epiphany by the river. For Mary, as for other budding biologists, it turned out to be one thing to love "the republic of beasts" at a slight remove and another to deal with their working parts in the lab.

Her enthusiasm stayed high all that summer and into the fall. She girded herself for a course in dissection. Then, in November 1872, she was invited to see a lecture by Dr. Corydon Ford, professor of anatomy and physiology. The lesson: The human viscera as seen in a dissected cadaver.

Mary brought two female friends with her. Before the presentation, Dr. Ford—"a grandly built man with a clear, kindly, searching blue eye"—beckoned to the women for a word. He wanted to give them an idea of what he was about to do.

"So we followed him," Mary wrote to Mary Alling a few days later, "and not until today have I in the least recovered from the horror of the next few minutes. Remember, dear, that I never saw in all my life but one corpse and that of a beautiful boy with a white rose in his hands. . . . I went into the lecture room . . . and sat down. The body had already been brought in covered, of course. The gentlemen kept coming in, literary boys who knew me very well. No other ladies came. I sat in my seat and finally when the Doctor came in with his great checked apron on and his dissecting instruments, I could not stand it and said 'we must not stay' and beat an ignominious and shameful retreat . . .

"I kept saying to myself, 'pretty scientist you are, to run away from a dissection by one of the finest anatomists in the world . . . .'"

A friend advised her to face her fear by taking a course that would force her to do dissections, but she said, "I shrink from it as I never shrank from anything before."

She stayed with science a while longer. But she gave up "beasts and birds and creeping things" in favor of physics, chemistry, mineralogy, and botany.

++ ‡ ++

One morning that fall, there was an announcement: All women students were invited to meet at 4 pm in the old chapel.

"What are those girls going to do now?" a few of the men asked—then added "some brilliant conjectures," one of the women scoffed.

Several women wanted a chance to know each other better. "Each class ... was interested in its own work," one of them recalled, "and with most of us, our work took all our time and thought. We learned each other by sight in chapel, but there was no crowded waiting room, no chance for introductions. Our acquaintance was limited to those few whom we met every day in recitation and even this acquaintance was slight. Surely it was time for us to be something more than so many disconnected human machines."

They met that afternoon but couldn't settle on a plan. Then, after the meeting adjourned, "some of the more zealous ones remained in the room and our brilliant little friend, Miss Sheldon of '74, moved that we ought to 'be something.'" The motion carried unanimously.

The club they formed became known as the Quadrantic Circle. It was the first women's organization at Michigan, forerunner of the Michigan League and the sororities. Members included Alice Freeman, who would become one of Michigan's most distinguished alumnae, the first woman president of a nationally known college (Wellesley); Olive San Louie Anderson, who would publish a novel based on her experiences at Michigan, *An American Girl and Her Four Years in a Boys' College*; Mary's first-year study partner, Sarah Dix Hamlin, who would found an important girls' preparatory school in San Francisco; and Laura Rogers White, whom Mary called "the finest mathematician in college."

Laura White had followed her older brother to U-M from Kentucky just to take a few courses. Well over six feet tall, she had been saddled with a dreadful nickname—"Alba Longa," after a Greek isle. President Angell had recognized her brilliance in mathematics, and Mary had persuaded her to pursue a diploma. She became the first woman to earn a Bachelor of Science degree from Michigan.

College life, then as now, forged friendships out of students with divergent backgrounds and clashing values. Mary was the daughter of a Yankee intellectual; Laura White the daughter of a Kentucky hill farmer. But the larger difference between them was religious, and it caused Mary pain.

"There is a great deal of interest here in religious questions," Mary wrote home, "and the deepest things are brought out boldly and discussed openly."

Mary, brought up as a firm Presbyterian believer, found her childhood faith challenged by these discussions, and she came to think it "dangerous" for parents and preachers to "conceal the real difficulties of our creeds," such as the inerrancy of the Bible. Yet she held fast to foundational Christian doctrine, and she was shocked to learn that Laura White believed in "a bad

God who . . . delights in Creation as a mere amusement"; that "there was no improvement in the human race" and "no praise or blame to be attached to any deed . . . I can't bear to think of her state of mind following such horrible beliefs . . . I have talked with her but one can do nothing with one who denies moral responsibility and the goodness of God."

On some days she could scarcely believe that her best college friend was "a rank infidel," another housemate "a regular scoffer," and "all the gentlemen at [my] table perfectly willing to joke on very sacred subjects."

But of course her world was being enlarged by these clashes of belief and background. It was enlarged, too, by friendships with men.

In those days before men's and women's dormitories, it was not at all unusual for male and female students to share a boarding house, and Mary became close to several male housemates, especially a Cuban, Mr. d'Aubique, "just the light of the house, so merry and cheerful is he," and Mr. Mills, whom she came to think of as "just the same as a brother." By her senior year, she commanded two or three "dear little innocent freshmen" who ran her errands and thanked her for the privilege.

As for romance, Mary had her share of invitations to "sociables" and sleigh rides. She accepted happily, and at least once she pronounced herself drunk at a party. She indulged in a few deliberate flirtations, but only for fun. By the middle of her second year, she had sworn off matrimony altogether.

The evidence is scattered in fragments through Mary's college letters and journals, but it appears she nourished a deep-seated and unrequited love for one man for a long time. It's not clear whether he lived in Ann Arbor or at home in New York, and she never referred to him by name in writing, even to her closest friend, Mary Alling, saying only that "it will be impossible for me to care for any man except _____."

But this attachment warred with another impulse, just as strong, toward an independent life as a woman working for the good of other women.

A century and a half later, we tend to associate early feminism with the voting-rights campaigns of the early 20th century. But currents of feminism were moving in the U.S. long before that, and they played a powerful role in Mary's years in Ann Arbor.

She listened, fascinated, to feminist sermons from her second landlady, a formidable woman named Foster, who lectured "her girls" on "the slavery of women to the lust and drunkenness of men, on the power of the ballot and education, especially the former, to free them, and on the millennial epoch when man and woman, husband and wife, should be *one* in counsel, *one* in action, and *one* in love." (When one of Mary's housemates, a young married woman, asked Mrs. Foster whether a wife couldn't persuade her husband to reform himself, Foster replied: "Persuade him? Persuade that stove!")

Mary had long talks with the women considered the most radical on campus, "strong, free women," most of them medical students, and became friends with two of them, Clara Armstrong and a Miss Lee. For a time, their zeal intimidated her: "Although I admire their strength and freedom with all my heart, yet I cannot pray for it without fear and trembling. It seems to me that life is not so beautiful to them and through them as it ought to be." But in the fall of her second year Mary was following their example, resolving to forgo marriage in favor of full-time devotion to her chosen work, whatever that might turn out to be.

"When I resolved to become a scientist," she wrote her parents in the fall of her second year at Michigan, "I had little idea where it might lead me or what other resolves must follow it surely." Now, she said, "I am resolved not to marry at all. I know right well that, if I should marry, I should devote myself fully to making a model home and to exerting the widest possible influence in the homes of other women. Although I could do this, yet I felt as if God had fitted me by nature and education for a different work; and that work must not be half-way done but I must devote my whole mind and soul to it, or not at all."

She knew such talk sounded melodramatic. But her commitment to put her work first and her "fierce devotion to my own sex" only deepened and matured over the next two years.

A critical moment came when she heard a horrifying report of a woman whose surgery was botched by a male physician who apparently misunderstood the nature of the case. "I see now that there are deeper reasons why women should be in the professions than that it is their preference," she wrote. "There is a stern necessity, for the good of humanity, that women should be able to meet injustice, cruelty, bestiality and falsehood, not only on the ground of humility, simplicity and purity, but that, not losing these powers, she should also meet them from the standpoint of knowledge, sagacity and power."

She was now "in rapport with some of the strongest, most radical and earnest women here," she told her mother. This was when she admitted that upon coming to Michigan, she had held secret doubts about women's intellectual equality with men. "But now everything is changed . . . I have come to believe that everywhere our *ability*, other things being equal, is equal to that of man. College education alone has given men an immense intellectual advantage over us. The culture and discipline of business has given him a still greater one. But we will soon stand on equal ground and give man that intelligent love and trust which he has rarely known . . . ."

As commencement approached in the spring of 1874, she was overcoming any lingering "fear and trembling" about devoting herself to the advancement of her sex. Her father hoped she would return to his Oswego Normal school to teach young women, and she embraced a plan to do so for two years, then take advanced training in science. "I am thankful that at last I see a way clear to doing some actual good," she wrote Mary Alling. "Just now, I could do no better nor find a larger field of work than in our Normal [school]."

"I no longer feel so deeply the need of love. My soul's motherhood shall be satisfied by the dear girls God will give me strength to save."

In her last days at the University, she wrote, "I cannot think of it without tears . . . Now that I am leaving it, I realize fully how much I have loved it all, the very campus ground is dear, the college walls and walks are well-beloved friends; all things are glorified in the near farewell."

On June 24, 1874, Michigan's 30th annual commencement, President Angell handed Mary her diploma.

Sarah Dix Hamlin, Mary's first-year housemate and study partner, taught at a high school in Detroit and a mining camp in Nevada before helping to found a school for child widows in India. In 1896 she took charge of what became the Hamlin School in San Francisco. As its leader for nearly thirty years, she built it into a leading independent academy for girls.

Early in her medical career, Mary's friend Ruth Hull suffered a nervous breakdown; moved to a commune of radical reformers in New Jersey; took up alternative medicine and vegetarianism; and rejected the restrictive conventions of Victorian dress, including her corset.

Laura Rogers White studied architecture at MIT and a leading school in Paris. "I expected to be a teacher of mathematics, or possibly an architect, and prepared for that," she wrote many years later. "My father's death made that not best for the family, so to be with my mother and do best for my sisters, I relinquished those ambitions. But my college education has helped me to help others in many ways … and has broadened my views and given me the power to enjoy the best in literature and art."

After leaving Ann Arbor, Mary Sheldon taught at the Oswego academy for two years, then became a college professor, first at Wellesley, then at Stanford University.

She became not a scientist but a historian. Using the hands-on approach to teaching she had learned as a girl, and perhaps inspired by her first hero at Michigan, the historian Moses Coit Tyler, she became a pioneer in inquiry-based learning—the use of original historical documents that students studied to explore the past and solve questions on their own. She wrote and published several books.

In 1885 she married Earl Barnes, a former student, who went with her to teach at Stanford. They had no children. Her impact on students can be guessed from a letter one of them wrote to her. The young woman thanked Mary for her help and asked: "Do you know that you save[d] me from being a coward?"

Mary died of heart disease in London in 1898. She was 48.

11: Women Apart

Mary Sheldon and her comrades were pursuing careers, and they lived largely free of the University's supervision. This meant they led very different lives at Michigan than my mother led in the late 1930s. I wondered why and how that change had come about. With more research, I was able to answer those questions with a story about deans of women who, as the number of female students grew, tightened restrictions on their freedom and discouraged thoughts of any careers but the traditional ones for women. They set the terms of my mother's era at Michigan, when families who could afford college for their daughters thought of it chiefly as a step toward a well-heeled marriage and child-rearing.

In 1924, a widowed woman in her sixties named Ora Thompson Ross—living alone after raising three sons, all of them launched into business as sellers of bonds and securities in big cities far away—sat down at her typewriter to fill out a questionnaire from her alma mater.

Mrs. Ross had spent nearly all her life in the small town of Rensselaer, Indiana. The exception was her four-year term as a student at the University of Michigan in the early 1880s.

The questionnaire had come in the mail from the U-M Alumnae Association. Fifty years had passed since the first women students graduated from Michigan. Now the University was asking all female graduates to send back notes about "the extent of their influence and service" since leaving Ann Arbor—their occupations, achievements, and "public offices held."

In the blank for "occupation," Mrs. Ross typed: "Home keeper."

As for public offices, she said she had been a trustee of the Rensselaer

In the early years of coeducation, women and men often shared Ann Arbor boarding houses like this one. One woman who graduated in that era recalled: "The intermingling of boys and girls in the same home brought about a democratic and broadminded outlook upon life." (*Bentley Historical Library*)

Public Library for 25 years, an officer in the Indiana League of Women Voters, and chair of the Women's Section of the Jasper County Council of Defense during World War I.

The final question was: "Won't you add a few of the outstanding memories of your college days?"

Mrs. Ross knew all about the fine new women's dormitories at Michigan—Helen Newberry, Martha Cook, Betsy Barbour—and the sororities and "League houses" with the house mothers checking their watches and peering over girls' shoulders and making sure that "gentleman callers" got no farther than the "social parlor."

Then, thinking back on the early years of co-education at Michigan, Mrs. Ross wrote: "I cherish the memory of . . . the free and uncensored existence led by women students in those days. The idea then was that a young woman old enough to go to college was old enough to be self-reliant. They seem so much younger now!"

In Ann Arbor, staff members opening completed questionnaires at the Alumnae Association read more than a few remarks like Mrs. Ross's. All came from women who had gone through Michigan without supervision, living on their own, often with male classmates down the hall.

Ruth Weeks, who had graduated in 1913, just a decade before the survey, remembered "the absolute freedom of the Ann Arbor life—an informal social life of the students in which men & women of congenial interests met & mixed." That had been "the chief value of the university," she said, and "the recent tendency to formalize social life at Michigan . . . strikes me as under-cutting the intellectual aspect of co-education . . . I have heard many a Michigan girl say, 'The men I knew educated me.'"

"A healthy and hearty relationship and honest rivalry between young men and women exists," wrote a graduate of 1876. "It is a stimulating atmosphere and develops in good stock a strength and independent balance which tell in after life."

It was not that way anymore.

Year by year, the situation of women at Michigan had been transformed. The change was well underway by 1900 and quite complete by 1920. Where women students had once fended for themselves and mixed freely with men, they now lived in a segregated, regulated, and tightly supervised sphere marked "Women Only." The pattern of women's lives outside the classroom that would prevail until the 1960s and '70s had been set.

✢ ✣ ✢

In the early years of co-education at Michigan, women students enjoyed a striking degree of freedom. With the early contingents of women numbering only in the dozens compared to more than one thousand men, the male majority regarded the newcomers as a curious but inconsequential minority.

Some on the all-male faculty applauded their presence. Some opposed it. But either way, professors left women students to lead their own lives outside the classroom. In the era before dormitories, women and men alike found their own housing in Ann Arbor's dozens of boarding houses, and the sexes often broke bread together under the same roof, coming and going as they pleased.

"The intermingling of boys and girls in the same home brought about a democratic and broadminded outlook upon life," recalled Genevieve O'Neill, who earned undergraduate and graduate degrees at the turn of the century, "as well as mutual understanding between the sexes."

"I never saw a girl 'fall,'" she said, "or knew a boy to demean himself by attempting to lead a college girl astray."

But as the proportion of women on campus marched upward—10 percent of students by 1880, then 20 percent by 1890—their situation drew increasing attention, especially from adult women who thought changes were needed.

✢ ✣ ✢

A renowned feminist issued the first call for change, in a speech delivered in Ann Arbor in 1890.

The speaker was Alice Freeman Palmer, the University's most distinguished woman graduate to date. She had been one of the earliest female students, and she became the first female president of the all-women Wellesley College at the age of only 26. She would soon be appointed the first dean of women at the new University of Chicago. No voice had been stronger for the cause of women's education.

But while Palmer valued the independence that women had enjoyed at Michigan so far, she also believed something was missing. Women students, she said, needed closer association with each other and with older women who might serve as role models, chiefly wives of male faculty members. The girls needed an organization to bring them together and promote their interests.

Many agreed. Independence was good, but its flip side—isolation—left too many women students lonely and unhappy.

"We frequently hear of girls who have been here in Ann Arbor through the entire four years of the college course, being good faithful students, and yet going away without having made any friends," wrote Mary Markley, a graduate of 1891—yes, *that* Mary Markley—"or being one whit the richer for the superior social advantages which must always be found in a university town."

The upshot was the organization of a Michigan Women's League. Sarah Caswell Angell, the wife of President James Burrill Angell, presided at the first meeting of eighteen students and three faculty wives. The group soon swelled in membership and influence.

In later years, many women students spoke fondly of their friendships with faculty wives. But the wives were not exactly progressive. One year, when the student president of the League invited the feminist leader Susan B. Anthony to address the group, she got a sharp talking-to by faculty wives. They said the student should have checked with them first, since the invitation to Anthony might look like an endorsement of Anthony's movement for women's rights, including the right to vote.

By the mid-1890s, with the new Waterman Gymnasium filled mostly with men, the League secured support and funding for a separate gymnasium for women. Barbour Gymnasium, completed in 1896, became the center not just of women's athletics but of all women's activities on the campus, with meeting rooms and an auditorium, not to mention a dozen bathtubs much valued by women accustomed to sharing a single washbowl in a boarding house.

The construction of Barbour Gym was hailed as a milestone for women at Michigan. But it also represented a large step toward a sphere separate from men.

And the gym housed an office with a new title on the door—"Dean of Women."

President Angell had been uneasy about the idea of a dean of women, a new post at a number of schools that competed with Michigan for students. He thought the position might foster an atmosphere more like a girls' finishing school than a university. But as the number of women students continued to grow, he felt the pressure of public opinion. Surely, it was thought, so many single young women on a campus teeming with men needed adult supervision.

Dr. Eliza Mosher, an 1872 graduate of U-M's Medical Department, accepted Angell's appointment as the first dean of women. (At her insistence, she also became the University's first female professor. She taught courses in hygiene, a forerunner of the field of public health, in LSA.)

As it turned out, Dr. Mosher had little interest in her charges' social lives. She focused on health and physical fitness. It was Myra Beach Jordan (LSA 1893), succeeding Mosher as dean in 1902, who tightened the boundaries of the separate sphere for women.

Energetic and conscientious, Jordan made it her business to learn the name of every girl on campus. In her view, this new generation of "co-eds" were not only younger than the first women students but also not as serious about their studies. They would need a stronger hand, in her opinion.

✣ ✣ ✣

By the start of Jordan's long term as dean (1902–1922), more than 700 women students were attending classes among some 2,800 males. Along with the men, all but the small number of women living in sorority houses were competing for space in Ann Arbor's overtaxed rooming houses.

The houses themselves were getting an unsavory reputation. Reports of tainted water and poor sanitation were not uncommon. Many were crowded and run down. Not a few owners had reputations for either tyranny or negligence.

In 1905, the *Michigan Alumnus* voiced a rising concern. The editors wrote: "The time-honored custom of throwing the students of the University, men and women, or rather boys and girls, upon the good will, or tender mercies, of the townspeople for home and food has resulted in a system which, while it has been accepted with more or less equanimity by the residents and authorities of the University—because it has worked—has undeniably brought criticism upon the University."

Dean Jordan was already working on it.

She instituted a system of certification. Rooming houses for women would receive the dean's personal seal of approval if they were women-only; if they met standards of safety and sanitation; if a supervising "house mother" lived on the premises; and if male callers would be restricted to an approved "social parlor."

The system was developed with the cooperation of the Women's League, so the houses were soon called "League houses." Year by year, more and more owners signed up to follow the dean's rules, and by the time of World War I, there were dozens of League houses in town.

But that still didn't solve the problem. There were still not enough sororities and League houses to provide quarters for the growing numbers of women students.

The League houses begat the obvious next step. "As this idea of group life and responsibility developed," Dean Jordan wrote later, "all thinking Michigan women saw that dormitories were the real solution for living conditions."

Many students agreed. "For anyone who has made a study of student life," wrote the editors of the *Michiganensian* yearbook, "the need of better housing conditions is apparent."

Again, the Women's League took the lead, hiring two recent graduates, Myrtle White and Agnes Parks, to mount a campaign of educating alumni and soliciting donations for women's dormitories. President Harry Burns Hutchins signed on. While White and Parks toured the country to speak with wealthy potential donors, Dean Jordan spread the word with visitors to the campus.

To their surprise, the idea of women's dorms was no easy sell with alumnae who had gone to Michigan in the early years of co-education.

"It seems difficult to believe it possible now," Myrtle White wrote from the vantage point of 1930, "but our first great problem was to convince the majority of our alumnae that halls of residence were needed at Ann Arbor."

But the campaign hit on a winning theme: They would urge prospective donors to imagine their gifts to the University as tributes to their mothers. That idea made a strong impression on the children of Helen Newberry, widow of a wealthy manufacturer in Grosse Pointe; on Levi Barbour, a Detroit real estate developer, the son of Betsy Barbour; and on William Wilson Cook, a native of Hillsdale, Michigan, who had become one of the wealthiest lawyers on the East coast.

When Myrtle Wilson suggested that Cook might honor his mother by giving money for a dormitory, Cook replied: "Little girl, that idea strikes a sympathetic chord in my heart. I'll tell you now that I'll give $10,000 toward this project, and it may be a great deal more. Tell your president to come to see me." Wilson's pitch would lead not only to the Martha Cook Building but to the Michigan Law Quadrangle, which Cook funded as well.

Within ten years, four dormitories for women were built—the Helen Newberry Residence, housing 78 women; the Martha Cook Building (120 residents); Alumnae House (later Henderson House), built for women paying their own way through college; and Betsy Barbour House (80 women).

Each was run by a social director answering to Dean Jordan. Curfews were enforced. Rules of decorum were observed.

"By 1920," wrote Ruth Bordin, a historian of U-M, "women's role at Michigan was well set in the patterns it was to follow until the second feminist revolution in the late 1960s and 1970s . . . The organizational life of the university's students, including athletics, student government, living quarters, and social and philanthropic organizations, were almost completely segregated by gender. Women and men students met only in classes, and then chiefly in the College of LSA, and in the dating game."

Four much larger dormitories for women would follow—Couzens Hall (1925), built to house nurses and nursing students; Mosher-Jordan Hall (1930), named for the first two deans of women; Madelon Stockwell Hall (1940), named for U-M's first officially enrolled woman student; and Alice Crocker Lloyd Hall (1949), named for the fourth dean of women.

Many of the first women at Michigan had subscribed to principles of the earliest wave of American feminism. By the 1920s, that wave had led, after a long struggle, to the Nineteenth Amendment—votes for women—and now a new era of feminist thought and action was underway. One of its adherents was Ruth Wood, who earned her BA in 1921 and a graduate degree in 1922. On her own Alumnae Survey questionnaire, she said just what she thought of the new sphere for women on the campus.

She excoriated "Michigan's sentimental and antiquated attitude towards women. Her students . . . and her officers, can conceive of no relationship between men and women other than that sentimentally devout or quasi-sexual. Her publications reek of it, the managing of class affairs, frat functions, is controlled by it. . . . Officers as well as students are unable to recognize professional intellectuality in women. Discrimination made in the medical school, and discrimination made against women for the faculty are two examples, infuriating beyond words. . . ."

But it would be half a century before Wood's view of the role of women would be taken up by a new generation of campus feminists.

12: "A Lot of 'Ordinary' Women"

The *Michigan Daily* was founded in 1890. The first woman to lead the staff was named Marion Ford. She held the editor's position in 1943–1944, when most men were away in the armed services. The second was Evelyn Phillips, who succeeded Ford for the 1944–1945 academic year. Then World War II ended, and no woman held the job again until Sara Fitzgerald in 1972–1973.

Fitzgerald broke the men's lock on the position. When I started as a cub reporter at the *Daily* in the fall of 1974, the newsroom teemed with women who, I am sure, never entertained the notion that a man by right should run the *Daily*.

I coveted the "editor-in-chief" slot. Ten, twenty, thirty years earlier, I probably would have gotten it simply because I was a male. But in my cohort at the *Daily* there was a woman named Ann Marie Lipinski. She became perhaps the most renowned of all *Daily* alumni—a winner of the Pulitzer Prize; executive editor of the *Chicago Tribune*; and, finally, curator of the Nieman Foundation for Journalism at Harvard. Suffice it to say that I was just lucky to be picked as her co-editor. And, come to think of it, maybe I got that "co-" slot only because I was a man.

This new state of affairs at the *Daily*, and at the University in general, came about in large part because in 1970, a few women challenged male supremacy across the campus. My mother's era at Michigan was now over for good.

In 1964, Jean Ledwith King—a forty-year-old secretary, mother of three, and active Democrat—attended the Democratic National Convention, the one that nominated Lyndon Johnson for a full term in the White House. At the convention in Jersey City, King happened to overhear a male delegate from Michigan, a well-heeled man in his midforties, make a patronizing joke about a female delegate, a woman named Millie Jeffrey, who was in her midfifties.

The male delegate was a lawyer from Ann Arbor. In recent years he had supported civil rights and worked for affordable housing in Washtenaw County. Now he was active in the local party organization.

Millie Jeffrey had a little more experience. As a white student at the University of Minnesota in the Great Depression, she and a Black friend had fought the racial segregation of Minneapolis restaurants. After college, she organized clothing workers in Southern textile mills. During World War II, she was a consultant to the War Labor Board. After the war, Walter Reuther tapped her to start the Women's Bureau of the United Auto Workers (UAW). In the 1950s, she helped to forge the UAW's alliance with the civil rights movement, ran the union's radio station, and became head of its community rela-

Barbara Newell, U-M's first female executive officer, presides at an early meeting of U-M's Commission for Women. She was later president of Wellesley College and the first woman chancellor of the State University System of Florida.(*Bentley Historical Library*)

tions department. She helped elect John F. Kennedy president, marched with Martin Luther King, Jr., and registered Black voters in Mississippi under the nose of the Ku Klux Klan.

So when Jean King heard the lawyer make his little joke about Millie Jeffrey, a major figure among progressives in the U.S. but not a lawyer and not a man, it was one of those moments of clarity. Later she remarked: "That was when I knew I would never be taken seriously as a woman unless I earned a law degree."

And she did. That set her up to initiate one of the great sea changes in the University's history. It started early in 1970, when King and a handful of other women asserted that Michigan should treat women the same as men.

✢ ⁂ ✢

When she was a student in the Law School, Jean King worked part-time as a secretary in several academic departments. She learned the rules, saw the standard practices, and generally developed a sense of how the place ran and who ran it. In the Psychology Department, she got to know Elizabeth (Libby) Douvan, one of the few full professors among the women on the faculty.

King was elected to the *Law Review* for three straight years. At her graduation in 1968, the American Trial Lawyers Association recognized her as "the outstanding student in her class for her 'scholarship and academic achievement, responsible leadership in student affairs, and demonstrated concern for the problems of American society.'"

Upon graduating, she hung out her shingle as a lawyer in Ann Arbor.

Early in 1970, King went to New York for a conference. She heard a talk by a woman named Bernice Sandler, an educational psychologist who had been rejected for a faculty position at the University of Maryland. Sandler was looking for help. She had discovered an obscure federal regulation forbidding sex discrimination in hiring by federal contractors. Sandler thought she had a case to make against universities that depended heavily on federal research grants. But she needed allies.

Jean King went home, called Libby Douvan and a few other women friends from around the campus, and said: "Would you come by my house on Saturday?"

✤ ✤ ✤

" M aybe the hardest thing to understand about 1970," Jean King reflected many years later, "was the lack of contact between women at the university— staff as well as professors. So they couldn't share with each other what was happening to them. They just sort of individually got angry. It wasn't a move- ment at all."

But a movement of sorts began that day at King's modest house on the far west side of Ann Arbor, where—by a cosmic coincidence—the terrain slopes down to two ponds called First Sister and Second Sister Lakes.

The discussion began. The women talked about a fact that each of them knew on their own—that the University did not pay them as much as it paid men of comparable qualifications. But now, perhaps for the first time, they began to see the pattern, and that it amounted to systematic and illegal dis- crimination on the basis of sex.

Interviewed in 1999, Libby Douvan remembered how, in the 1950s and '60s, women on the U-M faculty tended to take their second-class status for granted.

"Because there were so few women and because the atmosphere was chilly," she said, "we were just glad to have a place where we could do our work." She recounted a chat she once had with two "dear friends," a married couple, one of them later "a world-famous historian," who were both on the faculty. (Douvan didn't give their names in the interview, but this was almost surely the prominent historian Natalie Zemon Davis and her husband, the mathematician Chandler Davis, fired by U-M in 1954 for past Communist ties. The Davises were close friends of Douvan's.)

Douvan remembered the conversation this way: "He said, 'Doesn't it really get you that you don't get paid what your male colleagues get?' And she and I looked at each other and laughed and said, 'Not really.' It didn't bother us. I mean, we were so grateful to have a place where we could do good work and enjoy our students and do our research that the fact that we didn't get paid very much didn't really seem to count for much with us. Now, that does seem really crazy . . .

"We were so used to it being so bad that we didn't really see it."

Also at Jean King's house that Saturday was Mary Yourd, the wife of an administrator in the Law School but not herself a U-M employee. Douvan remembered Yourd as "the most charming, warm, loving—and angry—woman. I mean, she was pissed off!"

The group decided to file an administrative complaint with the federal government, alleging systematic discrimination by the University against women on its staff. But it would be signed only by Jean King and Mary Yourd, neither of them officially connected to U-M. They all believed that U-M employees might be vulnerable to retaliation if their names appeared on the complaint.

They declared themselves an organization and took the name Ann Arbor Focus on Equal Employment for Women—FOCUS, for short.

Focus quickly found an important ally in Kathleen Shortridge, a graduate student in journalism who'd been collecting data on the status of women at U-M.

Just as King and Yourd were planning their strategy, Shortridge published her results as a long article in the magazine of the *Michigan Daily*. She found, among other things, that:

Thirteen percent of U-M PhDs were earned by women, but only 7 percent of the faculty were women, and the hiring trend was going down, not up.

An undergraduate taking a random assortment of forty courses over four years was likely to encounter only two professors who were women.

The Office of Admissions deliberately skewed its offers to ensure that women students, despite higher grades and test scores overall than men, would not exceed 45 percent of the student body.

Even more revealing were Shortridge's conversations with male faculty and administrators, who were unabashed about their bias in favor of male scholars.

"We considered hiring a woman," a professor of political science told her, "but in the crunch, it came down to: 'Do we really want to do this to the Department?'"

A high-ranking administrator in admissions told Shortridge that concerns had arisen when, about 1960, it became clear that a good many more qualified women than men were applying to U-M.

LSA, in particular, wanted to guard against an "overbalance" of women in each entering class. So men with worse grades and test scores were given the nod to keep the split at about 55 percent men, 45 percent women.

Shortridge took her questions about this to John Milholland, a professor of psychology on LSA's admissions committee.

"We just felt maintaining parity was a good policy," Milholland told her. "It was just a feeling in our bones. I don't know that we ever discussed it at all."

He reflected on this, then added that men applying to U-M were at a disadvantage. They matured more slowly than girls, didn't do as well in high school, and didn't please their teachers as much. So they deserved a leg up.

"Men need the education more," Milholland said. "They're more likely to go into jobs that require a college education. They're the breadwinners."

Jean King and Mary Yourd salted their complaint with the data that Kathleen Shortridge had gathered. On May 27, 1970, they sent it to the U.S. Department of Labor. It was soon rerouted to the Department of Health, Education, and Welfare (HEW). The women also sent the complaint to the newspapers. Eventually it landed on the desk of Robben W. Fleming.

Fleming, president of U-M since 1968, had just weathered a tortuous encounter with students of the Black Action Movement, who had brought off a highly publicized shutdown of many classes for two tense weeks. He had engineered a settlement by promising, among other things, to allot enough financial aid to bring the percentage of Black students to 10 percent. Now he was weathering political blowback from conservatives around the state, and he was in no mood for another fight.

This complaint about sex discrimination was nothing to worry about, he told his staff. It would blow over.

It did not blow over.

Twice that August, the Chicago office of HEW sent investigators to Ann Arbor—a response that came at "the speed of light in federal investigations," Jean King remarked. They held a series of talks with administrators and gathered reams of files.

Fleming, who said he was "not alarmed" by the HEW inquiry, gave the *Ann Arbor News* a chilly evaluation of the FOCUS complaint.

"It is clear statistically," he said, "that in professional fields the personnel is overwhelmingly male, and that is the preference of the market. The question arises whether in a supposedly free economy, market preference should have any weight."

That sounded more like an analysis from a labor economist than a humane response from a sympathetic leader who meant to right a wrong. After all, "the preference of the market" for men was precisely the problem that women were pointing out.

More women working for U-M began to speak up, and a number of them formed a group called PROBE to support King and Yourd's complaint.

In makeup and tone, PROBE was much more moderate than bra-burning students demanding "women's liberation." Yet "the deeper any of us got into this," one PROBE member said later, "the more radicalized we became." They soon published a fact-filled booklet titled "The Feminine Mistake: Women at the University of Michigan."

The feds quickly demonstrated they had been entirely persuaded by King and Yourd's case. Just weeks after visiting Ann Arbor, HEW's lead investigator, Don Scott, sent Fleming a twelve-page letter listing multiple ways in which U-M was violating federal executive orders forbidding discrimination on the basis of sex. He liberally cited the data that Kathleen Shortridge had provided to Jean King, combining it with his own analysis of individual personnel files.

Scott documented these facts, among others:

Men on the faculty were paid more than women with comparable training. (One table pointedly showed that the male members of eleven married couples on the faculty enjoyed significantly better status and pay than their wives. In Forestry, for example, Henry Townes, a professor, earned $20,000 a year while his wife, Marjorie, a "research associate," earned just $10,950. In Geography, John and Ann Kolars, both associate professors, earned $17,900 and $14,600, respectively.)

Discriminatory hiring practices handicapped women who applied for faculty positions, resulting in hugely lopsided male-female ratios all across the campus. The letter blamed academe's habit of hiring via the "grapevine" used at male-dominated professional conferences.

Far fewer women than men were studying for PhDs, with academic advisers actively discouraging women applicants.

Differences by gender were at least as obvious in the non-academic staff. Of more than three hundred job classifications, full- and part-time, that HEW reviewed, twenty were made up almost entirely of women, with an average wage of $595.49. In the 25 classifications held almost entirely by men, the average wage was $1,049.52.

Women made up two-thirds of the non-academic staff, yet there were no women on the non-academic staff's grievance committee.

The University advertised for low-level jobs with such headlines as "Attention: Student Wives."

HEW's letter concluded with a bracing list of orders.

Among other steps, Scott said, the University must equalize the hiring and pay of comparably qualified men and women, award back pay to women who had been discriminated against, improve gender ratios in all PhD programs, and give priority in promotions to women on the non-academic staff.

And the letter demanded action within thirty days, or the University would face the cancellation of millions of dollars in federal research contracts.

Fleming's response was brief and cold. "We do not differ with respect to the principle of equal treatment for women," he said. But "there are extraordinarily difficult problems in establishing criteria for what constitutes equal treatment, and we believe they are quite different from the now familiar problems in the field of race."

And even if U-M accepted all of HEW's analysis—which it did not, Fleming noted—the administration could not possibly comply with the department's order in just a month.

A stalemate ensued. HEW demanded immediate action. The Fleming administration stalled and refused to make HEW's findings public.

Watching this play out in the press, more and more Ann Arbor women found their consciences aroused by the sight of a few gallant women challenging a massive male bureaucracy.

❖ ⋮ ❖

In his settlement with the Black Action Movement, President Fleming had acknowledged the University's past wrongs in the treatment of Black students and faculty, and he had promised to make things right. Yet now he seemed unmoved by claims of bias against women. The discrepancy awakened a new sense of grievance among women at U-M. And they began to speak up about what their lives on the campus were like.

One of them was a Bryn Mawr College historian named Mary Maples Dunn, later president of Smith College, who was just finishing a year as a visiting professor at Michigan. Departing Ann Arbor, she wrote to Fleming about her experience. It had been fine overall, she said. "[Yet] at Michigan, I have had a claustrophobic sense of living in a man's world, despite the fact that the Department of History has been generous but not patronizing. I have missed the companionship of women who share my professional commitments and the problems they bring, and I have become defensive about the professional potential of women who should not need my defense any more than men do . . . Until there are more of us, women may not be entirely comfortable on this faculty.

"My relations with students have also been interesting to me, and I think more important than my personal reactions to the University as a man's world. In the first weeks of the summer term, many girls came to talk to me. Most of them volunteered the information that I was the first woman professor they had met and studied with, and they were intensely curious about me. They wanted to know how and why I had decided on such a career, whether I am married and have children, whether I neglect my children, how I cope with these multiple roles. It was a novel experience, and I concluded that at Michigan the students have far too few models to suggest to them the wide range of intellectual and professional choices they can make. Furthermore, my conversations with them led me to think that beyond a narrow range of acceptable professional training (principally . . . teaching and social work) they have only the vaguest ideas about the purpose of women's education in general and their own educations in particular."

Libby Douvan remembered older women professors who, like herself, had once written off discriminatory treatment as simply the way of the world, to be accepted without protest. Now, she said, "little by little, these . . . wonderful women who [had] done such stellar work said, 'Well, maybe it was really discrimination. The fact of the matter is I *didn't* progress as quickly as my male colleagues.'"

Fleming received a letter from a graduate student named Gloria Gladman. She was from a small town in northern Michigan, and she assured the president she was no radical but "an older student, a conservative and an engineer" who had "gone along with the University on most of its issues." "I don't usually get that angry," she said. "As a woman on campus for five years, I've been aware of discriminatory practices and attitudes of the University directed unknowingly and knowingly toward women. I've always kept my cool, feeling things would become better . . . .

"Unfortunately, I am finding your attitude and statements with regard to sex discrimination on campus exactly paralleling the administration's unenlightened stand years ago when the University was labeled by a government investigation as a white, racist university. It took rabble-rousing, sit-ins, and ugly headlines to get a semblance of justice for blacks . . . .

"Don't underestimate the feelings of women on this campus and the capabilities of current University policy and attitudes radicalizing a lot of 'ordinary' women on campus. When one wakes up and discovers the shackles on her own wrists and ankles it is a very frightening experience. . . . Don't radicalize me and for heaven's sake DON'T INSULT MY INTELLIGENCE with a paternalizing attitude."

In private homes around town, there were tense exchanges between husbands and wives. One was between Paul Federbush, a mathematics professor, and his wife, Marcia, who wrote to Fleming in "frustrated indignation" over his refusal to release HEW's findings.

In the Math Department, Marcia Federbush wrote, there were 89 faculty, all of them men. Yet "my husband tells me with complete seriousness that the Math Department does not discriminate against women.

"This is a period when women are suddenly becoming aware of the enormity of their debasement in all sectors of society," she added. "What hurts most of all is the realization that they have been living with obvious and subtle, purposeful and unintentional discrimination all their lives and have somehow either failed to recognize it or have not tried to change it."

She spoke, she said, for "a great many women whose lives are intimately entwined in the fabric of the University."

✢ ✦ ✢

President Fleming had made his reputation as an expert in labor law, especially as a master mediator. He was renowned for his ability to find common ground between antagonists, and in his tenure to date, he had shown time and again that he had a knack for calming roiled waters.

And he was hardly unfamiliar with claims of sex discrimination in the workplace.

In one of his cases as an arbitrator in the 1950s, he was asked to rule on a grievance submitted by women janitors who worked for a major manufacturer. A clause in the union contract mandated equal pay for equal work. The women proved they did the same work as male janitors, yet received ten cents less per hour.

The company insisted the differential resulted from a scientific evaluation system that looked at jobs, not individuals. If that was so, Fleming asked, why did the women always wind up getting ten cents less than the men? The managers were bewildered. "But women always get less than men," they told Fleming. "Therefore, there is a differential."

Fleming ruled in favor of the women. It just showed, he wrote later, "how blinded we can all be by prevailing attitudes and past practices."

Yet this was just what women at U-M were now accusing Fleming of—being blind to the power of traditional roles for men and women in academe.

✦ ✦ ✦

The women of FOCUS and PROBE conducted a mounting pressure campaign. Jean King blitzed her contacts in Washington, DC, with letters, and the response from Michigan's congressional delegation—including supportive women staffers—was encouraging.

On campus, members of PROBE distributed thousands of letters to women employees via the University's interoffice mail system—until the mail manager declared the move "illegal."

Then, in early November 1970, shortly after HEW's thirty-day deadline had passed, the *Michigan Daily* broke the news that federal officials had cancelled a $350,000 contract between the U.S. Agency for International Development and U-M's Center for Population Planning. Jean King learned from congressional staffers that more grants were being held up or cancelled—up to $15 million of the University's $66 million in federal contracts.

"At the present time the matter is of no concern to us," Fleming told the *Daily*. "We are concentrating on the broader problem of arriving at an agreement with HEW."

But Jean King believed quite the contrary—that this demonstration of the feds' firm intentions was stirring fear in faculty offices and labs across the campus.

"Knowing what I do about the inside of the University," she said later, "the faculty member who was applying for a grant would be notified when his grant was not going to come through and he'd complain to his dean and the dean would call Fleming. So I'm sure he sat there with deans on his neck for weeks. And he had to give in. That was a force he just couldn't deal with."

Meanwhile, Fleming sent appeals for support to other research universities and to his own contacts in Washington, DC, even as HEW prepared to take action against universities elsewhere. But the test case remained Michigan, the school that all eyes were watching.

As the Christmas break approached, Fleming began to moderate his position, indicating a willingness to meet HEW's demand for concrete "goals and timetables" to correct inequities. A key sticking point was admissions to graduate programs; Fleming insisted that was no business of the government's.

On December 21, Allan Smith, U-M's vice president for academic affairs, flew to Washington, DC. He met with HEW officials for two and a half hours.

Then on Christmas Eve, Stanley Pottinger, director of HEW's Office of Civil Rights, announced that an agreement with U-M had been reached. The issue of graduate admissions would be deferred.

The University then began to put in place what is now regarded as the nation's first affirmative action program to bring about equity between the sexes.

"It's a beginning," said Bernice Sandler, who had started the whole thing. "But we've got a long way to go yet, baby."

In eleven years as president, Robben Fleming appointed one woman to a high position among his top aides. She was Barbara Newell, who had worked with him when he was chancellor of the University of Wisconsin. As acting vice president for student affairs for two years, she was U-M's first female executive officer. (She was later president of Wellesley College.)

Libby Douvan recalled a meeting, several years after the HEW episode, when Fleming was preparing to appoint the geologist Frank H.T. Rhodes, then dean of LSA, as U-M's vice president for academic affairs.

Douvan and several women colleagues—including Regent Sarah Goddard Power and Nellie Varner, later a Regent, too, but then head of U-M's affirmative action program—went to Fleming to express their concerns. They were hoping a woman might compete for the position.

Normally mild and courteous, the president was uncharacteristically abrupt. Douvan recalled that he said: "That is none of your business . . . That's my appointment and I don't have to take the advice of any group like yours."

Douvan thought he regretted his tone immediately.

After a moment, he said it was simply unlikely that women candidates could be found with the experience necessary for such an important job.

"For example," he said, "when I brought Barbara Newell here from Wisconsin . . . you'll see that every time Barbara had to make a critical decision, she hadn't really had that experience before. I was there with her. I always backed her. I made a visible presence so that she had the support to go through it for the first time."

At that, Douvan said, Nellie Varner spoke up.

"Mr. President," she said, "that's all we're asking of you. That you should treat women now the way you treated Barbara at the time—that if we don't have the background, someone has to give us a leg up."

Douvan saw that register with Fleming.

"He thought about it," she said, "and was much more positively oriented toward us on the way out than he had been on the way in."

IV: SPIRIT AND SPORT

My dad was captain of Michigan's varsity tennis team, a defenseman on the varsity hockey team, and president of his fraternity, Phi Delta Theta. In short, he was what they used to call a "big man on campus," and thus a prime candidate to spend the rest of his life as a rah-rah "Michigan man," since he enjoyed a moment in the spotlight of college glory.

Instead, he always looked askance at Michigan mythology and privately grimaced at sentimental worship of the maize and blue. He might well have approved of Freud's theory of the narcissism of small differences—the tendency of populations very like and near each other to develop hypersensitive ideas about how greatly they differ—and observed how well the theory fits the students and alumni of Big Ten universities.

But if he was a doubter, he was also a believer. When he was about as old as I am now, we gave him a record album called "Songs of Michigan," performed by the Michigan Men's Glee Club. One day I saw him listening to "The Friar's Song" ("In College Days"), a lovely, sentimental song that includes these lyrics:

Then raise the rosy goblet high
The singer's chalice and belie
The tongues that trouble and defile;
For we have yet a little while
    to linger,
You and youth and I
In Michigan.

He had tears in his eyes.

I've always shared his mixed feelings.

I live a few blocks from Michigan Stadium. If I'm standing in my backyard when a Wolverine scores at the Big House, I can hear the Michigan Marching Band play "The Victors," and I feel the bittersweet pang of lost youth in my gut. But when a dear friend, my old roommate at East Quad, invites me to share his seats at a game, I always find a reason to turn him down.

When my daughters were at Michigan, I had to smile when, on football Saturdays, they waved their friends off to The Game, then stayed home for a quiet afternoon. Yet when they put on their caps and gowns for commencement, I felt deep pride, not only because they were graduating from college but because they were graduating from Michigan.

Any college fundraiser will attest to the power of intangible loyalties. As a reporter, I went to Los Angeles to write about Michiganders at the 1990 Rose Bowl (USC 17, Michigan 10). Between posh events for wealthy alumni, I chatted with Walter Harrison, U-M's chief of public relations. I asked why it took a football game to raise a lot of money for Michigan. "Excellence in football—I think people want to identify with that," Harrison said. "It's that sense of: 'I'm with a winner.'"

An obvious truth, I guess, and why object? But I do. It pains me that U-M's image, even its essence, is so deeply imprinted by sport, which has essentially nothing to do with the place's mission. I believe U-M, like nearly all its peers—not the University of Chicago, which found a different path—veered off course in the early 20th century when it crowned football king. But of course that wrong turn in the University's evolution can never be undone now. The mutation had its way with campus culture, and now it is fixed in the University's DNA.

Several times I was drawn to write about all that—the maize-and-blue intangibles. The mix of stories reflects my mixed feelings.

13: Rhapsodies in Blue

One day Deborah Holdship, my editor at *Michigan Today*, forwarded an email to me. It was sent by one Bob Neir, class of 1951, who told Deborah: "You must tell alumni how 'Go Blue' came about."

Well, that was intriguing. So I pulled on the thread and discovered not one or even two tales about "how 'Go Blue' came about," and wrote a romp through the whole business of Michigan blue in its most famous manifestations.

There was once a popular professor of Greek named Albert Henderson Pattengill. He joined the faculty soon after he graduated from Michigan in 1868 and taught until his death in 1906. His tenure at U-M was the longest of any professor to date except his colleague in classics, Martin Luther D'Ooge.

He left a number of marks on Michigan. A tall and husky fellow, he once batted a baseball from a point just south of North University onto the roof of the old Medical Building on East University, a distance of several hundred feet. His love of the classics enthralled several generations of students. And it was said that Pattengill once persuaded Coach Fielding Yost to turn down a better offer from a competing football program and stay at Michigan.

Those were singular contributions, no doubt. But his longest-lasting service to his alma mater may have been a small duty he performed in the fall of his senior year, when he signed his name to the document that first sealed Michigan's devotion to the color blue.

✣

The origins of that devotion lie lost in the years before the Civil War. All that's known for sure is that a few surviving diplomas are decorated with a ribbon that colorists today would call cobalt—at least that's how the ribbons look now, more than a century and a half later.

Some early U-M ribbons were not only blue but yellow, too. The lighter shade was consistently "the characteristic corn color" known as maize, according to an early account.

But the shade of blue varied. Sometimes it was "a dark blue" near navy. In other decorations, it was "a very deep and a very brilliant blue." In still others, it was "sky blue," and in later years, early graduates attested that "sky blue" was "regarded as the standard color." That variety of blue was often called azure.

So when Albert Pattengill and two classmates named Jackson—Milton, of West Grove, Pennsylvania; and Joseph, of Ann Arbor—were named as a committee of students charged with choosing Michigan's colors, they returned on February 12, 1867, with this report:

"Your committee . . . unanimously agree in presenting as their choice, AZURE BLUE AND MAIZE, and recommend that the following resolution be adopted: Resolved, That Azure Blue and Maize be adopted as the emblematic colors of the University of Michigan."

As it was recommended, so it was done.

But what exactly was azure? Even lexicographers couldn't agree.

In 1888, the *Oxford English Dictionary* said azure was the color of the gem lapis lazuli, which is more royal blue than sky blue. In 1895, the *Century Dictionary* said azure was the same as cobalt, while the *Standard Dictionary* said it was more like ultramarine or even a ceramic pigment called smalt.

Imagine what might have been: *Maize and smalt. Let's go smalt. Hurrah for the yellow and smalt.*

On this point, the Latin professor Charles Mills Gayley, who wrote the words to "The Yellow and Blue" in 1886, is no help at all. His lyrics compare Michigan blue to no fewer than six varying shades—*"the billows that bow to the sun"* (sounds pretty pale); *"the curtains that evening has spun"* (definitely darker); *"blossoms to memory dear"* (actually, blue flowers are all but unknown in nature); *"the sapphire [that] gleams like a tear"* (a saturated blue approaching royal); a maiden's eyes *"brimming with blue"* (not specific); and *"garlands of bluebells"* (closer to purple than sky blue).

But who was looking up azure in the dictionary, anyway? U-M people of the late 1800s used any old blue they wanted, and over the years, Michigan azure faded to a washed-out baby blue, at least in official University documents and decorations.

On the playing fields, it was different. Starting in 1879, when Michigan's first football team wore uniforms of white canvas with blue stockings, athletic uniforms showed blues of bolder and bolder hue over time.

By 1912, the bifurcation of the blues—baby and bold—was no longer entirely trivial. The University's 75th anniversary had arrived. (This was when 1837 was still recognized as the year of U-M's founding.) Robes and flags and printed programs were needed, and the shade of blue had to be consistent.

So the Regents appointed a faculty committee "to determine the exact shades of maize and blue which should be suitable for the official colors of the University and embody them in some lasting form."

The committee chair, Professor Warren Lombard of the Physiology Department, took his charge so seriously that he sailed to Norway in search of craftsmen who could make a ceramic tile that would hold the right blue forever. They couldn't guarantee it. So Lombard sailed back home and settled for heavy silk ribbons of "a rich, deep, pure blue," in the words of the U-M graphic designer Liene Karels, who found the ribbons buried deep in the Bentley Historical Library.

From then on, Michigan blue waxed and waned, sometimes paler, sometimes deeper, until a version recognized by every true Wolverine came into general acceptance—a blue that is definitely darker than the sky on a sunny Michigan day but at least a shade lighter than navy.

In 1995, the University tried to fix that exact hue in a permanent ink. But, like Professor Lombard's tiles, it was a will-of-the-wisp. Inks and papers simply varied too much for designers to make a Michigan blue capable of foolproof replication.

Nearly twenty years later, in 2013, U-M's branding chief, Steve Busch, did a careful survey and found no fewer than twelve shades of Michigan blue in use—"way too many." So he went in search of just one "intelligent, inventive, and noble shade of blue." He got thinking about the dark blue panels he used to see when he was a kid selling frozen treats on the concourse of Michigan Stadium, and he found out the Athletic Department had brought it back, using a hue in the Pantone Color Matching System called Pantone 282 c. It's a combination of one hundred parts cyan (a greenish-blue), sixty parts magenta (a light purple), and sixty parts black.

"I liked it," Busch said. "It's a very deep blue which I think helps connect today's U-M with our 200-year history and harkened back to the shade of blue I recall as a kid in the '70s. It had longevity."

And that was that—the final word on the color blue in Ann Arbor.

But the use of the *word* blue has a longer story.

✧ ⋮ ✧

It's hardly surprising that Bob Neir couldn't remember every detail of that long-ago Michigan hockey game. It had been nearly seventy years, after all. He couldn't remember the exact date or even whom Michigan was playing. But he remembered what his roommate, Paul Fromm, did that night—which means that Bob Neir was pretty surely an eyewitness to the moment when the word *blue* was given its most famous usage in America.

It happened on a cold night in the winter of 1950–1951.

Neir (pronounced *near*), a native of Queens, New York, was a senior in business. His buddy, Paul Fromm, was a senior in engineering from Buffalo, New York.

They were serious students, not rah-rah types. But now and then they would get dinner at the Old German or the Pretzel Bell, then trudge down to the Coliseum to watch a varsity hockey game.

Those games weren't like Michigan hockey today, with thousands of raving fans crammed up to the ceiling of Yost Arena (formerly the Yost Field House). Admission was free. You sat wherever you wanted in the Coliseum bleachers.

Fromm was a good guy, Neir said. "Independent. Very smart. He was a fun guy but he was not a back-slapper, ha-ha-ha kind of guy. Very serious student."

So the Wolverines were out on the ice against somebody or other, hustling up and down the rink. Fans were watching and cheering for this or that—the usual thing.

Then, with no preface or pronouncement of any kind, Paul Fromm stood up.

"He felt good about Michigan and up he went," Neir said. "I think it was absolutely spontaneous."

And Fromm shouted two words with a pause in between:

"Go ... blue!"

Then he shouted the words again. And again.

At first, people nearby just looked up at Fromm and laughed a little. Nobody had heard anybody say that before. Everybody knew, of course, that Michigan's colors were maize and blue. But nobody yelled "go blue!"

"Go Michigan!"—sure. But not "go blue!"

Fromm kept going. After a minute, people began to pick it up. It became a crowd chant, two words over and over, in rhythm:

"Go ... blue! ... Go ... blue! ... Go ... blue!"

Bob Neir was chanting along.

"It was absolutely amazing how two words like that would elicit so much emotion from the crowd," Neir said. "We were part of the team with 'Go blue!' One thing that's nice about it is that it's just two words. Any idiot can say two words."

After a while, Fromm sat back down and that was that.

Fromm went on to a successful career as an engineer at Bell Helicopter. He died a number of years ago. Neir became an executive with Boeing Aircraft.

Neir can't remember if they did the cheer at other hockey games that year. He just knows that "Go Blue" is now heard at every Michigan sporting event and that it's the universal slogan of U-M loyalists everywhere.

"I just can't believe it," he says. "It's all over the country now."

❖ ❖ ❖

So that's how "Go Blue" was coined.

Unless it wasn't.

The thing is, in a 1998 letter to *Michigan Today*, Margaret "Peg" Detlor Dungan, an Ann Arbor native, said that Paul Fromm, who was a friend of hers, was the inventor of "Go Blue," all right. But she says Fromm first yelled the words, not at a hockey game, but at the home football opener against Michigan State in the fall of 1950 (a 14-7 loss, sorry to say).

So that clears that up. It was Fromm, but earlier. At a football game, not a hockey game.

Unless it wasn't.

Because Charles J. Moss, of Midland, Michigan, in another 1998 letter to *Michigan Today*, claims to have invented and introduced the "Go Blue" cheer at a U-M baseball game in the spring of 1947. He says the cheer was picked up at Michigan football games the following fall, and thus was history made.

Not by Paul Fromm. Not at a hockey game. Not at a football game. Not in 1950. Not in 1951.

As any historian will tell you, the past is seen, at best, through a glass darkly.

❖ ❖ ❖

The way Ken Burke remembers it, the conversion of "Go Blue" into a jingle that swept from Michigan Stadium to Hollywood started with some tuba players in the University of Wisconsin band.

It happened some time in the hockey season of 1973-1974. Burke, a junior in the Business School, was hanging out with a couple friends in his apartment at the corner of Tappan and Oakland.

One of them was Tom Blaske, a law student. He and Burke had both played tuba in the Michigan Marching Band.

The other guy was Robbie Moore, a neighbor of Burke's. He was the All-American goalie on Michigan's hockey team.

Moore always got a kick out of the pep bands that played at hockey games. That night he got talking about a tune he'd just heard on a road trip to Madison.

Burke and Blaske both remember what Moore said: "There's this cool thing the Wisconsin hockey band does."

And he sang a catchy little tune that had stuck in his head, with three staccato notes at the end—*bup-bup-bup*.

That was it. Ken Burke thought no more about it until the following fall, when the Marching Band traveled to Madison. There he heard the Wisconsin horns play that ditty with the *bup-bup-bup*, the same one Robbie Moore had sung.

A couple months later, Burke walked down to Yost Arena to see a hockey game.

In the stands, he spotted the hockey pep band, a ragtag bunch of volunteers who pumped up the crowd with jingles and Michigan songs.

Burke walked over to a tuba player he knew named Joe Carl, one of the pep band's unofficial organizers.

He said: "Hey, Joe, give me your horn for a minute."

And he played the little tune that Robbie Moore had sung in the apartment.

Burke told Carl: "You guys should play that, and then after the *bup-bup-bup*, you could shout, 'Let's go blue!'"

And they did.

✦ ✠ ✦

Now, Joe Carl's memory of what happened is slightly different. But he remembers that Wisconsin's band was somewhere in the mix.

"The band traveled to Wisconsin for the football game," Carl said recently. "And the Wisconsin band—they're kind of rowdy, kind of interesting—and I do remember them doing something that ended with a *bup-bup-bup*, you know?

"It was their sousaphones as they're marching into the stadium. We were waiting there to come in the stadium, and here comes the Wisconsin band, and they were doing something. I couldn't recognize what the piece was . . . but I do remember it ended with this *bup-bup-bup*. I remember hearing that."

That something with the *bup-bup-bup* came back to Ann Arbor in his head, Carl said, then to that hockey game at Yost.

"I don't remember how that came around to 'Let's Go Blue,' other than it was just kind of: *They* seemed to be goofin' around, then we started goofin' around."

And that certain tune began to pop out of Michigan tubas that night.

Then, just after the *bup-bup-bup*—if Joe Carl's memory serves—an alto horn player named John Endahl yelled: "Let's go blue!"

And the crowd loved it.

"Yeah, the crowd picked it up, absolutely," Carl said. "And you get a crowd there in Yost Arena and it sounded like 10,000 people. It was really cool. It certainly caught us by surprise."

By the following football season, George Cavender, director of U-M bands, had heard the "Let's Go Blue" tune and cheer, and he loved it, too.

So one day he buttonholed Albert Ahronheim, who had been the Marching Band's drum major. Now he was Cavender's graduate assistant and the band's principal arranger, and he had studied with Jerry Bilik, the U-M-trained composer, arranger, and musical director who conceived "M Fanfare."

Cavender said: "Hey, Al, there's this tune that this tuba player's been playing at the hockey games, and it goes like this . . . "

Cavender sang it.

"I want you to do a full arrangement for the Marching Band."

So Ahronheim sat down at a piano and got to work—singing notes, playing notes, and scribbling on a blank score.

Gradually, the arrangement emerged. He started with the original tuba bassline—the low, thumping notes—and added trombones. Then he wrote a new melody to burst in at a higher octave—trumpets playing a scrambling Dixieland kind of thing. Then all the instruments ascended together into a riot of melody and counter-melody, punctuated at the end with those three popping periods—*BUP-BUP-BUP!*

Ahronheim got it down on paper. He handed it to Cavender, who looked it over and scribbled in the margin, at the appropriate point: "Yell let's go blue."

"It's arranging more than composition," Ahronheim said, "but the two are intimately related. . . . What I did was an arrangement based on this bassline. I came up with that new melody, so I guess that was composition. But I don't want to make too much of it. It's not Beethoven."

Maybe not. But it approached the half-century mark with no signs of age. It was a Michigan calling card, of course, but it was also played all over the country. It popped up in movies from *The Big Chill* to *Remember the Titans*. (In the credits of *Titans*, Carl and Ahronheim are the very last names listed, thanks in part to George Cavender, who urged them to get the tune copyrighted.)

"It's a lot of fun, there's no question," Ahronheim said. "I had no idea how much fun it was going to be."

So who gets the credit?

It looks like everybody deserves a piece of it, small or large—Robbie Moore, Ken Burke, Joe Carl, Michigan's hockey fans, George Cavender, and Albert Ahronheim. And maybe especially those tuba players at Wisconsin, even if Michigan loyalists would rather not admit it. Ken Burke's friend Tom Blaske put it this way: "As they used to say of the Panama Canal: 'Stolen, fair and square.'"

And who's to say Wisconsin didn't swipe the tune from somebody else?

14: Two against Football

The patron saint of the maize-and-blue creed is Fielding H. Yost, the football coach who led the Wolverines to an extraordinary record of victories in the early 1900s. So my little streak of iconoclasm was activated when I heard that one student and one young professor had stood up for one moment against Yost's drive to build the nation's biggest stadium—a project, the rebels said, that would be "a permanent concession, set in concrete for years to come, to the notion that college is nothing more than a Roman holiday." That put the case against the supremacy of football better than I ever could.

"At Ann Arbor is an institution called a University. What does this mean? It means first and foremost that here is a social structure dedicated to the improvement of human life through the acquisition of knowledge."
—ROBERT COOLEY ANGELL

The University of Michigan *Chimes* was a little student weekly that published sketches, essays, poems, and literary reviews. Nobody paid much attention to it, at least not until a senior named Neil Staebler took over as editor in the autumn of 1925.

Staebler had grown up in Ann Arbor at a time when the biggest man in town—arguably the biggest man in the state—was the football coach Fielding H. Yost. In 1905, the year Staebler was born, the Yostmen—as the *Michigan Daily* liked to call the varsity team—had an off year, for Yost. They went 12-1. (From 1901 to 1904 the team's record had been 43-0-1.) In the twenty years of Staebler's youth, Yost's teams tied 9 games, lost 29, and won 114. Yost was widely seen not only as a great coach but also as a great man, a builder of character in the young, and a champion of athletics for all—all men, anyway ... well, all white men. (The son of a Confederate soldier, Yost allowed only a small handful of Black athletes to play for Michigan, and only in sports less conspicuous than football.)

Now Yost was also Michigan's athletic director. In the fall of 1925, at the age of 54, he was working crazy hours and running all over the state in pursuit of a huge new achievement.

Most people in town were rooting for him. Neil Staebler was not.

Americans had gone nuts for college football, and a stadium race was under way. Colossal palaces had been built or planned at Yale (70,896 seats), Ohio State (75,000), and Illinois (92,000), among others.

Michigan students, Michigan alumni, and people with no direct connection to the school mobbed home games. In 1922, half the entire student body of 11,000 went to the Ohio State game—in Columbus. When Michigan played at home, special trains discharged carloads of fans from across the Midwest, and every Ann Arbor bedroom was crammed with extra cots, bunks, and blankets.

But Michigan's Ferry Field, beloved as it was, held only 37,000 spectators in the early 1920s. The demand for seats was estimated at twice that number or more, and a cry was rising for some solution to the uproarious demand for tickets.

At first the University's governing Board of Regents (some of whom requested up to sixty tickets a game for family and friends) said no to any new stadium; the cost would be too high. Maybe more stands could be built at Ferry to meet the need. They were—and the demand for tickets only grew.

When the Wolverines compiled an 8-0 record in 1923 and were named national champions, powerful alumni began to call for construction of a new stadium to seat up to 100,000 fans.

✢ ⁑ ✢

Coach Yost had an idea to defuse the Regents' fears about the prohibitive cost of a new stadium. To fund construction, he would sell twenty-year bonds with a guarantee of two season tickets to every buyer. No student would pay extra. No one would be asked for a donation. No new taxes would be levied. And Yost said football revenue would pay for a grand new complex for other sports and intramurals.

It was brilliant. Alumni were delighted. Students were ecstatic. Marion LeRoy Burton, the University's popular president and a great friend of Yost, appeared to be on board. The Board in Control of Intercollegiate Athletics (where Yost enjoyed a strong majority of alumni and students) sent it up to the Regents.

Then, early in 1925, President Burton died of heart disease at the age of only fifty.

His interim replacement was the scholarly Alfred Henry Lloyd, dean of the graduate school, a professor of philosophy. Dean Lloyd was not the friend of football or Fielding Yost that President Burton had been, and he called a screeching halt to the stadium charge. He appointed a faculty committee headed by Edmund Day, dean of the School of Business Administration, to study the entire question of athletics at Michigan. After the Day committee had studied and deliberated, Lloyd said, a thoughtful decision about any new football stadium might be made.

When Fielding Yost (at right, with an aide) proposed the biggest football stadium in the U. S., nearly everyone applauded—but not young Neil Staebler, who said the construction would be "a permanent concession, set in concrete for years to come, to the notion that college is nothing more than a Roman holiday." (*Bentley Historical Library*)

At this, Yost went into overdrive. All that spring and summer he gave speeches from Monroe to Marquette to Kalamazoo, to Rotary Clubs, Kiwanis Clubs, Chambers of Commerce. On the faculty, there might be snooty nay-sayers, but among outstate alumni and just plain fans, he had thousands of allies. Michigan was behind in the stadium race. The state had to compete.

"Whether the stadium is crammed to capacity or almost empty," he told audiences, "the desire to win by students and alumni is present just the same. It will be a sad day for the youth of America when they no longer want to win. They will become a limp, listless set of boys and girls."

Yost came off the stump to start the 1925 season. The Day committee met, asked questions, met some more. The Regents appeared to be coming around. "You made a mistake when you went in for football instead of the law," Regent James O. Murfin wrote to Yost. "As an advocate either orally or in writing you have no equal."

That was when Neil Staebler, twenty years old, became the editor of *Chimes*.

As his classmates marched down to games at Ferry Field, waiting and watching for what now seemed all but inevitable—an announcement that the Yostmen would soon play in the country's greatest stadium—Staebler got in touch with Robert Cooley Angell, a sociology professor who was barely out of graduate school, one of the youngest members of the faculty.

Knowing the impossibly long odds, and the poisonous treatment they would get from their friends, Staebler and Cooley decided to object.

❖ ❖ ❖

Robert Cooley Angell was a reluctant recruit to Neil Staebler's hopeless cause.

If there was such a thing as U-M royalty, no one had a better claim to it. Angell's paternal grandfather was James Burrill Angell, Michigan's president from 1871 to 1909. His maternal grandfather was Thomas McIntyre Cooley, a great dean of the Law School. His father was Alexis Caswell Angell, a Michigan law professor. One of his uncles was the Michigan sociologist Charles Horton Cooley; another was James Rowland Angell, then president of Yale. In 1919, *that* Angell had almost been appointed president of Michigan—until he stated plainly that he thought intercollegiate athletics should be done away with.

This new Angell was anything but a musty-headed old professor looking down his nose at students' fun. He was barely 25 years old. Only a few years earlier he had been sports editor of the *Michigan Daily*. He had played varsity tennis for Michigan and was "a thorough believer in athletics." And he knew the student mind better than anyone. His doctoral dissertation was about student social structures in Ann Arbor, soon to be published as *The Campus: A Study of Undergraduate Life in the Contemporary American University*.

In the *Daily* and the *Ann Arbor News*, he already had spoken out against the excesses of college football, saying "the complete abolition of intercollegiate athletics" would be "the quickest solution to the problem."

For that, he said, he had been "pronounced inhuman, devoid of emotion, incapable of feeling thrills and disgustingly academic." So many people had stopped him to say, "What's the big idea?" that he had resolved to keep his mouth shut on the subject.

But Neil Staebler persuaded him to take one more swing at big-time college football.

Angell sat down to craft a careful essay in the vein of an introductory lecture in sociology.

"The easiest way to approach the problem at hand," he began, "is to go back to fundamentals.

"At Ann Arbor is an institution called a University. What does this mean? It means first and foremost that here is a social structure dedicated to the improvement of human life through the acquisition of knowledge."

No one would dispute that statement, he said—not even the fiercest Michigan fan.

So the logical question about football should be: "Does the present system of intercollegiate football promote or discourage the acquisition of knowledge?"

If it promoted knowledge, he said, then everyone should rally around Yost and build a bigger stadium. But did it?

As for the players themselves, Angell said, only a few did more in class than maintain their eligibility. Nearly all their time and energy went to the sport. "Their diplomas cover a multitude of intellectual sins."

But the athletes were only "a few drops in the bucket of university life." What harm could football possibly do to the thousands of other students who simply showed up to cheer?

Well, said Angell, every autumn, football became a kind of addiction for students, "many but mildly, some seriously." The sport seized "a monopoly of undergraduate conversation . . . A scientific theory or a piece of fine poetry has not a chance to squeeze in edgewise.

"Around the dinner table, in one another's rooms, walking to and from classes, the chief topic for discussion is the team's makeup, its powers, its chances for the next game . . . ."

And all this talk hauled students' attention away from the real purpose of college. Their focus was not the mind but the muscles, not clashing ideas but clashing bodies on a field of battle. "The worship of the man who can throw a forward pass thirty yards . . . is not likely to turn . . . impressionable youngsters towards the fascinating problems of science, history and literature."

And beyond the campuses, Angell said, big-time football was exerting "a subtle degrading influence" on the public's opinion of education.

Because of press attention to football, he said, now "the 'college man' is proverbially an individual with little to do but drink, make love, and cheer for the team." That influence, in turn, was attracting "pleasure seekers with no intellectual interest"—and "how can we hope to stimulate a love of knowledge in students like this?

"I enjoy watching a football game almost as much as the next man," he said. "Time was when I enjoyed it more. But that does not alter the unmistakable fact that students could still be allowed this pleasure without the contests becoming a great public spectacle. That is what turns a fine thing into a degenerating one. The university has certainly no duty to furnish public entertainment to its own detriment."

And "all the harmful conditions which I have suggested as flowing from intercollegiate football in its present form would be made worse if Michigan were to build a larger stadium.

"A university, if it is to be a university at all, must preserve its intellectual standards at all costs; to cater slavishly to the [desires] of the general public is but to invite destruction."

When Fielding Yost read that, he saw red.

❖ ⁑ ❖

What infuriated Yost was that Angell was biting the hand that had fed him.

"This same Robert C. Angell is a former member of the Varsity Tennis Team," Yost fumed in a letter to the press. "He played with racquets and tennis balls purchased by the Athletic Association. He played on tennis courts built and maintained by the Athletic Association. He went on out-of-town trips and had all his expenses paid by the Athletic Association. He wears the 'M' Hat and 'M' Sweater awards he received from the Athletic Association. The money for all these items was taken from the earnings made by these horrible football men."

The *Daily*'s editors rushed to Yost's side.

"What are the objections?" the paper's lead editorial asked. Angell was attacking intercollegiate football as a whole, they said, not the proposal for a bigger stadium. And that was plain nuts, since "football is here to stay."

In that case, they said, "one finds it hard to understand how a stadium of 75,000 seats will have a more detrimental effect on the student body than one of 45,000."

If there were any good reasons not to build a bigger stadium, the *Daily* taunted, the critics should state them, "but the mere fact that freshmen idolize the Varsity man is hardly a valid objection."

The *Daily*'s volley was published on Tuesday, October 13, 1925, two days after Robert Angell's essay in the *Chimes*.

That gave Neil Staebler the rest of the week to polish his own arguments for the *Chimes*' next assault on the stadium plan.

Angell had opened the argument. But he spoke as a faculty member. That left out a lot that Staebler wanted to say from a student's point of view. If the *Daily* wanted to hear more objections, he was happy to oblige.

❖ ⁝ ❖

On October 20, the *Chimes* carried Staebler's own essay, titled "Stadiumania."

He began by saying the stadium debate amounted to competing theories of "what college should be."

Opponents of a giant stadium, he wrote, "conceive college to be primarily a place for those who are interested in study, a place in which distraction shall be minimized."

The other view, "sponsored by convivial alumni and accepted by what is unquestionably a majority of students," was that "college is a place to acquire a minimum amount of knowledge and technical skill required to earn a fair living, at a minimum sacrifice of amusement and pleasure."

Construction of a giant stadium would be a monumental endorsement of the latter view, he said. It would be "a dedication of Michigan to the proposition that sport—which is the representative college amusement—deserves even a greater place in the minds and lives of students, alumni and the public than it now occupies."

Angell had attacked the stadium plan on academic grounds, Staebler said, but he opposed it more for "its deleterious social influence."

He didn't mean gambling, he said, or drinking, or "the other debaucheries so common during football season."

What really troubled him was the sheer fatuousness of student culture under the influence of football—"the fellows that boast about their beer parties and hot times and that seem to be hangers-on in the University only for the amusement they derive . . . a disgustingly Babbittish crowd to whom the true purpose of college is as incomprehensible as the Dialogues of Plato."

So what did that have to do with a bigger stadium?

Consider basketball, Staebler said. Just as exciting a game, but played in a small arena, it generated none of the obsessive chatter or boorish behavior that football did. If the size of the football phenomenon had been capped early on, it "would not have grown into the parasite it has become."

A stadium twice the size of Ferry Field would double the trouble—twice the monopoly on daily conversation; twice the pre- and post-game brawls; twice the publicity and its attendant pressure for winning above all.

Finally, he said, "Michigan, by building a larger stadium, will be setting its stamp of approval upon an institution and a set of conditions inimical to its own best interests; it will be a permanent concession, set in concrete for years to come, to the notion that college is nothing more than a Roman holiday."

✛ ✛ ✛

In all, Staebler published more than a dozen substantial pieces by various authors on the stadium question. Most were against a vast new football palace; several wrote in favor. The series concluded in January 1926, just before the Day committee released its report on athletics at Michigan.

The committee said Michigan should dampen the fierce emphasis on winning, reduce the imbalance between intercollegiate and intramural sports, and put more faculty on the Board in Control of Intercollegiate Athletics. The University was "an institution of higher learning, not a purveyor of popular entertainment," the committee said. "Intercollegiate athletics seem to have grown out of all proportion to the importance of the purposes which they serve."

But few people paid attention to any of that. Instead, headlines trumpeted the Committee's grudging admission that there might as well be a new stadium of perhaps 60,000 seats.

The Regents soon approved the report, saying "a stadium of seventy thousand would not be objectionable."

A year and a half later, on October 1, 1927, with 72,000 seats, Michigan Stadium hosted its first game, a 33-0 victory against Ohio Wesleyan—though heavy rains kept the day's attendance to under 40,000. The official dedication was held three weeks later on a fine Saturday afternoon when the Wolverines defeated Ohio State, 21-0.

Over the years, many more seats were added—13,752 in 1928; 12,187 in 1949; 3,762 in 1973; 1,500 in 1992; 5,000 in 1998; and (after 1,300 seats were lost in 2008), 3,700 in 2010. With an official capacity of 109,901, it became the largest football stadium in the United States.

❖ ✛ ❖

After Angell's essay appeared in the *Chimes*, his friends and foes alike took delight in reporting his presence at Michigan football games. But he had one consolation prize: In 1926, he was appointed to the Board in Control of Intercollegiate Athletics, and thus enjoyed a small measure of influence over U-M athletic policy.

Angell went on to become one of the most prominent sociologists of his generation. He published several notable books and served as president of the American Sociological Association. He became chair of Michigan's Sociology Department and helped to found the Honors Program, which he directed for several years. He retired in 1969—though he continued to teach for a number of years—and died in 1984.

Fielding Yost was not head coach for the Wolverines' first season in the new stadium. He had stepped down just before the season began, saying he simply had too much to do as athletic director. He retired as athletic director in 1941 and died in 1946, the most honored figure in the history of Michigan sports.

Neil Staebler graduated from Michigan just as Yost's architects and engineers were drawing plans for what would much later be called "the Big House." He was the last editor of the *Chimes*, which folded the following year.

He earned a law degree, joined the family business in Ann Arbor, then went into politics. After World War II, he became the power-behind-the-throne to four major Michigan Democrats—G. Mennen Williams, who served a record seven terms as governor; Gov. John Swainson; Sen. Patrick McNamara; and Sen. Phil Hart. (Like Staebler, all but Swainson were Michigan alumni.)

In 1962, Staebler was elected congressman-at-large from Michigan. In 1964, he ran for governor against the popular Republican incumbent, George Romney, and lost. For many years thereafter he was the grand old man of Michigan Democrats. He lived and worked in Ann Arbor until his death in 2000.

And he was an enthusiastic fan of Michigan football, holding season tickets for decades.

Once, at the peak of the civil rights movement in the 1960s, Staebler wrote to a Michigan faculty member of the 1920s about their mutual support for a controversial student organization called the Negro-Caucasian Club. The fight for Black equality had been one thing, Staebler remarked, but "no present protest has approached the obloquy that the community poured on us for trying to subvert football."

15: The Mystery of Belford Lawson

Another email: An old colleague from the *Daily*, Rich Lerner, wrote to me about a photograph of Michigan's football team in Fielding Yost's heyday. The coach had an unwritten rule that no Black man would ever play football for Michigan—yet there, unmistakably, was the image of a Black man in the team photo. I pulled on that thread, too, and discovered a Wolverine who failed to qualify for glory because he was not the right color.

Among the cognoscenti of Michigan football lore, it is well known that there was not a single Black letterman at U-M between George Jewett in 1892 and Willis Ward in 1932. This forty-year gap is commonly attributed to the attitudes of Coach Fielding Yost, the son of a Confederate soldier, who did not permit Black men to wear Michigan's football uniform.

In track and field, there were Black Wolverines in Yost's time, including the great William DeHart Hubbard, the 1924 Olympic gold medalist in the long jump. And there was a Black letterman in baseball, Rudolph Ash, who batted .405 in 1923. But in football Yost upheld a strict color line—or so it has long been assumed.

Yet a photograph in the U-M's Bentley Historical Library of the 1923 team—national champions, led by the All-American Harry Kipke—appears to show otherwise. There, second from the left in the second row, is a Black player. This was not the formal studio photograph of the team taken annually at season's end, but a field-side photo of men in uniforms and pads. Labeled "U. of M. Football Squad 1923," it was published in the *Michigan Daily* and several game programs. Captions identify the Black man simply as "Lawson."

The facts of his life are fairly easy to establish—except for his role on the Michigan football team. There, questions and ambiguities remain, not only about Lawson, but about the permeability of Yost's color line and the experience of Black athletes before the civil rights era.

The player in the picture was Belford Vance Lawson Jr., originally from Roanoke, Virginia. The son of a railroad switchman and a schoolteacher, Lawson went briefly to Ferris Institute (now Ferris State University) in Big Rapids and then enrolled at Michigan in the fall of 1920. He was a member of Alpha Phi Alpha, a leading Black fraternity, and of U-M's varsity debate team. He won awards as an orator. In 1924, he graduated from LSA.

After coaching football for a time at the all-Black Morris Brown College in Atlanta, Lawson got his law degree at Howard University, then went into private practice in Washington, DC. In the 1930s, he helped found the New Negro Alliance, an early force in the fight for civil rights. He was a member of legal teams that argued two successful civil rights cases before the U.S. Supreme Court. He served as national president of Alpha Phi Alpha from 1945 to 1951. As a Democratic Party activist, he became, in 1956, the first African American ever to address its national convention. Lawson retired in 1977 and died in 1985.

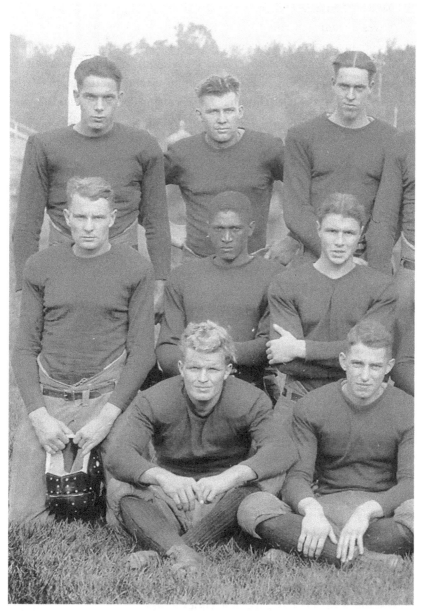

Was he on the team or not? This photo, labeled "U of M Football Squad 1923," shows Belford Lawson Jr. in the midst of his teammates. But an assistant coach later said of an unnamed black athlete, apparently Lawson: "We decided it was not worth the friction that would have resulted to have him on the squad." (*Bentley Historical Library*)

His wife, Marjorie McKenzie Lawson, also a U-M grad (LSA 1933, MSW 1934), was a campaign aide to John F. Kennedy and later became the first Black woman appointed to a federal judgeship. She died in 2002.

The Lawsons had one child, Belford V. Lawson III, who became an attorney with the Federal Communications Commission in Washington, DC. In the early 1960s, at the elite Groton School, alma mater of Franklin D. Roosevelt and other pillars of the American establishment, the younger Lawson was one of the first Black football players named to the All-New England prep squad. After graduating from Harvard, he followed his parents into the law. As he approached retirement, he wanted to learn exactly what happened to his father at Michigan in the 1920s.

It was a staple of Lawson family lore that Belford Jr. had been a member of the Michigan team under Yost. In the home, there was a navy blue blanket trimmed in maize with a foot-tall letter "M" in the middle. Yet he never spoke much about his experience on the team.

"My father was just so remote, so close-mouthed about his Michigan career," Belford III said. "I always speculated that maybe he didn't want me to find out that he did not formally win a varsity letter. Or maybe he played enough to get a varsity letter, but Yost decided not to give it to him because it was not the time, not the custom.

"I'm content just to find out if there are any records of him actually having been on the field."

So far, no such record has surfaced. The Athletic Department records in the Bentley Library show that Lawson won varsity reserve letters in his sophomore, junior, and senior years. That meant he was a member of the team but not a starter or a regular substitute. Nor is there any mention in the *Michigan Daily* or the *Michigan Alumnus* of his playing in a game. In that era, the *Daily* published thorough, play-by-play chronicles of most games, noting all starters and substitutions, and the *Alumnus* also carried game accounts.

So perhaps Lawson simply wasn't good enough to play for a national championship team. There would be no shame in that, either for the player or the university. And Lawson's presence on the squad, even as a reserve, would suggest that Yost's color line was not a brick wall.

Yet it appears the truth is more complicated than that.

✢ ⁛ ✢

In 1928, four years after Lawson's graduation, Elton "Tad" Weiman, Michigan's football coach that year, exchanged letters with an Indianapolis lawyer and U-M alumnus named Herbert Wilson. Wilson was trying to assist a young Black student who had hopes of making the Michigan football team. He asked Weiman if he would accept a qualified Black player. Wilson said: "I know while I was in school, Coach Yost would not permit it."

Coach Weiman replied that he had recently talked things over with the student:

> There were certain complications that would be difficult for all with a colored man on the squad; that because of this I did not think it advisable for a colored man to be on the squad unless he was good enough to play a good part of the time. In other words, unless he were a regular or near regular, the handicaps to the squad would be greater than the advantages to say nothing of the difficulties that would encounter the individual, himself. I assured him, however, that any man who could demonstrate that he was the best man for any position would have the right to play in that position.
>
> During the time that I have been at Michigan we have never had a colored candidate for the team who was good enough to play regularly. At one time we did have a backfield man who, had he been white, would probably have been on the squad as a second or third substitute. In a case like that we decided that it was not worth the friction that would result to have him on the squad. I do not know of any other case where a man's color has in any way affected his standing in athletics at Michigan.

It seems very likely that the "backfield man" was Belford Lawson. By "the squad" Weiman probably meant the first team—the starters and the small cadre of regular subs in the era when men played both offense and defense and substitutions were few.

It appears, then, that Lawson was made a reserve, not a "second or third substitute"—which likely would have allowed him some playing time—because of the risk of "complications" and "friction." He rode the bench because the coaches would not stand up to racists—on the team, among the alumni, or in the programs of opposing schools—who would object to a Black man playing football as an equal to white players.

In any case, Weiman's letter is unusually clear evidence for the contention that it was not enough for a Black athlete to be as good as a white player in order to be treated as an equal. He had to be better.

Just one press account referring to Lawson has been found—a *Detroit Free Press* article in September 1923 about a preseason Michigan scrimmage between a "blue" squad and a "red" squad. The article said: "Lawson, colored halfback on the red, demonstrated his ability at breaking up passes, knocking them down with great regularity."

Good enough to knock down passes thrown by the quarterback of a national championship team but not good enough to take the field in a regular-season game?

Belford Jr. once told his son about an incident that occurred early in his sophomore year. He said he had played well enough as a freshman to win his class numerals. (The numerals—such as "1924"—were a recognition of achievement on the frosh team, usually to be worn on a letter sweater.)

The following fall, needing money, he took a job as a waiter at a campus dining club used by the football team.

The younger Lawson recalled: "An assistant coach—this is what Dad told me—came up to him and said, 'Belford, what are you doing waiting on tables in the Varsity Club?' Dad said: 'Nobody said anything to me about coming out for the varsity, so I assumed you didn't want me back.' And the coach said, 'Belford, that's ridiculous. Everyone knew you won your freshman numerals. Everybody knew you were coming back.'"

So Lawson began to attend practice and made the reserve team. His son isn't sure what to make of this.

"Perhaps the situation was that no assistant coach wanted to be the one who might incur the displeasure of Yost, a notoriously racist guy, by asking if Belford could be invited back," he says. "And so everybody said, 'Well, you do it.' None of the assistant coaches wanted to invite my father back without getting Yost's formal approval, which is one of the classic examples of how racism worked in those years. It's just a hunch on my part. I have no evidence to support it.

"Maybe Dad just didn't know that because he'd gotten his numerals, that was the invitation. Dad was kind of proud that way. He would have wanted to be asked rather than to presume. And I think maybe as a Black person in that era, he would not have wanted to presume that he had been invited, and then return and be told that he had not been invited back."

In fact, press accounts from the era refer to players invited by Fielding Yost to come out for the team in the fall. So it's plausible, at least, that Lawson had been correct in waiting for an invitation, and that he was not merely imagining a slight when an invitation did not come.

Belford Lawson Jr. told his son other stories, too—stories that appear to have been untrue.

Lawson told his son he once had tackled the great Red Grange of Illinois. And he said he had been proud to take the field against Iowa, which had defied racial mores by playing Duke Slater, a Black player who was named a first-team All-American in 1921.

But Grange didn't play for Illinois until the fall of his sophomore year. That was 1923, Belford Lawson's senior year, and Michigan did not play Illinois that year. So Lawson could not have tackled Grange, at least not in an official game between the two schools. And there is no record in the play-by-play chronicles in the *Michigan Daily*, which nearly always included lists of substitutions, that Lawson entered any game against Iowa.

"Dad's recollections of his on-field exploits seemed so concretely detailed and so vivid, and his body language so animated when he talked about his game appearances, that I had no reason to disbelieve him on the rare occasions when he reminisced," Belford III said when asked about the inconsistencies. "All I can do is speculate. Maybe he made up a few stories in order to hide from me the fact that he never played. Maybe he did play a bit, but there was an unwritten rule among sports journalists not to mention a Black player."

Finally, the younger Lawson wondered why his father never took him to a game at Michigan Stadium.

"It was such a mystery to me. Here's a guy who played varsity football for the University of Michigan on the national championship team and didn't want to take his son, also a star football player, to Michigan to see a game? That heightened my curiosity. I could never understand that."

Raising their son in Washington, DC, in the 1950s and 1960s, his mother and father had sent him mostly to private prep schools.

"They didn't want me in a segregated environment," he said. "They wanted me to go to Groton. They wanted me to go to Harvard. They didn't want me to have to go through anything of what they did.

"So maybe the idea of taking me back to Michigan was associated in the minds of my father's generation with: 'He might find out something about what it was like to live under extreme segregation.' He might have thought that if I started to find out information about the twenties and how Black students lived and where they lived and where they ate, it might be traumatic. And it wouldn't have been just preventing me from finding out about the harshness of life in segregation, but preventing me from finding out about the emotional difficulty of enduring the ambiguity."

With his father gone, Belford Lawson III could only wonder about those long-ago seasons. What seems most likely is that his father—unquestionably a highly accomplished man in every other part of his life—did what countless fathers have done before and since: He told his son a few tall tales of past athletic glory and then dodged a situation in which he might have been forced to admit that those few stories were more fiction than fact.

But even if that is so, Belford Lawson Jr. was not quite the same as the average father making up stories to impress a son. He was making up stories about what really might have been, had it not been for the racism of his time and place. Perhaps, as he told his son those tales, he was for a few moments escaping the necessity, as his son put it, of "enduring the ambiguity" of being accepted yet not accepted, good enough yet not good enough.

V. THE WORLD THE
STUDENTS MADE

In the early years of his long presidency, James Burrill Angell was called upon now and then to decide where a gravel walkway should be laid on the Diag. It was never a difficult decision, as he explained one day while speaking to students about the reliance of U.S. law on precedent. "One of the finest examples of the value of precedent that I have ever seen," he said, "is one of the paths which you fellows make across the grass of the campus. We take that as clear proof that a walk should be there, and set about building one."

The analogy to the University as a whole is exact. As much as Regents, presidents, deans, and professors, students have made the University of Michigan. This is true across every realm of campus life. It was students who rebelled against mandatory attendance at morning chapel in the 1800s. Students started the fraternities and sororities. Students' semi-violent "rushes" fostered the invention of college football. Students demanded their own gymnasia. Students created and regulated the rituals of campus social life, from "smokers" and "mixers" to pot parties, keggers, and day-drinking. Students overthrew the regime of in loco parentis. Students have done much of the actual work in research labs and much of the actual teaching in classrooms.

Soon after I started writing for John Lofy at *Michigan Today*, he and I began to see a certain theme crop up often. We called it "students behaving badly." I wrote about the Michigan boys who started the national craze for "panty raids" in the 1950s, students racing around town in cars in the 1920s, and students breaking the rules of Prohibition. Who could resist writing these tales? They made up many of the most vivid memories of alumni.

But I thought it was important to show that mere sophomoric behavior—and many of the miscreants were sophomores, after all—makes up only a fraction of the students' impact on Michigan. It has never been an institution that students simply passed through, changed by it but not changing it. The place has been shaped at every turn by what students demanded and what they did.

16: The Rise and Fall of J-Hop

I'm always surprised when I mention the term J-Hop around Ann Arbor and get a puzzled look in response—"Did you say 'jay hop'? What's that?" That's how familiar the term was in my house when I was growing up. My mother spoke of it with a mixture of adoring nostalgia and deep respect. My dad, too. When they went to school in the late 1930s and early '40s, it was *the* social event at Michigan in an era when big dances filled the campus calendar nearly all year long. For my parents, it had mostly to do with the music, and when I thought to write about J-Hop, it was mostly to tell how the biggest swing-jazz bands in the U.S. played in Ann Arbor every year. But as I did my research, I learned that J-Hop's history had to do with more than music. It represented the long rise and long fall of a particular way of going to college that changed for good, like much else, in the 1960s.

The hard decision had been put off for as long as possible. Now, on a chilly night in May 1960, the existential question of J-Hop—whether to keep it on life support for another year or let it die—had finally landed on the weekly agenda of Michigan's Student Government Council.

Since its founding almost a century earlier, the mid-year social event that became known as the Junior Hop, then simply and universally as J-Hop, had swelled into a glittering three-day-and-night festival of big band dances, house parties, hayrides, and morning-after breakfasts. To generations of living alumni, the spectacle of J-Hop occupied a pedestal in Michigan tradition just one level lower than varsity football itself.

So this would be no easy decision for sixteen student politicos barely out of their teens and with no great store of respect among their peers. The prevailing view of student government was voiced by a critic who said student government was "run by a bunch of hams for a lot of don't-give-a-damns."

Indeed, not to give a damn was very much in vogue just then. Dressing for dinner was out. Creased pants were out. Rah-rah was out. The new place to go for live music was the Promethean, a coffee house on Liberty with dark gray walls and deliberately mismatched furniture. No dance music there, just mournful folk songs, and the beverage of choice was muddy espresso.

J-Hop? In this age of apathy?

One student said J-Hop was "so OUT even the OUT people won't touch it."

As recently as 1955, there had been the usual fierce competition for 1,350 J-Hop tickets, one ticket per couple, the maximum crowd that could squeeze into the Intramural Sports Building's giant gymnasium.

But since then, ticket sales had dropped by nearly two-thirds. By 1959, said Murray Feiwell, that year's forlorn J-Hop chairman, "we did everything but line people up at the administration building and take seven dollars out of their pockets."

In desperation, the 1960 affair had been downsized and shifted to the smaller ballroom at the Michigan League.

"Oh, let it die," begged a *Michigan Daily* editor. That was "the most merciful thing you could do to the fine old Michigan tradition, J-Hop."

So the members of the Student Government Council trudged upstairs to their office in the Student Activities Building and started the debate about what to do. They had a lot of history to consider.

In the 1930s and '40s, J-Hop's attendees danced to the music of the great bandleaders of the swing era, sometimes two bands in the same night—Duke Ellington, Benny Goodman, Count Basie, Tommy and Jimmy Dorsey. (*Bentley Historical Library*)

✦ ⁑ ✦

The holding of a mid-year student dance—a private affair with no special sanction from the University—had begun in the misty past of the late 1860s, just before women were admitted to U-M. (Male students invited sweethearts from home, paying their railroad fare and putting them up in chaperoned digs.) From one year to the next, the event moved from the Gregory House, a hotel on the city's old courthouse square, to Hank's Emporium, then Hangsterfer's, both downtown saloons.

The organizers of these early affairs were U-M's nine original fraternities, known collectively as the Palladium. In the early 1890s, they moved the dance to the larger setting of Waterman Gymnasium, just constructed at the southwest corner of North and East University Streets.

That changed things. Putting the dance on University property meant faculty had the final say over how the dance would be run. The nine original frats rebelled by holding their own dance in Toledo in 1896. But they came back a year later, upholding their honor by sponsoring elaborately decorated booths emblazoned with their emblems, a practice that lasted for decades.

As the student population swelled, so did the Junior Hop. (Off and on, juniors were in charge of organizing the dance, with the idea of honoring the outgoing seniors. Even when that tenet waned, the name "J-Hop" stuck.) By the early 1900s, it was firmly in place as the crowning event of each year's social calendar.

One night of dancing expanded to two, with parties before and after. Each year, more tickets were sold. Decorations and lighting became more elaborate. Programs were printed. Faculty "patrons and patronesses" were invited and feted. Favors and keepsakes were handed out. Then "the Hop itself comes, and what a reign of bliss it brings!" wrote a student satirist in 1906. "There is the blare of music, the glare of lights ... There is My Lady Talcum, vivacious, in her new gown. And by her stands My Lord White-Gloved Discomfort, brilliant in patent leathers, wash tie, and a coat with most expressive long tails...."

At the start of the 20th century, J-Hop combined a restrained romantic ambiance with visual spectacle. Overall, it was a decorous affair of which even a concerned parent might approve.

Then came the ingredient that turned J-Hop into a craze.

The ingredient was jazz, in one form after another, developed largely by successive generations of southern Black musicians and seized upon by successive generations of northern white youth.

In 1913 the decorative theme of J-Hop was "a shrine to Terpsichore," the Greek muse of the dance. But old Terpsichore never saw some of the steps students were doing out on the floor of Waterman Gym as the hour grew late.

In fact, "fancy holds" and "feature dancing" had been raising chaperones' eyebrows for several years. Ragtime, the irresistible new music that encouraged wild departures from the Victorian holds of the 1880s and '90s, had brought a nationwide fever for such steps as the Bunny Hug, the Grizzly Bear, and the Turkey Trot, all of which required varying degrees of hugging and grinding.

Most scandalous of all was the "clutch hold" of the tango. Student authorities had already been talking about banning it just to preempt a crackdown
by the faculty.

As midnight approached, something rowdier than dirty dancing was
brewing outside the gym.

For some years, J-Hop organizers had allowed people not attending the
dance itself to gaze upon the spectacle from Waterman's upper galleries.
Then, as the dance came to a close, the doors would be opened for the spectators to walk through and admire the decorations.

But this year, the J-Hop Committee had decided to keep the gallery off-lim-
its and the doors locked. This did not go down well. A number of well-oiled
men outside now decided to attend J-Hop by force. With a heavy length of gas
pipe, they battered the doors open. Once inside, they found themselves facing
a phalanx of intrepid campus janitors and a U-M purchasing agent named
Loos. Wielding make-shift clubs and at least one fire extinguisher, Loos and
his men held off the unarmed intruders for twenty minutes, long enough for
eight of Ann Arbor's finest to arrive and bring the skirmish to an end.

Outrage grew over the next few days. Newspapers, alumni, and the University's out-state critics seized on the brawl as only the most flagrant of
J-Hop's excesses.

Finally, the faculty senate voted to do away with J-Hop altogether "until
such time as the university authorities are satisfied that all objectionable fea-
tures will in the future be eliminated."

They intended not only to prevent more violence but also to curb J-Hop's
extravagance, "ragtime and low vaudeville music," and "objectionable dancing."

Poor Willis Diekema, general chairman of J-Hop that year, said no mere
committee could have resisted the J-Hoppers' determination to dance the
tango in 1913.

"Because of the extreme popularity of the tango," he pleaded, "the objectionable dancing could have been checked only by the action of police."

The faculty stuck to the ban for only one year. J-Hop was reinstated in 1915,
then rolled along as ever through the years of World War I.

In 1920 there was more trouble. Unescorted "flappers"—young women
who insisted on their rights to pleasure, self-determination, and cigarettes—
crashed the affair, displayed "scantily clad forms," and engaged in "drinking,
smoking and individual caddishness."

There was another one-year ban and another reinstatement, this time with a long list of rules. But the demand for tickets only grew.

Then, in 1928, the giant Intermural Building on Hoover Street opened its doors. When J-Hop's organizers saw the cavernous main gym—252 feet long, big enough for four basketball courts—they reserved the space with stars in their eyes.

This was where J-Hop would enter its golden age.

✛ ✛ ✛

The kingpins of the J-Hop Committee now did some figuring.

With the IM Building's huge gym for a venue, they could sell tickets to many more couples at the long-prevailing rate of $7 per ticket—enough to pull in $7,000 to $8,000 in revenue. That was enough to hire the best bands in the U.S., and not just one great band but two, even three.

Ragtime was out. The new music was swing jazz. It was as hot on college campuses in the 1930s as rock and roll would be twenty and thirty years later.

Now J-Hop put students on a dance floor within a few yards of their musical deities—Duke Ellington, Benny Goodman, Count Basie, Tommy and Jimmy Dorsey. This was like having the Beatles play for your high school prom in 1965. If you loved swing and you could scratch together seven dollars, Depression or no Depression, you would fight like hell for a J-Hop ticket.

Typically now, two bands would set up, one at each end of the gym. They would trade off, each playing half-hour sets, each fighting the other to whip the crowd to a higher plateau of excitement. It drove U-M's swing aficionados into raptures.

"Twenty years from now," a swing worshipper told *Daily* readers in 1941, "Goodman may be remembered only vaguely as the beginner of a movement known as swing, some mad, senseless rhythm that died out . . . ." Not likely, the reviewer said. Instead, "he may be lauded as the father of . . . something more moving and beautiful than has ever before been found in folk music."

Every year now, students would wait for weeks to hear which bands the J-Hop Committee had landed. In 1931, the Detroit radio station WJR began to broadcast the spectacle live from 11:30 pm to 1:30 am, with Professor Waldo Abbot of the Department of Rhetoric offering song-by-song commentary. By the time the swing era began to fade in the mid-1950s, J-Hoppers had danced to virtually every big-name band in the country.

I f swing was king in the court of J-Hop, fashion was queen. Intense attention and no money were devoted to the question of what to wear. For men, that was easy. Tuxedos and tails were standard. Women had to choose not only their gowns but also accessories, jewelry, and the proper arrangement of one's hair.

Fashion took center stage at J-Hop's Grand March, where the couples lined up to circumnavigate the floor. The J-Hop chairman (always a man) and his date led the procession. All this would be written up in the *Daily* as if it were a royal wedding, with the closest attention to descriptions of what the leading ladies wore.

The *Daily's* reporter intoned in 1935, "The climax of the evening, the grand march, was led by Winifred Bell, '36, and Edward Litchfield, '36, general chairman. Miss Bell selected a charming robin's egg blue uncut velvet formal, made in the Empire style. It featured a short bodice and a full skirt, with a short train, while the neckline was trimmed with a draped collar, shirred at the front which outlined the V-neck. She wore a rhinestone clip at the neck, with matching earrings and bracelet. Her shoes were white velvet, trimmed with silver, and she wore a black velvet wrap with a white lapin ascot collar."

And that was just one of twenty women's outfits described for readers of the next day's *Daily*, from Miss Bell's rather complicated ensemble to Jean Greenwald's raspberry waffle-weave crepe to Margaret Mustard's flowered satin with a high Peter Pan collar.

"The dark blue of the ceiling decorations provided an effective background for the vivid colors and dainty materials. Glittering trimmings of lame and sequins and accessories of gold and silver reflected the maize colored lights"—a spectacle that made that year's J-Hop, like every J-Hop, "the most brilliant social event of the year."

There were big dances at U-M all year long in the '30s—the Freshman Frolic, the Senior Ball, and many more.

But J-Hop was much more than a single big dance. It stretched across three days and nights. Associated meals and parties spread across the campus and beyond. Virtually every fraternity held at least one house party, and many gave breakfasts that began shortly after the last dances of the night. A big breakfast was served at the Union starting at 1 am, organized chiefly for "independents"—students not affiliated with fraternities or sororities. That, too, was a reservation-only affair. Cost: 75 cents.

Hayrides, sleighrides, and sledding expeditions got the revelers out for some fresh air in the Arboretum or along the Huron. After the after-dance breakfast, J-Hoppers rolled from one hamburger joint and bar to another until the breaking of dawn.

The sheer physical ordeal left many a survivor exhausted. In 1939 a J-Hop veteran named Roy Heath compared it to fifteen rounds in a championship boxing match. "To say I don't know anything about J-Hop is to say Max Schmeling doesn't know anything about Joe Louis," he told readers of the *Daily*.

Heath offered point-by-point advice for neophytes.

First: The cash needed.

"C'mon ... cough up that watch. Don't kid yourself, it will cost just double what you think it will."

Then, "on the night of the battle," for courage, "you should prepare a sort of a pick-me-up to sip when the going gets rough. It consists of six parts Scotch, one part pure alcohol, three parts extract of Tiger blood and four parts iron pyrite."

Thus fortified, one could proceed to the main event. But only the bravest souls, Heath advised, would let themselves in for the full four hours. It was much wiser to save two hours of strife by arriving at midnight. But then you had to prepare for a deafening assault on the eardrums.

"There is a band playing no matter what anyone tells you and if you don't believe it just go up to the hospital and ask someone who got there early and saw it before the crush of the crowd got them ...

"As soon as the band starts to play a piece the news is relayed back. When the message gets to you, just whistle it softly to yourself and jiggle up and down."

Afterward, there must be time to recuperate. "You will be as good a man as your grandfather was at the age of 90 in two months at the outside."

✤ ⁑ ✤

B eneath the courtly surface, there was a predictable mixture of drinking and sex—or attempts at it.

In 1939, *Daily* reporters sought out local cabbies for their take.

"There ain't much petting going on early in the evening during J-Hop," one confided. "At least, I don't see any. No, man, when I'm driving, I'm driving. But I can't help hearing things. And early in the night, the boys do get their faces slapped once in a while, and from the sound of things, some of those babes sure pack a mean wallop.

"Maybe it's drunkenness or just plain appreciation, but the slapping sort of wears off later in the night."

Appreciative or not, a woman was expected to send her escort a "bread-and-butter letter"—a thank-you note describing the wonderful time she had had. In 1935, the *Daily* prepared a handy cheat sheet with multiple choice offerings that suggested the romance of J-Hop was more often an ideal than a reality:

Dearest:
  1 Tom
  2 Dick
  3 Harry
  4 Phineas

I had a wonderful:
  1 hangover.
  2 cleaner's bill.
  3 time with . . .
    (a) your roommate;
    (b) the chaperone;
    (c) Uncle Joe [Joseph Bursley, dean of students, who kept a stern watch from J-Hop's sidelines]

I adored your:
1   *house party.*
2   *brawl.*
3   *cocktails.*

It was all so:
1   *divine.*
2   *tiresome (speaking frankly).*
3   *exhausting.*

And now I feel like:
1   *you looked.*
2   *Hell!*
3   *another Tom Collins.*

A comparable note from the male point of view had been written years earlier by none other than Avery Hopwood (LSA 1905), who became the most popular American playwright of the 1910s and '20s and bequeathed part of his fortune to start U-M's prestigious Hopwood Awards.

In a short story, "After the Hop Is Over," published in the *Inlander*, Hopwood's fictional U-M man jots a diary entry about the morning after at one fraternity:

"The girls have gone. I'm almost dead. So are we all. The house smells of perfume, and there's powder in the air . . . I got a crush on Miss Evans—Ratty's girl. She made Jean [his own date] look like two cents. I'm in love, in love— and dead broke . . . . Thank God the damned thing is over."

✤ ⁝ ✤

For some, J-Hop was just a hubbub in the distance—someone else's party.

Especially during the Great Depression, plenty of students could barely cover the cost of tuition and food. There was no J-Hop for them.

Others, by an unspoken understanding, simply were not welcome. William DeHart Hubbard, the Black track-and-field star who won a gold medal at the 1924 Olympics, told an interviewer years later that the tiny circle of

Black students at U-M in the '20s barely noticed the shindigs that were not "whites-only" by law but might as well have been.

"They would have the big—what do you call it? J-Hop or something?" Hubbard said. "We just didn't bother about them."

And there were students who hoped to get in on the fun but never could. The *Daily's* classified ads one year carried this brief appeal: "WANTED: DATE FOR J-HOP. AM BLOND, 5'2", BIG BLUE EYES. NO. 2-2591. ASK FOR DONNA H."

Still, for the lucky and the privileged facing the cold, gray landscape of winter in Ann Arbor, J-Hop was a citadel of warmth and color.

"Didn't we come back with rings under our eyes, a collection of prize pictures and guest towels, to say nothing about the favors and the fraternity pin?" mused a columnist in the *Daily* who used only her initials, J.C.X. "And then we woke up Monday AM to the tune of the alarm clock played in the dismal key of C minor, gazed out upon the cold cruel world and decided what's the use anyway. Nothing exciting would ever happen again."

J-Hop's staying power was evident in the weeks after Japan's attack on Pearl Harbor in December 1941. It was quickly announced that the event would stay on the calendar for February 1942.

But in 1943, with thousands of U-M men away at war, J-Hop was downsized, combined with the Senior Ball, reduced from three days to two, and renamed the Victory Ball. So it remained through 1945, a shadow of J-Hops of the '30s.

With the war's end, the J-Hop Committee for 1945–1946 proposed a revival of prewar splendor—two dances, three big-name bands, house parties, breakfasts, the whole shebang. Total cost: $10,000, the highest budget ever.

There were qualms. The Student Affairs Committee, with its faculty majority, vetoed that plan on several grounds: It would strain Ann Arbor's already overtaxed housing stock; there was a shortage of willing chaperones; such a luxury-fest would "look bad out-state." The Committee approved a trimmed-down affair—one dance on a Friday; house parties on Saturday.

Some students diagnosed a more troubling flaw in the big-spending plan—a moral one. Did students really want to re-animate the make-believe luxury of J-Hop in the wake of a world war and in the shadow of the atom bomb?

"No one denies the delight of the proposed weekend," said a letter to the *Daily* signed by sixteen student critics. "Yes, and wonderful it would be to return to the gaiety of the old carefree days: to turn our minds from the sickening pictures of devastation and suffering abroad, to wrap our oceans around us more tightly, to preach not only America First, but Me First ... But our ears detect a false note in the old melody."

Nonetheless, in just one day the J-Hop Committee gathered 2,300 student signatures in favor of prewar J-Hop glory. A female graduate of 1945, married to a Navy man who had left Ann Arbor to serve and now was back as a student, demanded what she and her husband had dreamt of for four years—a real J-Hop.

"We feel most students want what we want: peacetime activities as soon as possible," she wrote the *Daily*. "Sure, J-Hop as a two-night affair would be a $10,000 dance. But if the students want it—well, they're paying for it, so let them have it!"

And they got it. In the late '40s and early '50s, J-Hop roared on. The great swing bands came back. The fashions became a little less formal, but the decorations were as lavish as ever, the parties as raucous as they'd been in the '20s and '30s.

But it was not to last.

++ ‡ ++

J-Hop had become so big partly because Michigan itself had become so big. By the 1930s the student body had topped 10,000.

When the tradition began to fade, that, too, may have owed something to Michigan's ever-swelling size.

In 1941 there were about 11,000 students. By 1950, thanks in part to the G.I. Bill, which brought crowds of World War II veterans to campuses across the country, Michigan's enrollment swelled to nearly 20,000. In the late 1950s the number jumped again, to nearly 25,000.

In 1959, Erich Walter, a U-M graduate of 1914 who became a professor of English and dean of students, remarked that the "problem of bigness" had caused profound changes in the student's experience of college life. An entering freshman on a campus so big felt tiny, even expendable. "The student is swept off his feet by the size of this place," Walter said. And it was so big that "there is nothing to bring this community together."

Football, maybe.

But not J-Hop. Not anymore.

"Especially in the past few years," a *Daily* editor named Faith Weinstein wrote in 1959, "a kind of sweeping lethargy has become practically the sole unifying force among the students of the University."

She blamed this on a rising "cult of the individual" and "a glorification of the personal, especially of the Personal Problem, and a deprecation of anything that concerns groups, with the possible exception of the group you drink with."

In the midst of a mood like that, a great communal ritual like J-Hop didn't stand much of a chance.

❖ ⁑ ❖

After a long discussion, the sixteen members of the Student Government Council voted 9-7 not to place J-Hop on the campus calendar for 1961.

A small irony was tucked away in that vote.

One of the seven who voted to save J-Hop was a student named Al Haber. He would soon stand at the center of forces that pulled students out of their apathy and swept them into a new era of campus energy quite unimaginable to the swing dancers of the 1930s and '40s. The following fall, Haber became the first president of the Students for a Democratic Society—SDS.

17: The Negro-Caucasian Club

My colleague Kim Clarke discovered the story of the Negro-Caucasian Club. When she told me about it, I all but begged her to hand it over so I could write it.

Readers of U-M history have rightly complained that so many stories about Black students in the University's past are stories of athletes. Here was a story about Black students who not only were not athletes, but who directly confronted the racism woven through the University's fabric long before the protest movements of the 1960s. Even so, a thin thread of hope ran through the story, too.

It began at the lunch hour one day in the fall of 1925, when there were perhaps 60 Black students at Michigan out of a student body of some 10,000.

A Black student named Lenoir Bertrice Smith had only a short break
between classes. There was no time to run home for lunch, and she hadn't
brought anything along.

So she and a white friend, Edith Kaplan, stepped into a restaurant near
Nickels Arcade and sat down for a quick bite.

They waited a long time.

Finally, a busboy came to their table and set a pile of dirty dishes on the
table between the two young women.

Lenoir Smith looked at the dishes, then rose from the table.

Before attending U-M, Smith's white friend Edith Kaplan had never spent
time with Black people. So it took her a moment to grasp what was happening.

Then she looked at Lenoir Smith, Kaplan recalled long afterward, and "I
trembled with rage when I saw her face, and knew that the dirty dishes had
not been accidental."

NEGRO-CAUCASIAN CLUB

Joseph Bursley, dean of students, authorized the Negro-Caucasian Club to discuss race
relations but not to work for "the abolition of discrimination against Negroes." (*Bentley
Historical Library*)

The two women went to see Oakley Johnson, a young instructor in the Department of Rhetoric. Lenoir Smith was taking Johnson's class; she knew him to be sympathetic to the difficult situation of Black students. The women asked Johnson what might be done.

Johnson took them to see John Robert Effinger, dean of LSA. They hoped he might bring the University's influence to bear on Ann Arbor restaurant owners who refused service to Black students.

Effinger's response was "correct, cold and unsympathetic," Johnson said.

"Why, I'm very sorry about this," Johnson recalled Effinger saying, "but, you know, the University has no control over the businessmen of the city. Our domain ends at the edge of the campus. We can't do anything at all."

"But can't you express the University's desire that its students be treated properly? After all, they're students here, regardless of color."

"No," Effinger said. "My grandfather owned slaves in Virginia, but you mustn't think I'm prejudiced. I would do something for you if I could."

"He seemed to think we were demented," Johnson recalled.

So the students and Johnson decided to do something for themselves. They gathered friends and declared themselves the Negro-Caucasian Club of the University of Michigan. It may have been the first such group on any U.S. college campus.

If not demented, they were certainly audacious.

The first two Black students had been admitted to U-M in 1868. But only a handful followed, and by the 1920s, Blacks still comprised only a tiny fragment of the student body. By University practice and informal understandings, they lived in a segregated sphere, joining white students only in classrooms.

In that era only women lived in University dormitories—but not the six or seven Black women enrolled at U-M. They lived in a boarding house arranged by the University. Black men generally lived in one of three Black fraternity houses—Kappa Alpha Psi, Omega Psi Phi, and Alpha Phi Alpha—or boarded with Black families. The Michigan Union would not serve Blacks. The University barred them from its swimming pools and University-sponsored dances.

"The colored were not part and parcel of the school," recalled Joseph Leon Langhorne, a Black graduate of 1928.

In this atmosphere, the Negro-Caucasian Club asked to be recognized as an official student organization. In their petition they declared their aim—"to work for a better understanding between the races and for the abolition of discrimination against Negroes."

The University's response: Not so fast.

✤ ⁺⁺ ✤

The Club's petition went to the faculty senate's Committee on Student Activities. But first, Joseph Bursley, the dean of students, wanted a word with Oakley Johnson, who represented the students as faculty advisor.

"Sometime at your convenience," Bursley wrote Johnson, "will you drop into the office so that I can talk over with you the application for recognition of the Negro-Caucasian Club. I should like to get a little more data on the matter before the petition is submitted to the Committee on Student Affairs."

Bursley apparently advised Johnson that it would be all right for the Club to meet and talk about race relations, but not to work for "the abolition of discrimination against Negroes"—not if it wanted official recognition.

As amended, the Club's articles of agreement included this paragraph, apparently amended to suit Bursley's advice: "The aim of the Negro-Caucasian Club is to encourage a spirit of friendliness and fair-mindedness between the races, and to study and discuss, impartially, the problems arising in relations between them."

Even this wording made the faculty nervous. After eight weeks and "very careful consideration," the Committee on Student Activities granted its approval, but only for a trial period of one year and only "with the provision that the name of the University of Michigan shall not be used in connection with the Club."

With that cold send-off, the Club began its business.

There were 26 student founders. Most were Black, including several of the tiny handful of Black women students then at U-M. About five were white.

The faculty senate had been dubious, but other faculty members stepped forward to support the Club as an advisory committee. These included Howard Yale McClusky, a young educational psychologist who would teach at Michigan for nearly fifty years and serve on the U.S. delegation to UNESCO; a mathematics professor named William Wells Denton; Eileen Erlanson, an instructor in botany; and R.C. Trotter of the French Department.

The Club sent one hundred surveys to white students with questions such as: "How many Negroes have you met other than your maid or butler?" and true-or-false choices such as: "All Negro men are drooling for the chance to rape white women."

The responses, tabulated by sympathizers in the Sociology Department, were appalling.

"We concluded that the problem was one of belief in the sub-humanity of Negroes and unfamiliarity," Lenoir Smith recalled later. "On this basis we decided to bring outstanding Negroes to the campus to show people that there were Negroes who were not 'hewers of wood and carriers of water.'"

The first to be invited was the Black philosopher Alain LeRoy Locke, a key figure in the Black cultural awakening called the Harlem Renaissance.

Locke's address in the Natural Science Building had the intended effect among white students. Julius Watson, a Black student from Detroit, remembered the reaction of a white teacher from Arkansas who was attending graduate school at U-M.

"After [Locke's] talk someone asked her if she was surprised," Watson said, "and she remarked that she was really shocked because she did not dream that there was a Negro who could say so many things that she could not understand."

More speakers came, including the great activist and writer W.E.B. DuBois, a founder of the National Association for the Advancement of Colored People, and the novelist Jean Toomer. Members of the club met with A. Philip Randolph, the labor leader who would organize the first march on Washington, DC, for civil rights; Frank Murphy, the liberal Detroit judge who would later defend minority rights as a U.S. Supreme Court justice; and Clarence Darrow, the fiery criminal lawyer who defended the Black Detroit physician Ossian Sweet in the most celebrated civil rights trial of the era.

✤ ✤ ✤

It's hard to know what the overwhelmingly white majority of Michigan students thought of the club. But one gets a glimpse of prevailing attitudes in a letter written to Oakley Johnson many years later.

It came from Nelson Ritter, a white physician who trained at Michigan in the 1920s. Ritter had read an account of the Negro-Caucasian Club that Johnson published in the *Michigan Quarterly Review* in 1969. He had been surprised to learn that Blacks at U-M in his day had been treated as inferior, and he sent Johnson his own recollections. The letter reveals something of the white myopia, the blind acceptance of stereotypes, and the gulf between Blacks and whites that prevailed for much of Michigan's history.

Ritter recalled Chester Chinn, "the only negroe [sic] to graduate in my class . . . He seemed to be a very fine person and I recall his being spoken of as more like a white than any of the other Blacks who started with us. By that I mean he had none of the other characteristics of his race which we commonly thought of in those days except his skin . . .

"I must confess that I and I think my friends, fraternity brothers and so forth had little or no awareness of a feeling on their part of not being a part of the human race . . . Among the northerners I am sure there were none who would have intentionally hurt their feelings. Actually to me they were simply another class of people as were the very rich, i.e. not part of my middle income life. If I had any feeling it was to be very careful not to let them know that we weren't all on a par. The cook and houseman in our medical fraternity couldn't have been more highly thought of . . . ."

✦ ⁑ ✦

Oakley Johnson, who was not only a champion of civil rights but a Marxist and a member of the Communist Party, left U-M in 1928, his bid for tenure denied despite the backing of his colleagues in the Department of Rhetoric. The Negro-Caucasian Club continued until 1930 with another faculty advisor, then faded as the Great Depression took hold.

The members went their separate ways, many to distinguished careers.

Because of her experience in the club, Sarita Davis gave up her plan to become a missionary abroad and instead became a social worker.

Lenoir Smith returned to Michigan for a master's degree in the 1930s. From 1953 to 1958 she was head of the serology section at University Hospital.

Smith's companion for lunch on State Street, Edith Kaplan, became an authority on ancient languages at the University of Chicago.

K.A. Harden became dean of the medical school at Howard University.

Armistead Pride became the long-serving chair of journalism at the historically Black Lincoln University and the nation's leading expert on the Black press.

In 1969, alumni of the Negro-Caucasian Club gathered in Washington, DC, for a reunion. Looking back at their time in Ann Arbor, it was their own informal gatherings they remembered most, usually at 620 Church Street, the home of Oakley Johnson and his wife, Mary.

"We sat on the floor and talked and ate peanuts," Lenoir Smith remembered. "We tried *not* to discuss the Race Problem, but everything else in order to prove that we *could*—that we were not sub-human, that we had ideas, feelings and aspirations."

"The Negro-Caucasian Club at Michigan helped relieve the Negro student's feeling of isolation," wrote Armistead Pride, "and to give him some portholes onto campus life other than those of the classroom and the *Michigan Daily*."

"I think the N.C. Club served a distinct purpose then," wrote Joseph Langhorne. "It was the only forum . . . for airing of Negro people's views and students' problems in Ann Arbor."

"For many of us this represented the first social contact with Caucasians which was of more than a casual degree," wrote K.A. Harden.

White members remembered a fundamental change in their outlook.

"Because of those associations, I lost my Black-white feelings," Sarita Davis recalled. "Ever since, a Negro has been another human being to me."

18: Panty Raid, 1952

The long-dead fad of "panty raids" was at best one part sophomoric comedy to two parts ugly male aggression. So some readers may think the trend is best forgotten. Still, I thought readers might like to know how the first such event in the nation unfolded at Michigan in the early 1950s. The more I learned about it, the more it seemed to prefigure the more potent waves of student unrest that would begin a decade later.

It had been another dismal Michigan winter. The gray and the cold had stretched well into March. But finally, as the earth approached the vernal equinox on Thursday, March 20, 1952—the eve of the first day of spring—the temperature in Ann Arbor crept up to 57 glorious degrees. Jackets came off. Windows opened.

At about 6:30 pm, Art Benford, a junior, finished dinner in the dining hall of West Quad. He went to his room in Allen Rumsey House and picked up his trumpet. Benford said later he had only meant to relax by playing a little music. But his impromptu rendition of Glenn Miller's "Serenade in Blue" set off a chain of events that gave the U.S. one of the most notorious fads of the 1950s—the panty raid.

Across Madison Street, in South Quad, an unidentified trombonist opened up with a loud reply to Benford's serenade, and the two began to duel. Guys began to shout, "Knock it off!" (Both dorms were all male.) Then someone began to blow a portable fog horn. Someone else put a phonograph up to his window and played "Slaughter on Tenth Avenue" at high volume. Two tubaists accompanied. Men began to run down the stairs and out onto Madison.

Stop here and review the ingredients: (a) the first comfortable night outdoors in four or five months; (b) a great deal of ambient noise; (c) a strict code of rules forbidding unsupervised mixing of the sexes; and (d) hundreds of eighteen-, nineteen-, and twenty-year-old males.

By the estimate of the *Michigan Daily*, about six hundred men were bellying up to a Quad-vs.-Quad imbroglio when the Ann Arbor police pulled up. This turned the quaddies' attention away from each other and toward the law.

Commenting the next day, Professor Amos Hawley, a sociologist, suggested the cops' arrival was the point of ignition. "Up to then it was a usual sort of thing," he told the *Daily*, "but that gave it a rallying point and set up a conflict situation."

Students jeered at the cops, who returned to their cars, whereupon scores of bodies swarmed over the cars and rocked them. The cops, vastly outnumbered, did nothing.

Perhaps the breaking of that one taboo—the defiance of police, unanswered—put the crowd in the mood to break more. Whatever the reason, the swelling mob began to move, first east on Madison, then around the corner and north on State toward the nearest concentrations of women, at Helen Newberry and Betsy Barbour Residences. There, the *Daily* said, men entered the women's dormitories, then "heckled excited residents and broke into the lounges."

Back outside, someone shouted words that would become a rallying cry for the next decade—"To the Hill!"—meaning, to the much larger and then-all-women's dorms on Observatory and Ann Streets. The crowd surged east on North University—first to Stockwell, then Mosher-Jordan. At each, they made incursions, ran up stairs and down corridors, then left. Women poured wastebasket-loads of water from the windows.

By the time the men got to Alice Lloyd Hall, women residents had locked the front doors. This apparently fueled the fire. The rowdies got in through side doors, raced upstairs and into women's rooms, and seized what the *Ann Arbor News* called "miscellaneous female unmentionables." The *Detroit News*, less squeamish, said the men took "items of lingerie as souvenirs."

After a rush through Couzens, the men streamed back down North University, where they invaded the all-women's preserve of the League. Others made it to the Michigan Theater, where they stormed the stage—interrupting, as chance would have it, a screening of *Behave Yourself*—and sang a verse or two of "The Victors."

By now it was 9 pm, and, for a moment, the storm seemed to have spent itself. But then the milling crowd of men spotted a counterattack heading their way: a horde of women flooding into Central Campus from the Hill.

The women aimed straight at the symbol of male privilege—the front door of the Union, which by tradition was never to be entered by an unaccompanied female. They surged through the Union, then into all-male West Quad, where "several quadders, caught unawares with their shorts on, were forced to scamper for safety," according to the *Daily*.

At South Quad, "pandemonium broke loose," the *Daily* reported. "While some men beckoned to the women, others formed a barrier at the front doors, but the screaming coeds broke through. In a moment, the lounge was cluttered. Hysterical staffmen called for order."

Here, at last, authority was reasserted in the stern form of Dean of Women Deborah Bacon, the enforcer of in loco parentis. Her appearance took the steam out of the women, who left and walked home before curfew.

Hundreds of men, still game and unrestricted by "hours," spread out for new assaults. Some went back to the Hill, where, at Alice Lloyd, a resident had mounted a flashing red light in her window; some to Martha Cook, where President Harlan Hatcher, venturing out of his house across the street, told the boys to go home, without much effect; some back to Betsy Barbour, where they were repelled by residents wielding a fire hose at a window.

Chuck Elliott, a *Daily* editor, detected a dark edge to the revelry, "the earlier, funny stages slowly changing as the night went on into unpleasant demonstrations of near-viciousness."

At about 1 am, it started to rain, and then it was over.

But only for that night. The "mass riot," as the *Daily* called it, drew a good deal of news coverage, even making the national newsmagazines. Within weeks, copycat episodes sprang up on other campuses, and a national "panty raid" craze ensued. The spontaneous swiping of women's underwear that night at Alice Lloyd became a standard, planned practice that went on for ten years—the ritual seeking of trophies by men raiding women's dormitories and sororities. Although the term "panty raid" apparently had been used earlier, it was the Michigan fracas that inspired the national fad.

The nation looked on with a mixture of amusement and disapproval. Some saw the panty raids as a replacement for the prewar fads of goldfish-swallowing and phone-booth-stuffing. Others were appalled by naughty frivolities on college campuses while soldiers were dying in Korea.

Exactly what had happened that night?

Dean of Students Erich Walter, announcing that no disciplinary measures would be taken, called the episode nothing more than "a form of spring madness"—though he noted, perhaps in a reference to male brutishness toward women in the dorms, that "a few of our students showed some pretty bad manners."

Dean of Women Bacon concurred. "Boys will be boys," she said.

Others didn't buy the "spring fever" theory. Professor Guy Swanson, a sociologist, pointed out that the University had seen many first days of spring come and go without 2,500 students running wild. To some who saw what happened—the mass breaking of rules, the flouting of the strict code of in loco parentis—there was a faint note of genuine rebellion, a hint, perhaps, of more serious things to come.

One of these was Professor Roger Heyns, a social psychologist who would leave Michigan in 1965 to become chancellor of the University of California at Berkeley. There he would see student rebellion in its full flowering, an awesome force that changed higher education and, one might say, U.S. society as a whole.

When the *Daily* asked his opinion about the "riot," Heyns said he had been thinking it over.

"I'd like to know whether I was sitting on a powder keg," he mused, "or whether I was just surrounded by normal, wholesome American boys."

19: Food Riot, 1956

If the panty raids were ugly, then a forgotten food riot at South and West Quads may seem simply trivial. Why tell about it at all, except to tickle alumni memories of god-awful meals in the dining halls?

Truth be told, I wrote this just to try to tickle those memories. But here, too, I see portents in reports of student revelry in the 1950s. They represent a dawning restiveness among students who were attending a much larger and more bureaucratic institution than the University of the prewar decades.

The playwright Arthur Miller, class of 1938, caught sight of the University's new and overwhelming size when he revisited the campus in 1953. "My memories of the place are sweet," he wrote, "and so many things that formed those memories have been altered. There are buildings now where I remembered lawn and trees. And yes, I told myself as I resented these intrusions, in the Thirties we were all the time calling for these dormitories and they are finally built." And it was not just new dormitories. There were new classroom buildings, new administration buildings, plans for a whole new campus to rise north of the Huron, and rules and programs and a thousand forms to fill out.

This was the University that students of the late 1960s would rebel against as the embodiment of a sprawling, all-powerful "Establishment," a mega-university that was hard to love as their parents' generation had loved U-M.

*S*unday, *December 2, 1956. 5:30 pm South Quad, the cafeteria line, Kelsey-Reeves Dining Hall*

First one man, then another, shakes his head at the main dish (Corned Beef and Swiss Cheese on Lettuce) and takes only the Fruit Salad in Lime Jello on Lettuce, the Pineapple-Graham-Cracker Refrigerator Dessert, and milk. Soon a dozen are standing at the end of the line, eyeing the tray of every diner who follows them. Those who have turned down the corned beef are cheered. Any man who has taken it is hissed and booed.

Out in the dining hall, knives and forks begin to beat a rhythm. A chant begins: "We want good food, no more dog food!" A little band tries to infiltrate the kitchen, shouting "Down with the dietitians!" They are pushed out and the doors are locked.

The protesters move out into the lobby, then through the doors onto Madison, moving toward West Quad across the street.

5:35 pm West Quad, Adams-Rumsey Dining Hall

At a single table, diners begin to pound in unison. (No direct evidence would be found to prove collusion between the two dorms, but the timing makes the inference all but incontestable.) The drumbeat spreads through the room and is taken up in the Chicago-Williams Dining Hall next door. Food and plates are piled on serving tables. The noise rises, starts to subside, then explodes as some two hundred yelling residents of South Quad pour into West Quad's courtyard. Snowballs fly toward open windows.

6:00 pm South Quad

Workers close the cafeteria lines fifteen minutes early. ("I feel we might have had extensive damage if the lines had not been closed," Joan Schwal, assistant dietitian, tells authorities later.) Hungry late-comers join the protesters in the street.

6:00–6:30 pm Madison Street

Students and their parents returning to South and West Quads from the annual holiday performance of Handel's "Messiah" at Hill Auditorium are pelted with snowballs.

A chanting mob of indeterminate size—later estimates range wildly from 150 to 1,200—flows up State Street to the front of the Union, then east in the direction of East Quad.

6:40 pm East Quad, North Concourse

Protesters from the western dorms are "received coolly" by diners in East Quad, according to the official report of the Inter-House Council, and add fewer than twenty to their number. Outside, four carloads of Ann Arbor's police keep their distance. The crowd makes a left at South University.

6:45 pm the President's House, 815 S. University

President Harlan Hatcher is not at home, says Dean of Men Walter Rea, who speaks to the crowd from the front steps. Take your complaints to your representatives, he says. The crowd disperses. Krazy Jim's enjoys an especially busy dinner rush.

Sunday evening

Freshmen David Gumenick, Jeffrey Mandel, and Roger Gottfried place telephone calls to reporters at three Detroit newspapers and the Associated Press.

Monday, December 3–Wednesday, December 5

Newspapers across the country publish news of a "food riot" at the University of Michigan. Officials declare they have received no complaints about food in the residence halls. Dean Rea assures anxious parents that the press has "grossly misrepresented the incident.... We readily admit our inability to compete with mother's cooking, but the quadrangle staff makes every effort to provide substantial, well-balanced and properly prepared meals."

Tuesday, December 4

The South Quad Food Committee, appointed several weeks earlier, announces the results of its survey of dorm residents. Among the complaints are smaller portions than the year before; fried eggs "cold, greasy and rubbery;" soft-boiled eggs served raw or hard-boiled; toast served soggy and cold; "extremely poor" coffee cake; "especially distasteful" ham balls; "extremely poor" hamburgers consisting mostly of filler; diluted ketchup, mustard, and salad dressing; "substandard" gravy; "poor" ice cream; and food served on dirty dishes.

Four years earlier, in the great panty raid of 1952, the hard-nosed Dean of Women Deborah Bacon had faced down a male mob far larger and more raucous than the food rioters of '56. She is unimpressed.

"Whoever heard of anyone being satisfied with institutional food?" she asks.

January 1957

The organizers are never identified. Gumenick, Mandel, and Gottfried are kicked out of South Quad for calling the Detroit papers and thereby doing "a definite disservice to the residence halls and to the University."

"The source of the articles in the newspapers [were] immature, irresponsible and sensation-seeking resident students who I hope are happier in their present quickly found accommodations than they were in our residence halls," says Leonard A. Schaadt, business manager of the residence hall system.

January–February 1957

Leonard A. Schaadt announces that the University will remove hash from residence hall menus, replace canned orange juice with frozen, and serve a higher grade of beef with "less tough meat and gristle."

March 2, 1957

The University announces that residence hall diners will have a choice of two meats at every evening meal.

20: The End of Hours

When I was at the *Detroit News* in the late 1980s, I applied for the vacant post of higher education reporter and got it. I wrote often about U-M controversies, U-M policies, U-M professors. But I hardly ever wrote about the everyday lives of U-M students as they went about the business of learning. So one semester I did nothing but hang out among the 1,382 students of South Quad to see what their education was actually like. (Executive summary: It wasn't quite what the admissions brochures promised.)

Rather to my surprise—since college administrators are notoriously tight lipped around reporters—one of my best sources turned out to be the popular and highly capable grown-up in charge of the residence hall, Mary Louise Antieau. As director of South Quad, she schooled me in the impossibilities of managing a domicile for hundreds of undergraduate students. Antieau also helped me understand the changes in law and public policy that strictly limited the University's ability to interfere with the laissez-faire lives of students in the 1990s. She was just old enough to recall the old regime of dorm mothers and strict visitation rules—a quaint time gone by.

The life I saw kids living in South Quad was pretty much like the life I had lived in East Quad fifteen years earlier—but much different from the college regimes my older siblings had known in the 1960s. How had all that changed? When I began to write about the University's history, I chose that question as one of the first I wanted to answer. I learned again that the students themselves, in their unruly power, were the ones largely responsible.

For more than a century, the University was every student's mother and father. By law and by custom, the school operated in loco parentis—"in place of parents." In theory, its mission was not just to train students' minds but to nurture their characters. In practice, this meant policing their conduct.

Decade by decade, deans, professors, and students built a system of written rules and quiet understandings that governed much of student life, especially for women and especially in the dormitories. The regime of in loco parentis told students what to wear for dinner; what time to be home at night; and where, when, and for how long they might receive guests.

Sex-segregated dorm life had rules about "late minutes" (the penalty for breaking curfew) and "open-opens" (the three-hour weekly window when dorms and rooms alike were open to guests of the opposite sex). There was

Critics of the proposed relaxation of dorm "hours" warned that if men and women were given free rein to visit each others' rooms, a sharp rise in promiscuity would follow. One resident advisor remarked: "Anyone who has stood in a women's lounge at closing has seen that privacy is not necessary for excessive displays of affection." *(Michiganensian)*

even a rule for how many feet had to be touching the floor when one male and one female occupied a dorm room alone—three.

Enforcement fell to live-in housemothers—many of them faculty widows tasked with chasing down rule-breakers less than half their age—and student resident advisors (RAs), who had to play cop with people scarcely younger than themselves. With winks here and nods there, the system creaked along from one student generation to the next.

Then, in a few weeks around Christmas 1967, everything changed.

Since at least the 1950s, with student numbers soaring, administrators had acknowledged that managing in loco parentis was like managing an empire in rebellion. Demands for student self-determination were rising all over campus, even in some circles of the faculty.

The fight was over two main questions:

1. At what times of day and for how long could dorm residents entertain guests of the opposite sex?
2. How late could women stay out at night? (For men, this was moot. They could stay out as late as they wanted.)

Year by year, small cracks appeared in the system. In 1962, curfews were abolished for senior women. Junior women followed in 1965, then sophomores. In November 1966, Thomas Fox, the director of South Quad, allowed residents to close their doors when entertaining a member of the opposite sex during visiting hours. (When professors objected, Fox had to retreat.)

In the fall of 1967, the whole system came under siege.

✤ ⁑ ✤

I t started with the women of Mary Markley Hall. First, members of the student judiciary of Van Tyne House said they would no longer adjudicate all cases involving alcohol in dorm rooms, but only cases in which a student "is infringing on the rights of others."

Then two other Markley houses decided to drop the penalty of "late minutes" against first-year women who broke curfew. The Honors Steering Committee "encouraged other women's houses to take similar action as a step toward entirely eliminating women's hours."

On November 13, the women of South Quad's Frederick House, asserting "the right of students to determine their own rules of personal conduct," voted to allow 24-hour visitation for a trial period of two weeks. To publicize the point, eleven women invited friends—female ones—to visit "after hours."

Then the Residence Hall Governing Board—a panel of five professors and two students—universalized the issue. They voted in December to allow all dormitory houses to set their own rules on visitation for one term, as an experiment.

"I visited dorms day and night talking to students," said board member Frank Braun, a professor of German. "I looked like a damn spy, but I came away convinced that our students are realistic and mature enough to handle this."

With that, higher authority stepped in. When students returned from their holiday vacation in January 1968, it was announced that the Board of Regents would hear public comment on the issues of visitation and curfews, then issue a new, campus-wide edict on the whole business.

✣ ✣ ✣

"The regents told me they are not prepared to let something so vital go by default," President Robben Fleming told the *Michigan Daily.* "I suggested the possibility of the hearing."

It seemed clear that the campus was about to move from one era of student life to another, either through flagrant rule-breaking or by a negotiated peace. What was at stake, as one resident director put it, was the entire question of "to what extent, if any, will the Residence Halls continue to keep company with that overworked but under-evaluated phrase: in loco parentis?"

Student leaders expected resistance from the Regents, so they mobilized.

"Power lies in numbers," Bruce Kahn, president of the Student Government Council, told students. "If you demand en masse your rights, the University will be unable to prosecute you." (That was overwrought; nobody was talking about prosecuting anybody.)

The housemothers, too, prepared for battle.

"Ethics, morals, practically everything has lowered somewhat in the last few years," one of them told her superiors in the Housing Division.

But on January 19, 1968, the Regents signaled that they, too, were ready for emancipation. They just wanted to make the momentous proclamation themselves.

They voted to allow each housing unit to set its own visitation hours, all in keeping with "the maintenance of good taste" in pursuit of "the goal of mature self-government." (Only Regent Paul Goebel voted no. "If my judgment is proved wrong," he said, "no one will be happier than I.")

And, at least for a trial period of one semester, the Regents struck down curfews for all women students in the residence halls.

But there was a catch. For a girl to have "no hours," her parents would have to give written permission.

Were mothers and fathers ready to turn their daughters loose, with no one acting in the parental role?

The letters from parents flowed in. Of 1,734 first-year women, the parents of 1,457 gave their permission. That may seem a surprisingly large majority until one hears the testimony of a male member of the class of 1968, who recalled that his girlfriend—a talented writer whom he later married—forged and signed letters on behalf of the mothers of "an astonishing number of her friends." It would not have taken many forgers of her quality to artificially inflate the number of women freed from "hours."

John Feldkamp, U-M's formidable director of housing for many years, was in no mood to surrender the final outpost.

"The policy that the University finds unacceptable pre-marital sexual intercourse continues in effect," Feldkamp wrote in a private memo to housing staff. "Further, the new policy sanctions only visitation, meaning the periodic visiting of guests. Specifically, cohabitation and overnight visitation will subject students to University discipline."

But when Feldkamp's memo was leaked, he gave ground. "I don't pretend to be an expert on pre-marital sex," he told the *Daily*. "Personally I can't imagine that any mature woman could have intercourse in a dormitory."

Roger Rapoport, editor of the *Daily*, could.

"Let's be honest about the whole thing," Rapoport urged readers of his weekly column. "You know the real reason why you cheered when the regents decided . . . to exempt freshman women from curfew and let students . . . set their own visitation hours. You were getting sick and tired of trying to sand-wich everything into those old-fashioned three-hour open-opens required under the old policy. No more of that 'I really do love you but I don't want to get any more late minutes' jazz. No more resident advisor stopping you to ask why that girl you said was only your 'sister' tripped the fire alarm at 5 a.m. Sunday morning while trying to sneak out of the building."

Responses from bona fide parents ranged from an expression of confi-dence that "the added freedom and responsibility placed in [the students] will contribute to their development, educationally and socially" to the belief that the Regents' decision "is in violation of a basic responsibility of a Univer-sity and violates good sense as well."

Most RAs supported the change. "Some attack this policy in that it encour-ages promiscuity," a Couzens Hall RA told the Housing Division. "I don't feel this is true. Anyone who has stood in a women's lounge at closing has seen that privacy is not necessary for excessive displays of affection."

Prophecies of a rush to lewdness and license failed to come true. There was not even a universal shift to 24-hour, seven-day-a-week visitation regimes. Some men's floors made that change—"more of a glandular response than a result of meaningful discussion," one Bursley Hall RA reported—but many chose to allow 24-hour visitation only on weekends. Only three women's floors chose the 24-7 regime. On men's floors, it was widely observed that noise decreased and civility rose during the hours when women were around.

On an East Quad men's floor with liberal visitation, an RA said "most res-idents have expressed their feeling that life in the house seems significantly more normal these days than in the old days when women were a sort of regulated taboo to be unleashed only on weekends—or, to be smuggled into one's room for a visit much the same as grass or acid might be sneaked in for insidious diversions. College men have no desire to look at their women friends as they do drugs."

If that was not quite what administrators wanted to hear, it said at least that students were adjusting to freedom in a certain spirit of moderation.

As for the specter of sex, housing staff judged that open hours had led to something less than a revolution. "A few students will have a girl in all night," reported South Quad Director Thomas Fox, "and many would like to. The general feeling of [resident directors] was that little, if any, sexual intercourse occurs. Occasionally, the couple may sleep together, but the staff was quick to point out: a) this would probably have occurred without the new hours; b) sleeping together does not imply sexual intercourse."

After a few months, Fox said, "Contrary to being the ultimate 'thing,' the presence of women during the week is now looked upon as passé."

So the die was cast. Before long there would be no limits at all on visitation and no curfews.

"With no rules to work with," said a housemother in Bursley, "I can't see the necessity for the kind of staff we have."

Nor could anyone else. The housemother's era soon ended. Only student RAs remained.

There still would be rules in the residence halls, of course, but they would grow from a new theory of campus life—that students were to be seen not as children under the supervision of a substitute parent, but as members of a community with obligations to respect the rights of others.

"People without knowledge have all kinds of fears," a resident director at Couzens Hall reflected in 1975. "Ten years ago they had lockup times, curfews, dress rules. They were all so sacred to many people, who fought to keep them. Now no one even thinks about those things. The greatest fears are not borne out by reality."

21: Earth Day Eve

In the spring of 1970, when I was thirteen, I came into a sense of myself as a responsible citizen with my very own cause to believe in. This was the time of the first Earth Day. I heard all about it in school. For weeks, I pored over the volume in the Time-Life Nature Library titled *Ecology*. I snooped around the house, looking for ways to make the family more ecologically responsible. I recycled. I wrote a speech about pollution. I signed up for a canoe trip in northern Ontario. I bought a copy of *The Environmental Handbook* and read the first two or three pages—several times.

That first candle of my idealism flickered but never went out. The first and most glorious Earth Day stayed in my memory, and the modern environmental movement it inspired has always struck me as our best model of mass action for the common good.

But it was many years before I learned that it all began with a few graduate students in Ann Arbor.

Even at the age of 25, Doug Scott knew how to project his voice to a crowd. For two summers in college, he'd been a guide for the National Park Service at Carlsbad Caverns in New Mexico. When you're standing in a gigantic cave, you learn to project or nobody hears you. So talking loud to a crowd was not the problem.

The problem was the spotlight that hit him in the eyes when he ventured out on the stage at Crisler Arena—that and the packed-in thousands of restless people he could hear but not see because the light was so bright, and the thousands more outside in the parking lot listening to loudspeakers, and the reporters from all over the country, and the senators and activists and superbrains waiting in line for their turn to address the crowd.

It was 8 pm on Thursday, March 11, 1970. Months earlier, when Scott and his buddies in zoology and natural resources had started all this, they had bravely said they intended to think big. But nobody had thought this big. Nobody had thought their little Teach-In on the Environment would look like Woodstock wrapped in the Democratic National Convention.

Now the moment had come, and Doug Scott was a little scared.

But somebody had to start it, so he squinted into the light and told the crowd the fire marshal wouldn't let people stand in the aisles, so would everybody please sit down? Then he said: "Ladies and gentlemen, the cast of *Hair* . . . ."

Then the Chicago cast of *Hair* ran out from behind a curtain and the lead singer started to sing those eerie first lyrics of "The Age of Aquarius."

"When the moon is in the seventh house . . . ."

And her microphone wasn't working.

For a second Doug Scott just about died. Then he came to and herded the actors back behind the curtain. In a minute, the sound guy hissed: "It's working now . . . it's working!"

So Scott sent the actors back out, and the microphone worked, and for the next few days the University of Michigan hosted what may have been the most influential single event in its history, an event that pushed on the wheel of history and launched the modern movement to save the planet from environmental disaster.

Michigan's Teach-In on the Environment was not the first Earth Day. It was the huge and spectacularly successful prototype of the first Earth Day, which happened five weeks later—"the most famous little-known event," one historian has written, "in modern American history."

⁘

When people tried to remember who had the idea, somebody said there had been a guy in the Center for Japanese Studies who remarked to a grad student in botany that Michigan ought to have a teach-in on the environment like the big U-M teach-in on Vietnam in 1965. The botany guy mentioned the idea to friends in the School of Natural Resources, who told other friends about it in a hallway in the Dana Building, and they had a brown-bag meeting in a classroom, and that was the start of it.

They formed a little organization—Environmental Action for Survival, Inc., or ENACT (every activist group needed a catchy acronym)—and picked two co-chairs. One was David Allan, a PhD student in zoology. The other was

In ENACT's cramped office, organizers scrambled to do two things at once—make a plan for Michigan's own early version of Earth Day while advising environmentalists on other campuses how to plan their own events a few weeks later. (*Bentley Historical Library*)

Doug Scott, who was working on a master's degree in forest recreation in the School of Natural Resources.

It was September 1969. Pollution was in the news, with TV images of seabirds dying in oil spills and the Cuyahoga River catching on fire in Cleveland. But the big issue was still Vietnam. People on campus were getting ready for a huge national protest on October 15 called the Moratorium to End the War. There was to be a giant rally in Ann Arbor.

In the midst of all this, the leaders of ENACT called a meeting.

Some in the room were radicals of the Students for a Democratic Society (SDS) persuasion. They wanted the teach-in to target their fellow student radicals; it should fire them up for a broader assault on industrial capitalism, the despoiler not only of Southeast Asia but of the entire planet.

Others in the room, a larger number, were not half so radical, including the original cadre of organizers from zoology and botany and natural resources. Some weren't students at all, but professors and people from the Ann Arbor community—teachers, lawyers, officials in local government. They believed you could do good with the conventional tools of politics and public policy, and they wanted the teach-in to educate the broader public in pursuit of specific actions to make things better.

The discussion got loud and tense, and finally Doug Scott told everybody to quit interrupting and talk one at a time, answering two questions: Who was the teach-in's main audience, and what was the desired outcome?

They went around the room. Scott took notes afterward:

> The radicals admitted that they did not mean anti-social, violent, or hopelessly irrational upheaval and shouting about environmental issues. Rather, it was their intent that the nature of the subject matter and its presentation during the teach-in would generate a sense of constructive outrage amongst the participants. Similarly, the anti-radicals admitted that they did not intend the teach-in to be merely a PTA-style presentation.

They all agreed the teach-in should target the University community as a whole plus influential people in government and industry—those were the primary targets. The general public was secondary.

"Constructive outrage"—that was a nice combination. Radicals and anti-radicals could get behind it.

✦ ✜ ✦

Doug Scott had fallen in love with the national parks. As a kid he had learned mountain-climbing in his native Pacific Northwest. During summer jobs at Mount Rainier and Carlsbad Caverns, he read the history and learned the lore of the National Park Service. He couldn't get enough of it.

But his personal life hit a bad patch. During his second year at Willamette University, his mother died in an auto accident. He fell into a sophomore slump. He went to a friend, the chief ranger at Carlsbad, and asked: "What do you need to do to go into the Park Service?"

"The best thing to do is get a degree in forestry or forest recreation," his friend told him. "There's just a few places in the country that have a really good program, and the very best is at the University of Michigan—the School of Natural Resources."

So, after boning up on basic sciences at the University of Washington, he set off for Ann Arbor. There he found a mentor in Professor Grant W. Sharpe, a pioneer in environmental education and a booster of the National Park Service. In courses such as tree identification and forest recreation, he did well, and after graduating he stayed on to pursue a master's in forestry—as much to avoid the Vietnam draft as to compound his schooling.

But then, like a lot of successful people who have a great experience in college, he found out that the most important learning often happened between classes—in chats with professors, or with fellow students over a beer, or in some project you got involved in almost by accident. College offered a crucible of smart people and intriguing opportunities. Some passed through it unchanged. Some were transformed.

For Scott, the key moment came when Professor Sharpe took a group of students to Isle Royale National Park, the wild rock left behind by the glaciers in Lake Superior. "It was eye-opening for a wilderness-loving kid from the Cascades to discover this astonishingly deep wilderness in the Midwest," he recalled. Because of that trip, he wound up testifying at the National Park Service hearing about the proposal to designate portions of Isle Royale as statutory wilderness. It was a taste of how federal land policy was made, and he liked it.

Soon he was doing work for the Sierra Club, the National Audubon Society, and the Wilderness Society—in Ann Arbor, New York, Washington, DC—while still in school. He was staying up half the night reading dusty old

Wilderness Society files for a master's thesis on the history of the federal Wilderness Act. In the summer of 1969, he took on more work in the office of U.S. Senator Philip Hart of Michigan, who was leading efforts to protect the Sleeping Bear Dunes as a national lakeshore.

All this work overlapped. Scott's knowledge of the National Park Service was handy in the Sleeping Bear planning. His knowledge of federal wilderness law helped Hart and his staff when they met with people from the Interior Department. At the Sierra Club office, he would draft a letter for Senator Hart's signature that would go out to Sierra Club members in Michigan to urge support for some piece of the Sleeping Bear campaign.

His heart was in the wild outdoors, but he was finding his true gifts in the offices and hearing rooms where wilderness policy was made. In New York, he told the head of the National Audubon Society that he no longer wanted a career in the National Park Service. He was hoping to make his mark in Washington, DC.

"Doug, let me give you some advice," a veteran advocate said. "I've tried both, and I find working *on* government a good deal more fun than working *in* government."

That stuck with him. He would be a lobbyist on behalf of the American wilderness.

In fact, between 1966 and 1969, still in his early twenties, he made himself into one of the canniest, hardest-working environmental advocates in the country, with deep, first-hand knowledge of the great environmental groups, the national parks, and the workings of Congress.

With those experiences in his pocket, he became co-chair of the Teach-In on the Environment in Ann Arbor.

Scott reflected on these events many years later in a long series of oral-history interviews conducted at the University of California at Berkeley.

"We went into this," he said, "with a common attitude . . . which was: 'We are going to set no artificial limits on our ambitions for this thing.'"

+ ⁝ +

Just after the Vietnam moratorium on October 15, 1969, ENACT's leaders saw a squib in *Time* magazine. It said Senator Gaylord Nelson, Democrat of Wisconsin and a leading anti-pollution voice in Washington, DC, was urging college students to organize teach-ins on the environment the following spring.

At first they were annoyed, as if someone had stolen their idea. Then they saw it differently.

Nelson had looked at the calendar and picked April 22, 1970, as the day of the mass teach-in. On most campuses, that date would fall between spring break and final exams.

But not at Michigan. By April 22, 1970, classes would be over in Ann Arbor. ENACT's planners had the middle of March in mind.

ENACT's treasurer, Art Hansen, was headed to a student conference on the environment in Washington, DC. When he got there, he dropped in at Senator Nelson's office, just then buried in mail from people asking how to put on an environmental teach-in. Nobody in Nelson's office knew.

Hansen told them who he was and said: "Hey, we're really doing this."

And he handed over Doug Scott's two-page memo. Point by point, the memo laid out ENACT's plan for the Michigan event. It was a template that other schools could follow.

Nelson was delighted. He sent a telegram to Ann Arbor just before ENACT's first mass meeting, which attracted so many people they had to move to the big multi-purpose room at the UGLI, and there still weren't enough chairs.

"I AM GREATLY ENCOURAGED BY THE INITIATIVE YOU AT THE UNIVERSITY OF MICHIGAN HAVE TAKEN IN THE PROGRAM," Nelson wrote. "WE LOOK TO YOUR EFFORT WITH THE FIRST SUCH TEACH-IN TO PROVIDE A PATTERN . . . WHICH CAN INSPIRE AND GUIDE OTHER TEACH-INS THROUGHOUT THE COUNTRY."

Then Doug Scott was named to Nelson's planning committee for the national teach-in. On December 1, 1969, Scott sent a letter to dozens of schools offering Michigan's help.

Momentum was growing. U-M President Robben Fleming said he approved of ENACT's plans, and the president's office put up $5,000 to help fund it.

Then Michigan-based Dow Chemical—a favorite villain of anti-war protesters and hardly a darling of the environmental movement—offered its own pledge of $5,000. Scott and the others, anticipating radical complaints about Dow, said all money was green and this was $5,000 Dow wouldn't spend on manufacturing defoliants bound for Southeast Asia.

They got other donations. When they made up a button saying "Give Earth a Chance," a thousand sold in the first week, and soon they were placing orders for 20,000 at a time. They made plans to sell tickets. The leaders drew up a budget of $50,000—a crazy figure for a student group in the '60s.

"By the end of November and December '69," Scott remembered, "we had a very large thing under way."

✣ ✣ ✣

In February 1970, students from some fifty colleges and universities came to Ann Arbor for a workshop on how to hold Earth Day teach-ins on their own campuses. ENACT passed out materials with point-by-point instructions.

Doug Scott sat in meetings and listened to fiery anti-establishment speeches by undergraduates who had never seen the Capitol dome, let alone watched a congressional committee mark up an actual piece of legislation. He had watched Sen. Phil Hart and U.S. Rep. Guy Vander Jagt, a liberal Democrat and a conservative Republican, come to terms on workable protection for the priceless Sleeping Bear lakeshore.

"My commitment to work within the system was pretty strongly fixed," he said later. "My sense was that radicalism was fine. If you had a radical commitment, I was prepared to be tolerant about it. But I thought you hadn't really earned the right to be radical and say the system sucks and it doesn't work and it won't save the earth unless you'd tried it. I'd tried it, and I had found it highly responsive.

"Now, I was trying it on relatively simpleminded things, but I had found that I, as one person, depending on how much energy I wanted to put into it, how hard I wanted to study and learn and . . . build my skills, that I could make the U.S. Congress do what I wanted it to on side issues. So I wasn't about to give up on that.

"Furthermore, I always had the theory that a society that turns to anarchy isn't a society that's going to stop pollution . . . If everybody's just looking out for themselves, it doesn't matter how radical they are if they're polluting the creek."

So Scott and the steering committee said: You want to take a sledgehammer to a car on the Diag? Go ahead. We'll sell tickets. And while you do that, we'll talk about how to get Congress and General Motors to cut poisonous emissions into the air you're breathing.

The syndicated columnist Joseph Kraft, of the *Washington Post*, came to Ann Arbor to nose around. Some SDS types told him ENACT and the whole Earth Day thing was a do-good diversion by the establishment, a trick to keep kids from protesting about racial injustice and Vietnam. But Kraft liked what he saw.

"Far from being a cop-out," he wrote, "the environmental movement looks like a way of involving straight kids in political issues—a cop-in, so to speak."

ENACT's leaders took pains to cover their left flank. When Black students said ENACT was paying only token attention to racial issues, Scott and Allan promptly apologized and reserved time in the teach-in schedule for discussions of race and the environment. When militants pooh-poohed ENACT's radical pedigree, ENACT asserted its own militancy.

"There are people in government, industry, and the offices of university presidents who think this is going to keep kids quiet on the campuses," Scott told the *Chicago Daily News*. "They are terribly wrong."

It was time to nail down speakers. They wrote down the biggest names they could think of. They figured a few would say yes; then they'd fill in the program from their back-up list.

Right away, Sens. Gaylord Nelson and Phil Hart said yes. William Milliken, the Republican governor of Michigan, said yes. Sen. Edmund Muskie, the frontrunner for the 1972 Democratic presidential nomination, said he couldn't make the opening rally but he'd like to speak at the wrap-up event.

The ecologist Barry Commoner had just been on the cover of *Time*—he said yes. The eminent environmentalist David Brower who had run the Sierra Club and founded the Friends of the Earth—he said yes.

They asked corporate executives and labor leaders. Herbert Doan, the CEO of Dow Chemical, said yes. So did Charles Luce, the head of Consolidated Edison. Walter Reuther, president of the United Auto Workers, said yes.

They asked radical activists and deep thinkers. Ralph Nader said yes. Rene DuBos, the microbiologist and environmentalist philosopher who would soon coin the slogan "Think globally; act locally," said yes. Kenneth Boulding, the Pulitzer Prize–winning economist who popularized the concept of "Spaceship Earth," said yes.

They asked Gordon Lightfoot, then one of the most popular singer-song-writers in the world. He said yes.

They invited mainstream TV stars who were popular with the Lawrence Welk set but also pro-environment—Arthur Godfrey and Eddie Albert. Both said yes.

After a while, they weren't asking any more. They were turning down politicians who wrote to ask if they could speak, too.

ENACT designed a four-day program for events all over the campus and the city. For the biggest event—a kick-off rally with speeches and entertainment—they booked Hill Auditorium, with 4,200 seats.

Then they started to think Hill wouldn't be big enough.

Nervously, they canceled the Hill reservation and booked the University Events Building—just renamed Crisler Arena—site of Big Ten basketball games and sold-out rock concerts, with a capacity of 13,609.

Could they fill it? Could they possibly attract 13,609 people to hear a bunch of anti-pollution speeches?

As Scott remembered, "We sort of thought to ourselves, 'Now what have we gotten ourselves into?'"

✦ ⁝ ✦

The crowd in Crisler Arena overflowed into the parking lots. Workshops and rallies were swarmed by Michigan students, schoolkids, retirees, and PTA parents. When it was over, the *New York Times* said Michigan's Teach-In on the Environment had been "by any reckoning . . . one of the most extraordinary 'happenings' ever to hit the great American heartland: Four solid days of soul-searching, by thousands of people, young and old, about ecological exigencies confronting the human race."

Measured against the extreme rhetoric and violent protests that set the tone of the era, it was an earnest, even quiet, event. A few speakers were heckled and a few showy demonstrations drew heavy media attention—the "trial and execution" of a 1959 Ford on the Diag; the dumping of 10,000 non-returnable pop cans at a Coca-Cola bottling plant (afterward students picked up the cans and threw them away, an irony not lost on reporters); the smearing of tar and feathers on a building where an oil company was interviewing job prospects.

But the other events were serious, sober exchanges of information and ideas taken in by rapt audiences.

By the *Michigan Daily's* count, there were at least 125 separate events. The Law School hosted authorities on the emerging specialty of environmental law. The Physics Department put on a computer simulation of how urban centers were expanding. With a crowd listening closely, an ecologist, a lakes scientist and an engineer discussed the future of the Great Lakes. There was a symposium on pesticides, a philosophical workshop on "the bridge between ideals and action," a panel discussion of "the root causes of the environmental crisis."

There were three or four big rallies, assemblies at the Ann Arbor high schools, and dozens of small workshops all over campus. Virtually every department held some sort of observance. On the final day, March 14, David Brower of the Friends of the Earth, arguably the leading figure in the entire environmental movement, led a mass walk along the Huron River.

Some Black students boycotted the event. Radicals were invited to vent their critique of environmentalism at an "Environmental Scream-Out," and several speakers warned that revolution, not a clean-up, was the only answer to industrial pollution.

But such "dissent," wrote Gladwin Hill, the reporter from the *New York Times*, "if not refuted, was systematically enveloped."

Edmund Muskie himself said: "I hope that the issue of environmental protection does not become a smokescreen that will obscure the overall crisis in America. The study of ecology—man's relationship with his environment— should finally teach us that our relationships with each other are just as intricate and just as delicate as those with our natural environment."

❖ ❖ ❖

"The Michigan teach-in was the first sign that Earth Day would be a stunning success," writes the historian Adam Rome, author of *The Genius of Earth Day: How a 1970 Teach-In Unexpectedly Made the First Green Generation* (2013).

Indeed, Earth Day 1970, observed in thousands of schools and communities small and large five weeks after Michigan's Teach-In on the Environment, was a spectacular experiment in public education that made millions of people aware that the planet was in danger. The national event has been credited with crystallizing scattered fears into a mass movement that brought about real change—curbs on water and air pollution, protections for wilderness and wildlife, the creation of environmental protection agencies at the state and federal levels. And that movement paved the way for today's awareness of the dangers of climate change.

"It wasn't that Doug Scott or Gaylord Nelson came up with some grand plan and pulled it over," Doug Scott said some twenty years later. "There was something going on in the drinking water or in the air, in the whole country, that mushroomed in the fall of '69 into the Earth Day movement."

Yet the event in Ann Arbor was not only a sign of the times but a prime mover of all that followed. There is no way to quantify the effect of ENACT's outreach to dozens of colleges and universities or of the aid that ENACT gave to Sen. Nelson's national organizing. But it was surely considerable. And Michigan's teach-in in March—superbly organized and mobbed with interested people—lent legitimacy to the looming national event in the eyes of news organizations and power-brokers. ENACT's big-tent strategy, incorporating all strains of opinion, made its own Teach-In an event of far greater long-term impact than many more militant protests of the 1960s that drew headlines, then were forgotten.

Early on the morning after the Teach-In's last day, a journalist named Luther Carter, of *Science* magazine, looked in at ENACT's compact office in the Michigan League. He had been around all week and made friends with the organizers. In the office, he found Doug Scott and a few others, exhausted but still buzzing with adrenaline.

Carter smiled and said: "You know, you guys are never going to organize anything this big again in your lives."

Yes and no. Long afterward, Doug Scott said: "We never in our wildest imagination conceived at the outset how big it was going to be." But the organizers undertook big things after Earth Day, too.

John Turner, who organized publicity for ENACT, was the Republican son of a Wyoming cattle rancher. The Teach-In steered him into politics. In the Wyoming legislature, he fought for environmental protections. Then he became director of the U.S. Fish and Wildlife Service in the first Bush administration, president of the Conservation Foundation in the 1990s, and assistant secretary of state for global environmental issues under the second President Bush.

Art Hansen, ENACT's finance chief, the one who told Gaylord Nelson's staff what was going on at Michigan, finished his PhD in natural resources. A Canadian, he became a professor of natural resources, head of the International Institute for Sustainable Development, and a leading adviser on sustainable development to governments in North America and Asia.

Among the organization's leaders, David Allan, co-chair of ENACT, was the most committed to pure science. But the Teach-In steered him toward studying the connections between science and policy. He became an authority on the impact of human activity on the ecosystems of rivers and streams—and professor and eventually dean of U-M's School of Natural Resources and Environment, later renamed the School of Environment and Sustainability.

Doug Scott became one of his generation's leading advocates for the protection of wilderness. Just in the ten years after Earth Day, he played key roles in such landmark laws as the Eastern Wilderness Areas Act of 1975, the Endangered American Wilderness Act of 1978, and the Alaska National Interest Lands Conservation Act of 1980. He was a lobbyist for the Wilderness Society, then for the Sierra Club (where he eventually became conservation director), then for the wilderness arm of the Pew Charitable Trusts.

22: The BAM Strike

As a sophomore in 1975, I was in the vaulted newsroom of the *Michigan Daily* when we heard that Black students had taken over the president's office at the Administration Building, just down Maynard Street. Several of us student reporters and photographers—nearly all white—went over to see what was going on. I stood in the tight quarters of the president's suite and listened to leaders of the occupation demand that the University make good on its promises of five years earlier, when the Black Action Movement (BAM) had slowed the University to something near a standstill for thirteen days. This, the leaders said, was BAM II.

As I stood there watching, a young Black man stepped in front of me and stared me directly in the face—and stayed there, inches away. It was a brilliant act of intimidation, and I was instantly as uncomfortable as I had ever been. I couldn't say anything. He neither said a word nor moved an inch. He just glared at me. I couldn't take it and moved away.

That was the first moment when I knew I was implicated in the University's abiding state of racial inequity. I was white. This kid was Black. It didn't matter what I might say. He held me responsible.

I found many things to write about the University's history without engaging with the problem of race in my own era at Michigan. Maybe I held it at bay because of some shadow of the discomfort I felt that day at the Administration Building. With the distance of many years, I finally got around to two stories in this realm—one about the first BAM strike, the other about the Michigan boys who for a century "played Indian."

One day in the spring of 1968, a few weeks after the assassination of the Rev. Martin Luther King, Jr., Robben Wright Fleming, president of the University, studied a letter he had received from Harry W. Wright, Jr., director of the Michigan Civil Rights Commission's regional office in the small Michigan city of Jackson.

Fleming saw that it was a complaint, polite but pointed.

Harry Wright was a white Presbyterian minister who had entered the field of civil rights advocacy some years earlier. He told Fleming a story about a student he had come to know—a Black high school senior in Jackson. She "expresses herself very well, both in speaking and in creative writing," Wright wrote. "She has drive and motivation, and pursues an end to which she is committed. My perception of her is that she has real ability which is now ready to fully express itself." But she had found little in her school to encourage her drive, nor was she counseled to choose college-preparatory courses. Her grades were not very good. And her family was poor.

Even so, she had recently come to tell Wright she was "ready 'to break out the trap' and seek a college education."

Picketers supporting the BAM strike of 1970 converge on the steps of Hill Auditorium. (*Bentley Historical Library*)

Wright said he knew many such Black youngsters, raised in struggling families and taught in inadequate schools: "Most do not reach the point where they can break out, but she wants to do this. I had heard of the University's program to recruit Black students and to provide the resources whereby they could attend the University." So, though it was late in the school year, Wright made an appointment for the student and himself to meet with an admissions officer in Ann Arbor.

Wright was referring to U-M's Opportunity Awards Program, which had begun several years earlier. The program provided financial aid to a small number of students regardless of race "whose economic and social background has been of deprivation," though its authors hoped it would help Black students in particular. In the program's first three years, Black enrollment at U-M rose from 0.5 percent to 1.65 percent.

"We were cordially and well received by your representative," Wright told Fleming. But as their host enumerated the requirements for admission to U-M, even under the special program, Wright said, "I saw . . . how unrealistic this attempt at recruitment of Black students really is." Many Black students he knew had "great potential, but due to a basically racist educational system, their creative possibilities are not fully realized as far as formal education is concerned."

The student saw the same thing, Wright said, and "we came away completely frustrated . . . . The young lady felt momentarily defeated, and in her mind she perceived the same racist system that she had known [all] along . . . ."

"What we both responded to was the seemingly inflexible demand of a college prep program for entrance and also the lack of a remedial program within the University which would allow a student to compensate for an inadequate background. It seems to me that if the University is going to be serious about recruiting Black students, its requirements will have to be different.

"I am not saying that the demands of the University should change for Black applicants," Wright told Fleming, but that to be fair to any and all applicants with sub-par preparation, "the University needs to be creative in its entrance procedures in order to compensate for secondary educational practices which have been destructive to Black students. I am proposing that minority students, for the most part, have been victims of a racist system. It seems to me that a public university has the responsibility to compensate for this, in ways beyond business as usual."

This student who wanted to "break out" was capable of succeeding at U-M, Wright said—he was sure of it. But to give her the chance to do so, the University needed "a procedure . . . whereby a student's potential could be pictured," and it should offer remedial courses to fill in what her school system had failed to give her.

President Fleming called the Office of Admissions to ask about the case. A note came back saying: "This girl just suddenly decided that she wanted to enter the U. of M. and no other school." She "had not followed a college preparatory program in high school; her grades even in non-college work were not good, perhaps 'C' average." The admissions officer advised her to seek more high school credits or try another college—perhaps the new community college in Jackson.

Fleming had been named president of U-M just a few months earlier. Trained as a labor lawyer, he had become a law professor, an expert on industrial relations, and a highly regarded arbitrator of labor disputes. As chancellor of the University of Wisconsin–Madison, he skillfully navigated the campus through several episodes of campus unrest, once paying from his own pocket to bail student protesters out of jail. By ideology and experience, he was inclined to favor the underdog. He was also devoted to the meritocratic creeds of the U.S.'s elite institutions of higher education.

He framed his reply to Harry Wright carefully. He conceded that "our present program is inadequate in a number of respects. We must, and will, do better. But our critics must also understand how thorny the problem really is." To admit a student like Wright's young friend—a student who would likely fail in U-M's demanding curriculum—would lead only to "further frustration." U-M's leaders had thought about just the sort of remedial program Wright proposed, Fleming said. But students who entered it might "reach a conclusion that they are inferior." And it would be expensive. U-M had applied to the Ford Foundation for funding but had been rebuffed.

"I do appreciate your letter and its constructive tone," Fleming said. "We will make progress, and we will do so within the next year. But I must repeat that the problem is enormously difficult."

✢ ✣ ✢

Two years later, in February 1970, U-M students who would soon identify themselves as the Black Action Movement (BAM)—akin to similar groups around the country—presented Fleming and the Regents with a list of demands, chiefly: a firm commitment to increase Black student enrollment from 3.4 percent to 10 percent, comparable to the state's Black population, by 1973; more financial aid for Black students; more Black faculty; more support for Black studies programs; and a center for Black students. (In his memoirs, Fleming, with tongue in cheek, noted that "labeling such matters as 'demands' was . . . entirely consistent with the actions of other student groups of the time. I always insisted on using the term *requests*, but this did not change their label.")

The Regents deferred to Fleming, asking him to prepare a response by the board's meeting the following month. BAM upped the ante by removing hundreds of books from library shelves, a signal of its willingness to use disruptive tactics.

Fleming and his aides already had calculated that the University could reasonably hope to increase the number of Black students to perhaps 7 percent in the next three years—though not without finding a lot more money. So he told BAM's leaders the administration would promise to aim for 10 percent, but only as a goal, not a commitment.

At their next monthly meeting on March 19, in a room crammed with angry student spectators—a combination of Black members of BAM and white supporters, including members of the militant Students for a Democratic Society (SDS)—the Regents approved Fleming's counter-offer on the key issues: a "goal" (not a "commitment") of 10 percent by 1973; doubling the money for the Opportunity Awards Program by 1973, enough to bring Black enrollment to 5 or 6 percent; and a promise to seek more funds to pursue the 10 percent goal.

That was not enough. "It makes no commitment to anything of major importance . . . ," BAM's leaders declared. "It is an attempt to dupe the people of Michigan, pretending to make a change when all it does is capitalize the same old message: 'S-H-I-T.'"

With that, they declared a strike. That afternoon, hundreds of students marched across the Diag. Protesters broke windows and blocked a police car. Ann Arbor police arrested four students, all Black, though most of the demonstrators were white. The next morning, picketers appeared outside classroom buildings.

The strike soon shaped up as the largest student protest in the University's history. Fleming deeply desired to manage the crisis without the intervention of police or the National Guard. But could he do so? Day by day, on both sides, the principals and everyone else waited to see if the strike would escalate from a mostly peaceful boycott to a violent clash between students and police, the sort of melee that had beset many other campuses, large and small, in recent months and years, amounting to a crisis in U.S. higher education.

What followed over the next thirteen days was, at base, an effort to change Robben Fleming's mind about the position he had taken in his letter to Harry Wright. His views undoubtedly represented those of most administrators and faculty. Their position was: (1) Blacks certainly ought to have greater access to higher education but (2) most Black students were badly taught in poor schools, so few could meet U-M's admission standards, and (3) if U-M lowered its standards to admit under-prepared Black students, many would fail and U-M's elite reputation would suffer. Fleming and like-minded leaders and faculty believed their hands were tied; the University could not, by itself, change the racist social structures that trapped Black students. They could act only in small, slow increments and promise to do better—a response that many Black students (and a fair share of white ones) interpreted as no more than racist resistance to just demands for equity. Fleming himself was well aware of this stark division in perception. "From their point of view," he wrote later, "those of us who represented the University could be expected to move only if forced to do so and, even then, unwillingly.... We looked at the matter quite differently. We wanted to be helpful, we wanted a society in which Blacks and whites were no longer separate and unequal, and the problem was not one of willingness, but of dealing with some very difficult practical problems. The problems had to do with finding qualified Black students in the numbers required the meet the goal, recruiting faculty and administrators who had the necessary background and experience, and then finding the money to support the effort."

Of course, Black students saw lots of University money going to programs peopled mostly by white students. They were asking for a reallocation—and a new conception of which students were "qualified."

+ ⁘ +

In the first couple of days, the picket lines made only a relatively modest dent in the number of students attending their classes. Support for the strike was highest in the College of Literature, Science and the Arts (LSA), the Residential College, and the School of Social Work. In other units—the Engineering College, the School of Business Administration—most students were going to class. Day by day, BAM and its white supporters became more disruptive. Protesters entered lecture halls and demanded that professors allow them to speak; they roamed classroom buildings, banging on garbage cans and tossing stink bombs; they hassled and threatened students trying to go to class. A few professors and more teaching assistants cancelled their classes. The empty seats multiplied. When white students staged their own demonstrations in support, BAM's leaders insisted on maintaining control, and the white students fell in line. But it was the absence of white students in classrooms that meant the strikers could claim a growing impact. Five days in, LSA attendance was estimated at 40 percent.

"It wasn't just a black strike or a white strike," Madison Foster, a BAM member, told the journalist Alan Glenn years later. "It was a *student* strike."

Meanwhile, Fleming was working on several fronts at once. He oversaw negotiations with BAM, then entered the talks himself. He spoke with the Regents, some of whom wanted him to call in the National Guard. (He counseled patience. A few more days, he said, and the strike would likely peter out on its own, with BAM accepting the University's best offer.) He reached out to the deans and leading faculty. (Although some 500 professors had quickly signed a public letter denouncing "the actions of the few who are driving the University community into chaos," the faculty's Senate Assembly voted unanimously to urge the University's schools and colleges to find ways to meet the 10 percent goal.) He demanded that BAM end aggressive picketing—apparently with a warning that he would bring in the Guard to enforce students' access to classes if he had to. According to Fleming, Black faculty and Black state legislators also quietly advised BAM's leaders to stick to peaceful picketing. BAM agreed. But the strike went on.

✦ ✠ ✦

BAM was applying televised pressure on Fleming on the sidewalks and in the buildings. But pressure on him behind the scenes was just as intense, and most of it was anti-BAM. Hundreds of letters and telegrams flooded the president's mailbox. Conservative alumni who had been steaming for years about televised protests on college campuses now perceived their beloved U-M to be under siege. They regarded Fleming as a soft touch at best, and they vented their rage at him. In a telegram to the Regents, who met during the strike at U-M's Dearborn campus instead of Ann Arbor, a member of the class of 1942 wrote: "You can be sure that countless thousands of Michigan alumni abhor the timidity and appeasement demonstrated by President Fleming. Let us have [the] guts to stand up to anarchy." A dentist who had graduated in 1927 excoriated Fleming for giving in to "mongrel madness . . . . Have you submitted your resignation as president? You are no compliment to the University of Michigan as it was in the past." Students, too, told Fleming he was letting them down. One who had been blocked from attending a particular class calculated what he had lost in tuition and sent Fleming a demand to be reimbursed for 75 cents.

If the key battle was to change the minds of Fleming and other leaders—the deans and faculty stars who wielded much of the power at U-M—then BAM made a strategic error when its tactics veered into intimidation and violence. However sympathetic the average faculty member may have felt toward BAM's cause before the strike, many got their backs up when the strikers got more aggressive. In their eyes, BAM was now putting paramount values at risk—the freedom of faculty to teach and of students to learn, as well as the principle of decision-making by reason and free deliberation. John Arthos, a professor of English, wrote a sorrowful note to Fleming, saying the University had negotiated with a knife at its throat: "When one permits the intimidation of the students in one's charge...one has contributed to the degeneration of a society that deserves sustaining as few societies ever have."

No objection to Fleming's conciliatory approach drew more attention than Professor Gardner Ackley's lengthy remarks at a mass meeting of LSA faculty in the midst of the strike. Ackley had been chair of the Department of Economics, one of the University's most prestigious units, a member of President John F. Kennedy's Council of Economic Advisors, and chair of the Council under President Lyndon Johnson. He had just returned to the faculty after his long stint in Washington and two years as U.S. ambassador to Italy. His credentials as an old-school liberal were obvious. But he was appalled by the BAM strike and said so with bare-fisted anger.

Even before BAM, Ackley said, the University in one encounter after another had capitulated to any students willing "to disrupt the life of the University." In such confrontations, "these lessons were taught and learned . . . that the Big Lie, loudly proclaimed, can become the truth; that the desires of the overwhelming majority of students, who only want to learn—and of the overwhelming majority of the faculty—who only want to teach and investigate—count for little or nothing." He had been deeply disturbed to see colleagues in Economics huddled in the chair's office to "discuss a demand that all classes in our building be shut down, or else . . . while the entrances to the building were sealed, and while the halls outside the room in which we were meeting were patrolled by men carrying pipes and clubs."

Now, he predicted, "we will submit in one way or another to all the demands of the BAM. In so doing, we will admit, explicitly or implicitly, that we are indeed a repressive, racist institution. *But that is still a lie!*"

Days later, in a private letter to Allan Smith, vice president for academic affairs and former dean of the Law School, Ackley said he had been more angry with fellow faculty who backed any radical student demand than with Fleming and his team, who had "confronted an almost impossible situation" and had "my fullest sympathy and support."

"I have been quite overwhelmed by the truly massive expressions of support I have received from members of the faculty following my LSA remarks," Ackley told Smith. "It came from all parts of the campus, from assistant professors to deans and distinguished university professors. What almost everyone said was 'you had the courage to say what we have been thinking.' This rather amazes me. What were they afraid of? The radical students? The Administration?" If the administration displayed a "more aggressive defense of what I think you and I agree are the traditional values of academic life," it might find "a degree of support that would surprise you."

Did Ackley gauge the mood of the faculty correctly? Or was he hearing from only a fearful minority? Was the Senate Assembly sincere when it endorsed funding for BAM's demands? Or, as some charged, was it responding to quiet pressure from the administration? Either way, the faculty as a body embraced no more than Fleming's ameliorative approach to Black demands. With exceptions here and there, they would have endorsed the president's reply to Harry Wright—that "we must, and will, do better. But our critics must also understand how thorny the problem really is."

On Monday, March 30, with BAM backing away from its aggressive picketing, attendance in classes crept upward. Some professors were moving their classes to churches, homes, or the Union, but they were teaching.

At 4:00 the next morning, in the midst of an endless meeting between Fleming and BAM leaders, one of the students asked the president to step into the next room. As Fleming recalled it, the young man "in a perfectly calm and friendly voice," said, "'We've got to get this thing over. What is the best offer you can make?'" Fleming repeated what he had said already, which was only slightly more than what he had proposed before the strike began—a goal (still not a commitment) of 10 percent, financial aid sufficient to reach the 10 percent goal (more than the five to seven percent funding promise that Fleming had made before the strike), and a commitment to meet most of the lesser demands. Okay, the young man said, "You repeat that to the others. I'll say we'll consider it. Then in the morning we'll shut the strike down."

That was essentially that. The next day, BAM suspended picketing and the Regents endorsed the agreement. BAM's leaders did the same and then addressed more than a thousand cheering students in the Union ballroom. "That wasn't the best agreement we could have settled on," a BAM leader named Dave Lewis told the crowd. "But it was a first step, a first substantial step."

❖ ⁑ ❖

By 1973, the University had fulfilled its commitments in the final BAM agreement—to create a Black student center, to expand Black studies and recruit more Black faculty, and to provide the funding needed to raise Black enrollment to 10 percent. But in 1973–1974, the year of the vaunted goal, Black enrollment stood at only 7.3 percent—the same figure the Fleming administration had considered a realizable goal, given the University's admission policies.

Black students and their allies mounted major protests in 1975 and again in 1987, when Black enrollment had fallen back below 5 percent. In the latter year, James J. Duderstadt, then U-M's provost and soon to be its president, initiated plans that coalesced as a broad initiative called the Michigan Mandate. Its thesis—that cultural diversity and education were not antithetical but intimately linked—was an early forerunner of ideas that soon would be taken for granted in higher education and other spheres of U.S. society. Michigan drew national attention for its new commitments—among other things, to allocate much more money to hire Black faculty, with incentives for academic units to raid other schools for the best talent, plus an aggressive new policy to punish racial harassment by students. By 1995, the new drive brought total enrollment of Black students to more than 10 percent, including 9 percent of undergraduates.

In 1997, three unsuccessful white applicants for admission to U-M—two as undergraduates, the third as a law student—sued the University and several U-M officials, claiming that affirmative action in admissions amounted to discrimination against white applicants. The University mounted vigorous defenses. Its lawyers argued that a good education depended on an ethnically diverse student body. Student groups seconded the University's arguments in friend-of-the-court briefs, as did such corporate giants as Microsoft and General Motors. Through a years-long battle, the cases rose to the U.S. Supreme Court, which struck down certain tactics in U-M's affirmative-action strategy but upheld others—and approved the University's contention that it was constitutional to admit at least a "critical mass" of Black and Hispanic students in the interests of a better education for all. The ruling meant that colleges and universities across the U.S. could consider race as one factor in its admissions decisions.

Then, in 2006, opponents of the Supreme Court's decision mounted a state ballot initiative to prevent admissions officers at Michigan's public universities from considering applicants' race, gender, or religion. Voters approved the measure, 58 to 42 percent, and the courts upheld it.

A long decline in Black enrollment at U-M ensued. By 2018, Black students made up just 5 percent of incoming first-year students compared to 17 percent of the state's population of those aged 18 to 24. Similar figures prevailed at many elite universities.

As President Fleming had said half a century earlier, "the problem is enormously difficult."

But what, precisely, was that problem?

In 2020, a historian named Matthew Johnson published an answer in the form of a book about U-M titled *Undermining Racial Justice: How One Uni-*

versity Embraced Inclusion and Inequality (Cornell University Press). Johnson studied U-M's long struggles over Black enrollment in depth, sifting and reading thousands of pages of documents, surveys, scholarly reports, and press coverage. In the end, he concluded that "institutional leaders incorporated black student dissent selectively into the University of Michigan's policies, practices, and values, while preventing activism from disrupting the institutional priorities that campus leaders deemed more important than racial justice." Those same leaders, with every good intention, declared the goal of establishing Michigan as a model multiracial community. Yet their strategies to meet that goal "led to social alienation and high attrition rates for Black students"—chiefly by channeling Black students' dissent into a minority-affairs bureaucracy that grew larger but had neither the authority nor the means to change the culture of campus life.

"Did U-M officials co-opt black student activism with the specific intent to perpetuate racial inequality?" Allen asks. "The simple answer is no . . . . The most powerful U-M administrators expressed sympathy for racial equity. In an ideal world, they wanted black students' representation on campus to match blacks' representation in the state population. They wanted black students to perform well in the classroom and thrive socially on campus . . . . It's clear that administrators would have celebrated a student body that reflected the racial demographics of the state of Michigan and a racial climate that made black students feel welcome—but only if that happened on administrators' terms."

If Matthew Johnson is right, then the "enormously difficult problem" remained much the same as it was when Harry Wright and Robben Fleming exchanged letters in 1968.

But if the student strikers of 1970 did not cut that Gordian knot, they did fix a vivid memory in the University's consciousness that has haunted it ever since. They elicited a promise—half-spoken, half-implied—that U-M would no longer be what Black students called "a white university." The University expanded and amplified that promise over many years and tried to keep it. But it failed. The failure was due in part to actors beyond the University's control—notably the citizens of Michigan who voted to ban affirmative action in state universities. Nonetheless, the promise was not kept, and the memory lingers.

23: Remembering Michigamua

In the summer of 2020, a "remember me?" email dropped into my in-box from a guy I'd known at Michigan in the late 1970s. He said he'd been gathering materials to document the history of the old senior honorary society called Michigamua, of which he'd been a member. He knew that just before World War II my father had been the head of it, so he was asking if my family had any memorabilia that I might share with him.

Michigamua (the "u" was silent) was best known for borrowing the imagery—the white man's imagery, that is—of Native America, circa 1901, when it was founded. For decades, the club enjoyed a prestigious place in student life, with secret meetings in a special room on the highest floor of the Michigan Union's tower. Members included Gerald Ford, the future U.S. president; Frank Murphy, a future governor of Michigan and justice of the U.S. Supreme Court; star athletes; leaders of student government; campus editors—all male. By the late 20th century, Michigamua's prestige had faded. I had a hazy memory that in some recent year, amid controversies over sexism and cultural appropriation, it had been thrown off the campus.

I could think of only one piece of Michigamua memorabilia that my dad had left behind—an old black-and-white photograph, torn at the edges and mounted on burlap in a heavy wooden frame. The photo shows forty young white men posing in two rows on the steps of the Michigan Union. All are shirtless. Half sit in the foreground, muddy and bedraggled, as if they've just been through some physical ordeal. The other half stand solemn-faced and superior behind the subservient row. Each man standing wears a headband with a feather.

Even in the monochromatic tones of the photo, the skin of all these young white men looks strangely mottled and discolored. I knew why—because they'd been doused with water and smeared with red brick dust.

One figure in the center stands out from the others—the "sachem," or chief, of the "Tribe" of 1940–1941. His cheeks are slashed with dark stripes. He wears an elaborate headdress of white-and-black feathers.

My dad.

He was president of Phi Delta Theta and captain of the tennis team—thus his Michigamua name, "Singing Strings." After his death in 2005, the old photo in its frame sat for a while in a box in the attic. Then we took it out and stood it up in a bookcase. It was a curiosity, an odd fragment of family lore from another time: "Look at this picture of Grandpa . . . this one here, in the headdress. It was 1941, just before the war, and there was this honorary society. . . ."

Now I looked at the photo with new eyes. If I sent it along for some online archive of all things Michigamua, someone from outside the family would soon be looking at it, too—someone who did not know that my dad was a kind and honorable man and anything but a racist as the word was understood in his time. Some stranger might soon be considering the parallel between this keepsake of ours and the repellant images of white men in blackface that had lately spread all over the digital universe, and of the Indian mascots and Indian names—the Washington Redskins and Cleveland Indians—that had been dropped in ignominy.

The more I stared at the photo, the stranger it seemed. What did those young men think about this weird spectacle they were making? Where had this business of masquerading as Indians come from?

My email correspondent knew one more thing about Michigamua and me—that as co-editor of the *Michigan Daily*, I, too, had been "tapped" for the Tribe, and I'd accepted.

So, along with pondering my dad's place in this prewar tableau, I was trying to remember why, as late as 1977, I had joined an all-male society that purported to honor the campus's leaders when I knew very well that many student leaders were women. What had I been thinking when I submitted to the water and the red brick dust—the red equivalent of blackface that my dad had taken part in?

And I was trying to remember why, just a few days after I was initiated, I quit.

✦ ⁝ ✦

On Rope Day, 1941, Michigamua's "fighting braves" and new initiates pose on the steps of the Michigan Union. The writer's father stands at the center in the sachem's headdress. *(Author's collection)*

I went to the digital archives of the *Michigan Daily*. In 1976, as a junior, months before I was tapped, I wrote two long articles about Michigamua. By that point in its history, many students didn't even know about it. But it was still around, and suddenly it was in the news. Two women in the student government had invoked the federal civil rights law commonly known as Title IX to bring a sex-discrimination complaint against the University for providing facilities to the all-male "Tribe." So a Native American student would launch a separate complaint. So I wrote this two-part story to explain what it was all about.

I told how, at the turn of the 20th century, a student club in the Philosophy Department had morphed into Michigamua with a declared mission of service to the University—to "fight like hell for Michigan," as the "Tribe" would always put it—and how the group adopted motifs and nicknames from whites' stereotyped imagery of Native Americans, even speaking in the "Injun" pidgin of potboiler western novels. I told about Michigamua's role in founding the Michigan Union—the association of male students that went by that name— and in campaigning for the landmark building on State Street that became the Union's headquarters. I told about the annual public ritual of Rope Day, when the "Fighting Braves" would corral new initiates in the Diag and smear them with water and red brick dust. I told how Fielding H. Yost, the legendary football coach, athletic director, and honorary sachem ("Great Scalper"), had arranged for Michigamua to take possession of the room at the top of the Union tower as its clubhouse, and how the room had been decorated as a "wigwam" for the sole use of Michigamua's weekly meetings. That was in the early 1930s, not long before my dad entered U-M as a freshman in 1937.

For those stories I interviewed Bob Ufer, the longtime "voice of Michigan football" and the quintessential "Michigan Man." A track star in his day, Ufer had been a member of my dad's fraternity and of Michigamua, though two years after Dad. In the *Daily* I quoted him accurately but perhaps not to his advantage. He said the women who brought the sex discrimination complaint about Michigamua "ought to be falling in love with a guy and raising some kids" instead of "getting all wrapped up with Title IX." And he added: "It's been said that life is 95 percent bullshit and five per cent fact, and you know, that's about the way it is with Michigamua."

At the age of 20 I thought that was a pretty funny thing for a guy like Ufer to say, so I put it in the paper. I soon had reason to wish I hadn't.

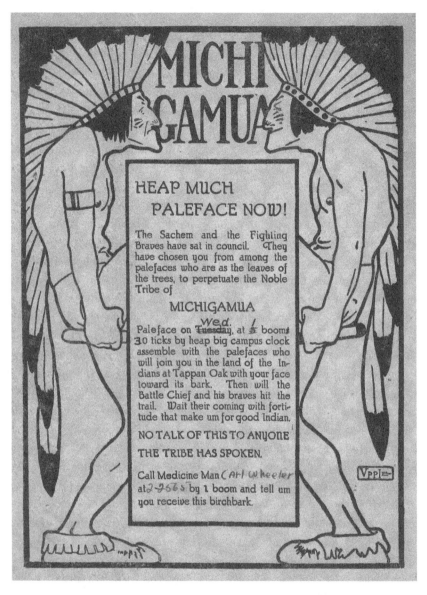

In the "Injun" pidgin of western movies, Michigamua's "birchbark" summoned initiates to be "tapped." *(Author's collection)*

✛ ⁑ ✛

I went back to the attic.

A few years before my parents died, my wife organized all the letters that my dad and his older brother had sent home to their mother during their years at U-M. In the files I found Dad's letter of May 14, 1940. (That was the day the Dutch government surrendered to Nazi invaders, another in a series of signposts to what lay ahead for his generation.) He wrote: "I was tapped for Michigamua last night and the initiation is all Wednesday afternoon."

My grandmother, divorced, had raised her two sons on her salary as a music teacher in the Detroit public schools. One of her brothers was helping to put the two boys through Michigan; in the family, the uncle's monetary gifts, along with my grandmother's own savings, were called "the fund."

At the end of the letter, Dad wrote: "Incidentally, as I guess I told you, the initiation fee for Michigamua is the sweet little sum of twenty bucks. Nice, eh? I guess the only thing I can do is to ask you to take it out of the fund and let me pay it back next summer. Okay?"

In another box I discovered Dad's "birchbark," the coveted invitation to join the "Tribe" that all "young bucks" received. It was printed on thick paper stock with words in the pidgin "Injun talk" of the westerns. "Heap Much Paleface Now!" it began. "The Sachem and the Fighting Braves have sat in council. They have chosen you from among the palefaces who are as the leaves of the trees, to perpetuate the Noble Tribe of Michigamua." Instructions followed about where and when to meet for the initiation.

The words are bordered by two cartoons—identical mock Indian chiefs in headdresses and moccasins. One grins; the other frowns.

The cartoons made me think of something I had just read in a book by the Michigan historian Robert F. Berkhofer. I had gotten the book, *The White Man's Indian: Images of the American Indian from Columbus to the Present* (1979) with the thought that it might help me place the Rope Day photo in context. Berkhofer's central message was this: From the earliest contact with indigenous peoples onward, Europeans and then Americans had always nourished two opposed stereotypes of the Indian—the Noble Savage, wise and serene, living in harmony with nature; and the savage Indian, a satanic denizen of the hostile wilderness. Here they were on Dad's "birchbark," the noble and the satanic, representations not of real human beings but of ideas harbored by white people.

I knew about another historian who, while at Michigan, had written a book called *Playing Indian* (1999). He was Philip J. Deloria, son of the Native American historian and activist Vine Deloria, Jr., whose book, *Custer Died for Your Sins: An Indian Manifesto* (1969) had provided intellectual fuel for Native American protest movements. *Playing Indian* includes no reference to Michigamua, but it does much to answer the question of where Michigamua came from.

Deloria traces two currents of Indian mimicry before 1900. Both represented efforts by white Americans to define their own identity in eras of anxiety.

The earlier movement started in the era of the American Revolution and spawned such groups as the Society of Tammany (the progenitor of New York City's political machine, Tammany Hall) and the Improved Order of Redmen. These were fraternal organizations, like the Freemasons and the United Ancient Order of Druids—semi-secret societies devoted to good fellowship and community service, with ideals drawn from idealized forerunners in a misty past. For the white Redmen, the ideal of the Noble Savage lent a distinctly American ethos to weekly conclaves in dim rooms.

The later current emerged in the late 1800s, when the indigenous peoples of the U.S.—those that survived viruses from across the oceans and wars with the U.S. Army—had been pushed onto reservations. Now, with the frontier closing and urban industrialism on the rise, some white Americans looked to the vanishing Indian for ideals that might preserve the nation's connections to nature and provide worthy lessons to modern American children in comfortable white families. Native American mythology was packaged into instructive collections of Indian tales and legends. These ideas brought forth a constellation of Indian-themed summer camps and children's organizations that drew on woodlore and a cult of the outdoors—the Boy Scouts, the Girl Scouts, the Campfire Girls.

The founders of Michigamua drew on both of these currents. The early documents of the "Tribe" make it clear that the founders, like others who sought a connection with indigenous cultures that had been wiped out or pushed away, believed in all sincerity they were enacting uplifting rituals of respect for the "noble savage," however ignorant they were of the actual peoples they meant to honor. Even more powerful, perhaps, was the fraternal urge. When I looked up what "Old Braves" said about the "Tribe" later in life or spoke to them in person, I found one after another attesting that it was a joyful part of their time at Michigan, a forum for making friends they would never have met outside the "Tribe" and one of the bonds with their alma mater that would never break. In some eras, Michigamua members took hold of particular projects and causes, such as the establishment of the Union and, much later, the founding of Dance Marathon, a major annual charity event. It was often a forum where senior leaders of disparate organizations exchanged views on campus controversies. So whatever Bob Ufer had meant about Michigamua being "95 percent bullshit," it was clear that he and probably most of his brethren found it to be a rich, rewarding experience. My dad occasionally called it a "mutual admiration society." But he also cherished his memories of it.

The guy who sent me the email was Steve Carnevale. At Michigan he'd been president of the University Activities Center (UAC), which planned major events like rock concerts at Crisler Arena. It was a big job and he was good at it. He and a guy named Scott Kellman—president of the Michigan Student Assembly, also tapped for Michigamua with Carnevale and me—had persuaded the University to undertake a major renovation of the Union. Carnevale had gone on to much success as an entrepreneur in Silicon Valley.

He and I got to emailing back and forth. "It's funny," I told him, "but I don't remember much about exactly why I quit Michigamua. It wasn't really because of concerns about Native American objections or the all-male thing. Mostly I just remember being kind of irritated by the football players' dominance of the group, though they seemed like perfectly nice guys."

"Your quitting was mainly about the women," he wrote back. "My close friend Jeff Baker quit as well."

Talk to Baker, he suggested. Kellman, too. They'd remember.

I'd known Scott Kellman pretty well. We were interns in Washington together. He was a smart, earnest guy. I knew he'd gone to Michigan Law and then into business. It turned out he lived just outside Ann Arbor, maybe five miles from my house. I called him.

He told me that in our first meeting as the new "Tribe," he and I and one other guy had sponsored a resolution to include women when the time came to tap the next cohort of members. We were voted down by a tally of something like twenty-two to three. A few days later, I quit. Kellman tried to talk me into staying, but I didn't.

Fragments of what Kellman said came back to me, but no more.

My wife said: "I can't believe you don't remember that. You told me all this forty years ago."

Here's one thing I did remember: During the initiation week, there was a cookout with a bunch of Old Braves, my dad among them. I remember him laughing with old friends from the "Tribe," and here I was, son of Singing Strings, joining the fold.

And I remember Bob Ufer, the uber-Michigan Man, catching sight of me, favoring me with a direct and mocking smile, and shaking his finger. Whether he meant it this way or not, I understood him to be saying: "So here you are, you hypocrite. You wanted to make fun of me and Michigamua, but here you are."

⁜

I called Jeff Baker. He'd been a leader of UAC along with Steve Carnevale. After many years in telecommunications, he'd shifted to corporate training and finally to coaching the skills of leadership, mostly in companies with democratic governance—co-ops. I asked him what he remembered about Michigamua.

He said he never actually joined. He dropped out of the initiation process at the last moment.

"It was a really, really powerful, emotional time for me with Michigamua," he said.

Baker had never heard of Michigamua before a senior in UAC asked if he would accept membership. "I thought: 'What an incredible idea to bring together twenty-five seniors from different walks of Michigan life who otherwise wouldn't meet each other—bring them together for their senior year to do great things.' So I'm, like, 'Yes. Wow.' I was honored and excited. And curious."

He remembered getting the instruction to wait at a certain street corner late one night . . . a big truck rolling up . . . piling in back with other guys . . . a jolting ride...the door rolling up . . . being ordered to crawl through a shallow pool of mud . . . then over to a roaring fire . . . shirtless guys in charge, shouting . . . then the brick dust sprinkled over his head and shoulders. . . .

I now had the flimsiest memory of the mud. I didn't remember the brick dust. But I must have submitted to that, too.

A night or two later, the seniors put on a dress-up dinner party for the new initiates and their dates. Baker remembered a particular moment. One of the seniors began to pass out song sheets to the women. In the lyrics, "squaws" would promise to serve their "braves." Baker's date studied the lyrics for a second and then said to the senior: "Here, I'll pass those out to the women for you." He handed over the stack, whereupon she tore the sheets up and tossed the pieces over her head.

"She thought it was really funny," Baker said. "I was completely supportive of her."

Baker said he had been waiting for someone to explain Michigamua's mission, to set the purpose of service in motion. But that never came. When he asked one of the seniors about it, the senior said: "Baker, would you lighten up? Michigamua is just like a bowling club."

So when the night came for Baker to climb the stairs of the Union tower for the first meeting of the new cadre of members, he couldn't do it.

"I might have said something to you," he told me. "I might have said, 'Jim, I'm out of here . . . . This isn't the place for me.'"

So he walked away, and I climbed the stairs to the "wigwam."

That first meeting must have been when three of us made our bid to admit women and got voted down. Then I decided it wasn't the place for me, either.

Why?

I still couldn't remember. Certainly not because it had dawned on me that Michigamua was steeped at worst in racism and at best in a puerile form of cultural appropriation. I cringed at the "Indian" name I'd been given—"Type-Um Tales." I thought the Indian business seemed childish. But that wasn't why I quit, I'm sure.

It was true, as I'd told Carnevale, that I didn't like the way the athletes seemed to be in charge. But I'd gone all the way through initiation knowing about that, and it hadn't stopped me.

The only thing I can figure is that my true tribe at U-M was the *Michigan Daily*, where half my friends were feminist women and the other half progressive men, all of whom thought the average fraternity, let alone Michigamua, was sexist silliness. It would be a long senior year if once a week I had to hear somebody at the *Daily* say: "So how's Michigamua, Type-Um Tales?"

I remember one more thing. I went alone up to the "wigwam" and left my key on the table, then went back down the stairs, and didn't think about Michigamua any more.

Carnevale wondered if my decision had broken my dad's heart. If so, he never revealed it. My only memory of this part is as vague as the others—that he told me to do what I thought was right for me. That was his tendency—to back up his children, whatever they chose to do. I don't think he and I ever spoke about it again.

❖ ❖ ❖

I talked all this over with my wife. What did it mean? Why couldn't I remember these things?

"I think you wanted it both ways," she said. "You wanted to belong, and you wanted to be the critic."

That, maybe, is why I couldn't remember. There had been nothing honorable about my flirtation with Michigamua. I had been neither wholly in nor wholly out. I had just been the smart-ass kid who wanted to thumb his nose at the jocks, the clique, the elite, the insiders, but who also craved a key to the secret boys' clubhouse, no girls allowed.

It was the hypocrisy that Bob Ufer, of all people, had spotted in me. He had me pegged.

❖ ❖ ❖

The Title IX complaint was settled in 1980 when the University created a senior honorary society for women called Adara (later renamed Phoenix), which joined Michigamua under a new umbrella organization, the Tower Society. By this stratagem the University achieved a kind of separate-but-equal compromise that appeased the federal government.

So Michigamua went on through 1980s and '90s. But women students and Native American students continued to raise objections. All references to Native American themes were dropped except for the name, and in 1999, the "Tribe" voted to admit women.

Then, just a few months later, in early 2000, a group calling itself the Students of Color Coalition occupied the entire Union tower, issuing demands for the University to condemn Michigamua and cut it off. For days, the occupiers offered tours of the "wigwam," displaying the Native American artifacts (only a few of which were genuine) that members of the "Tribe" had long since put away in a storage closet. The *New York Times* and the *Washington Post* covered the spectacle. The Rev. Al Sharpton arrived in Ann Arbor to speak on behalf of the occupiers. After 37 days, the demonstration was brought to an end, and after more protests and negotiations, the University closed the whole tower and eased Michigamua off the campus and out of its official good graces.

In 2007, after a running campaign of further protests and complaints, Michigamua, now divorced from the University, reconstituted itself as the Order of Angell, with both men and women as members. Members of the Order declared a renewed dedication to service to the University, to the cultivation of leadership skills, and to the recruitment of a truly diverse membership. They elected an Arab-American woman as their first leader. Year after year, its rosters reflected the 21st-century diversity of Michigan's student body. But because of its past, it remained the target of accusations and protests. In 2021, under fire on social media and in the *Michigan Daily*, a majority of the membership concluded that they could not escape the legacy of Michigamua. They voted to dissolve the Order of Angell for good, and they urged that no effort be made to resurrect it.

✦ ⁑ ✦

I often think of a little fable that one of my favorite professors at Michigan, Gerald Linderman, told us one day in a lecture. Linderman had been in the U.S. Foreign Service in Africa and India and then came home to study U.S. history. He taught courses in the modern era. I don't remember the context, but the fable itself went like this:

The 20th century says to the 19th century: "You evil bastard...you enslaved Africans, tore them from their homes, divided children from mothers and fathers." The 18th century replies: "We didn't think of it that way. It was natural. It was what we knew."

Then the 21st century says to the 20th century: "You evil bastard...you married our mothers, stuck them in kitchens, suppressed their creativity, consigned them to second-class citizenship and sexual penury." And the 20th century replies: "We didn't think of it that way; it was natural; it was what we knew."

Did the members of Michigamua cause pain to Native American people by "playing Indian"? Surely they did. Would any thinking person start the Michigamua of old in the 21st century? Of course not. But do we deserve to take a stance of moral certitude and pass judgment on the campus cultures of the past? We can do so, but not without first inquiring into them deeply to make sure we meet them on their own terms and see them as clearly as we can.

The University is the accumulation of decisions made by imperfect people in their imperfect generations. Each generation cast off elements of the past and replaced it with new creations, and so it went, era by era. So it must go if a worthy institution is to survive.

So what would I do with the Rope Day photo in its dusty old frame, with my father at the age of 21 standing somberly in his faux-Indian headdress? Should I throw it away as if it were shameful?

Many years ago, members of Michigamua placed a plaque inscribed with a tomahawk in the ground near the Tappan Oak on the Diag. Then, when Michigamua's use of Native American symbolism was declared to be unmitigatedly racist, the plaque was dug up and moved to a scraggly plot of grass behind the Bentley Historical Library on North Campus. Nobody sees it there unless they go and look for it. A few feet away, on the blank back wall of the library, you can see the 1948 bas-relief sculptures titled "Dream of the Young Girl" and "Dream of the Young Man" that used to be affixed to the facade of the LSA Building on State Street. "Dream of the Young Girl" shows a sleeping girl conjuring the image of a young woman with two children who takes the hand of a muscular pioneer by his Conestoga wagon. In the mid-2000s, administrators decided the image was anachronistic and sent it to the Bentley.

The economist Paul Courant, then U-M's provost, remarked at the time: "My own general view about anachronistic statements of value is that you ought to use them as opportunities to teach. When possible, you'd like to have a display that gives people opportunities to reflect on what the world was like when the art was created."

To me, Courant's point seems just right, especially at a university. The archivists of the Bentley Library don't honor such relics as the tomahawk plaque and "Dream of a Young Girl" by preserving them. But they don't burn them in a ritual of renunciation either. The relics document particular moments in the University's history, which is itself one microcosm of our history as a society—imperfect, troubled, always evolving.

The Rope Day photo represents a fragment of the world as my dad knew it in the spring of 1941. It was one slice of what he considered normal and natural. I loved him and I miss him. So I'll put the photo back in a place where I can look at it from time to time. It may remind me to take a dose of humility whenever I feel the temptation to pass judgment on the past.

Epilogue

"A Splendid Beneficence"

Here is an imaginary human web that stretches across more than a century and a half.

At the far distant end, in the 1850s, the first strand in the web is tied to Michigan's first president, Henry Philip Tappan.

Here in the present, there's a tiny strand tied to my little finger.

This isn't a web of causation, just of connection—one person connected to another, then another and so on, from Tappan to me.

So, here goes:

Henry Tappan became U-M's first president in 1852.

In 1858 Tappan hired a young historian named Andrew Dickson White. White became the first professor to teach modern history in U-M's original Department of Literature, Science and the Arts.

One of White's students was Charles Kendall Adams.

Adams graduated from U-M in 1861 and joined Andrew Dickson White as an instructor in history. When White left, Adams was appointed to fill White's vacant professorship.

Adams was one of the first American historians to use the seminar method of teaching. In a history seminar, students study and write about original historical documents, just as working historians do. Adams's colleagues picked up the seminar method and soon it became standard, not only at Michigan but in many other history departments.

In the late 1800s, the most influential historian trained by the seminar method was arguably Frederick Jackson Turner, author of the "frontier thesis" of American history—the idea that the nation's distinctive identity had arisen from the ever-receding experience of a wild frontier. He earned his PhD at Johns Hopkins, then taught at the University of Wisconsin and Harvard.

At Wisconsin, Turner had a deep influence on a young colleague, Ulrich Bonnell Phillips, who later joined the Department of History at Michigan, where he rewrote the history of slavery and the Old South.

One of Phillips's star students was Dwight Lowell Dumond, who joined the Department of History in 1930. He wrote important books on the anti-slavery movement.

One of Dumond's star students was Sidney Fine, who joined the Department of History in 1948 and later was named the Andrew Dickson White Professor of History. He taught until 2001.

Of the 29,000 students taught by Sidney Fine, my wife was one and I was another.

I was *not* one of Fine's star students.

But I learned how to study original historical documents in his graduate seminar—a seminar of the kind introduced at U-M by Charles Kendall Adams, student of Andrew Dickson White, hired by Henry Philip Tappan.

That gave me the tools to write three biographies and the stories in this book, among many others. So I feel a long-distance connection to Henry Tappan through seven degrees of separation, and I feel grateful for it.

Any Michigan alumnus can play this game. A biology major can string a line to Tappan through the great U-M bacteriologist Frederick Novy (1864–1957). A teacher's connection to Tappan runs through John Dewey (1859–1952), the philosopher and theorist of education. An information specialist's line goes through Margaret Mann (1873–1960), who helped start the unit that would become the School of Information. Graduates of the Honors Program have a very short route back to Tappan. The program's first director was Robert Cooley Angell (1899–1994), grandson of Thomas McIntyre Cooley, whom Tappan hired as a law professor.

This becomes more than a parlor game when you think about why these strands of human connection exist at all. They form a vast, complex web that is the University of Michigan as an institution—that is, a network of people reaching through time and space and united by a common purpose: To learn.

I remember Sidney Fine remarking that one of his purposes as a teacher was "to instill in my students a respect for my profession."

At the time that struck me as a mildly selfish motive. Shouldn't he teach just for the students' own good?

I see now he was thinking of how his work served institutions precisely *for the sake of* students—the institution of history as a profession and the larger institutions that supported that profession, namely, the University and higher education as a whole. Fine's work as a teacher depended entirely on the health of those institutions, and the teaching of history would outlive him only if those institutions were strong.

By the light of popular culture, American institutions look very powerful, even too powerful. Since the 1960s, at least, many of us have seen the institution qua institution as the enemy of the individual, and no doubt that's often true enough.

But in another light, the web of an institution can look delicate, even fragile.

President Tappan had something like this in mind when he said universities were like families. They were "maintained, not by legal enactments, but by the influences of predominant character, by the force of example . . . by the diffused spirit of the social life itself—the esprit de corps of the family or society and by principles breathed around from the intimate relations, the mutual dependencies, and common aims and pursuits . . . . Where eminent professors breathe around the spirit of knowledge and liberal culture, and give the example of a noble devotion to learning, they must...create a prevailing sentiment which . . . will prove more commanding than all written statutes, and without which written statutes are a dead letter."

The University wasn't standing on the strength of Regents' bylaws, and certainly not on the strength of mere bricks and mortar. It was held up by nothing more substantial than the breath of professors and students talking.

Recall Henry Carter Adams writing President Angell to ask for a permanent position, saying: "You have the men to talk to." The idea is the same now as it was in 1882—modified by the realization that a university composed only of men would be only half a university. The value in the institution lies in the quality of the talk and the questions asked—and so, by extension, in the freedom to talk and the eagerness to listen.

It's worth reflecting that this delicate web needs diligent care as much now as it did in Henry Tappan's time.

It's one thing, as an individual, to love learning—to be aware, curious, and questing.

It's quite another to support an institution whose whole purpose is to nurture and fulfill that love.

The institution is the purpose made permanent. It's a means of defying our own mortality. It connects all the University's faculty, students, and alumni to Henry Tappan, who said in his inaugural address, just before Christmas 1852: "We cannot entail estates in our country to our legal heirs. But an estate might be entailed in a great University as long as our country shall exist—a splendid beneficence—a monument worthy of the ambition of any man."

If you think our universities are too strong to be in danger, ask yourself this: If they didn't exist already, thanks to the generations that came before us, would our society be willing to make the massive investment that would be required to build them now, from the ground up? And if we would not build them—and I think we would not—will we at least sustain them?

Sources

Sources are listed roughly in order of their importance to the assembly of each story. I note the help I received from particular individuals at the end of several entries.

1: A Different Diag. Russell Bidlack, *John Allen and the Founding of Ann Arbor* (1962); Daniel Boorstin, *The Americans (vol. 2): The National Experience* (1965); Cornelia E. Corselius, *Some of the Early Homes of Ann Arbor, Michigan* (1909); *History of Washtenaw County, Michigan* (1881); *Regents' Proceedings, University of Michigan,* 1837–1864; Wilfred B. Shaw, *The University of Michigan* (1920); Jonathan Marwil, *A History of Ann Arbor* (1987); Orlando W. Stephenson, *Ann Arbor: The First Hundred Years* (1927); Wilfred Shaw, ed., *The University of Michigan: An Encyclopedic Survey*; and Nettie Idell Schepeler Van der Werker, *History of Earliest Ann Arbor* (1919).

2: Professor White's Trees. *The Autobiography of Andrew Dickson White*, vol. 1 (1905); Anne Duderstadt, *The University of Michigan: A Photographic Saga* (2006); "The Trees on Michigan's Campus," *Michigan Alumnus*, January 1923; "Campus Paths — Old and New," *Michigan Alumnus*, December 1922; Dr. W.F. Breakey, letter to the *Michigan Alumnus*, April 1901; and Elizabeth M. Farrand, *History of the University of Michigan* (1885).

3: When Heads Rolled. Margaret Leary, *Giving It All Away: The Story of William W. Cook and His Michigan Law Quadrangle* (2011); Ilene Forsyth, *The Uses of Art: Medieval Metaphor in the Michigan Law Quadrangle* (1993); Kathryn Horste, *The Michigan Law Quadrangle: Architecture and Origins* (1997); the papers of Walter Hulme Sawyer and Elizabeth Gaspar Brown at the Bentley Historical Library; Alexander Grant Ruthven, *Naturalist in Two Worlds: Random Collections of a University President* (1963); and Shirley W. Smith, *Harry Burns Hutchins and the University of Michigan* (1951). Several passages in the story are adapted from my short book, *Michigan Law at 150: An Informal History* (2004). Margaret Leary gave me crucial advice on numerous points.

4: Hangouts. *Michigan Daily; Ann Arbor News.* My conversation with Professor Zevi Miller of Miami University provided the basis of the story about Dominick's.

5: Tappan's End. Paul E. Lingenfelter, "The Firing of Henry Philip Tappan," student paper, 1970, Bentley Historical Library; *Review by Rev. Dr. H.P. Tappan of His Connection with the University of Michigan* (1864); Charles M. Perry, *Henry Philip Tappan: Philosopher and University President* (1933); "Andrew D. White on President Tappan and the University as Tappan Made It," *Michigan Alumnus*, March 1903; Howard H. Peckham, edited and updated by Margaret L. and Nicholas H. Steneck, *The Making of the University of Michigan, 1817–1992* (1967, 1994); *Autobiography of Andrew Dickson White*, vol. 2 (1906); Wilfred Shaw, *The University of Michigan* (1920); and *Proceedings of the Board of Regents*, 1871–1875.

6: The Making of Michigan. S. Lawrence Bigelow, Leo Sharfman, and I.M. Wenley, "Henry Carter Adams," *Journal of Political Economy*, 30:2 (April 1922), 201–211; A.W. Coates, "Henry Carter Adams: A Case Study in the Emergence of the Social Sciences in the United States," *Journal of American Studies*, 2:2 (October 1968), 177–197; Gary A. Cook, *George Herbert Mead: The Making of a Social Pragmatist* (1993); George Horton Cooley, *The Two Major Works: Social Organization; Human Nature and the Social Order* (1956) and *On Self and Social Organization* (1998); Jane M. Dewey, ed., "Biography of John Dewey," in Paul Arthur Schilpp, *The Philosophy of John Dewey* (1939); Andrew Feffer, *The Chicago Pragmatists and American Progressivism* (1993); Sidney Fine, *Laissez-Faire and the General-Welfare State: A Study of Conflict in American Thought, 1865–1901* (1956); George M. Marsden, *The Soul of the American University: From Protestant Establishment to Established Nonbelief* (1994); George Herbert Mead, "Cooley's Contribution to American Social Thought," *American Journal of Sociology* 35:5 (March 1930), 693–706; Steven Rockefeller, *John Dewey: Religious Faith and Democratic Humanism* (1994); Marvin Rosenberry, "Henry C. Adams," in Earl D. Babst and Lewis G. Vander Velde, eds., *Michigan and the Cleveland Era* (1948); James Turner and Paul Bernard, "The Prussian Road to University? German Models and the University of Michigan, 1837-c. 1895," in *Intellectual History and Academic Culture at the University of Michigan: Fresh Explorations* (1989); Brian Williams, "Thought and Action: John Dewey at the University of Michigan" (Bentley Historical Library *Bulletin* No. 44, 1998); and the papers of James Burrill Angell, Bentley Historical Library.

7: A War over Words. Michael Adams, "Sanford Meech at the Middle English Dictionary," *Dictionaries*, 16 (1995), 151–185 (the key source on the Meech/Knott imbroglio); "Phantom Dictionaries: The Middle English Dictionary before Kurath," *Dictionaries*, 23 (2002), 95–114; Dianne Williams, "Hope Emily Allen Speaks with the Dead," *Leeds Studies in English* (2004), 137–160; Frederic G. Cassidy, "Hope Emily Allen: A Personal Reminiscence," *Dictionaries* (1989), 149–151; John C. Hirsh, *Hope Emily Allen: Medieval Scholarship and Feminism* (1988); Warner G. Rice, "Thomas A. Knott, 1880–1945," *College English*, 7:5 (February 1946); and Simon Winchester, *The Meaning of Everything: The Story of the Oxford English Dictionary* (2002). I am grateful to Dr. Michael Adams of Indiana University, who unearthed Sanford Meech's role in saving the *MED*, for answering many questions about Meech, Knott, the *MED*, and dictionary-making in general.

8: The Fourth Name on the List. Documents that reveal many details of Lawrence Klein's departure from U-M, as well as the Davis-Markert-Nickerson controversy, are held in the papers of Marvin Niehuss, Harlan Hatcher, the University Senate, the U-M chapter of the American Association of University Professors, and the Economics Department, all at the Bentley Historical Library. The Department's papers include transcripts of Marjorie Cahn Brazer's interviews with members of the Department and her unpublished history, which deals with the Klein case. Praise for William Paton appears in Herbert F. Taggart et al., "A Tribute to William A. Paton," *Accounting Review* (January 1992). Key secondary sources are David A. Hollinger, "Academic Culture at the University of Michigan, 1938–1988," in *Science, Jews and Secular Culture* (1998); "2009 Postscript and Second Thoughts," Ellen Schrecker, *No Ivory Tower: McCarthyism and the Universities* (1986); and Peggie J. Hollingsworth, ed., *Unfettered Expression: Freedom in American Intellectual Life* (2000). Also revealing are interviews conducted with many of the surviving principals in the Davis-Markert-Nickerson episode by Adam Kulakow for the documentary he created as a student in the late 1980s, *Keeping in Mind: The McCarthy Era at the University of Michigan.* Videotapes of the interviews, as well as the documentary itself, are held in Kulakow's collection at the Bentley Historical Library.

9: The Warrior Scholar. This story is drawn chiefly from interviews with Yale Kamisar conducted by Enid Galler, who collected a series of oral histories with law professors now held by the Bentley Historical Library, and by the author. Other sources: Francis A. Allen, "Yale Kamisar: Warrior Scholar"; Eve L. Brensike, "Saying Goodbye to a Legend: A Tribute to Yale Kamisar—My Mentor, Teacher, and Friend"; Jeffrey S. Lehman, "Yale Kamisar the Teacher"; Ruth Bader Ginsburg, "Tribute to Yale Kamisar"; and Welsh S. White, "Yale Kamisar: The Enemy of Injustice," *Michigan Law Review,* August 2004. The author thanks Bruce Leitman, one of the Law students who yelled up at Hutchins Hall late one night in the mid-1960s, for details of the students' exchange with Yale Kamisar.

10: "Our Brilliant Miss Sheldon." The papers of Mary Sheldon Barnes, Sophia Smith Collection, Smith College, Northampton, Massachusetts. Mary's papers include her letters to her parents, siblings, and Mary Alling, as well as scrapbooks and memorabilia from her years at Michigan.

11: Women Apart. The papers of the Women's League (University of Michigan), Bentley Historical Library; *The Castalian; Michigan Daily; Michigan Alumnus; Michiganensian;* and Marian Swanson Wissenberg, "The Women's League," Wilfred Shaw, ed., *The University of Michigan: An Encyclopedic Survey.*

12: "A Lot of 'Ordinary' Women." The key sources for the story are in a rich digital collection of documents and commentary by Sara Fitzgerald titled "What Factors Led to the Success of the Historic 1970 Sex Discrimination Complaint Filed against the University of Michigan?" The collection was developed as part of a research project conducted through the University of Michigan Institute for

Research on Women and Gender. The Bentley Historical Library holds most of the original documents in the collection and many related materials.

13: Rhapsodies in Blue. Liene Karels, "Which Maize? Which Blue?" *Michigan Today*, Fall 1996; "Maize and Azure Blue," *Michigan Alumnus*, May 1912; Benjamin R. Kurtz, *Charles Mills Gayley* (1943); "Michigan Football Uniforms, 1879–1899," Bentley Historical Library; T.R. Chase, *The Michigan University Book, 1844–1880* (1880); and the author's interviews with Kenneth Burke, Albert Ahronheim, Joe Carl, and Tom Blaske.

14: Two against Football. *Michigan Chimes; Michigan Alumnus; Michigan Daily;* Fielding Harris Yost papers, Bentley Historical Library. After this story was published in its original form, Neil Staebler's grandson, Ned Staebler, told me that for all his early iconoclasm, his grandfather was a lifelong fan of Michigan football.

15: The Mystery of Belford Lawson. Belford V. Lawson III shared extensive recollections of his father. He was also exceedingly generous in sharing with me his own reflections about his father's life. Other sources included records of the Athletic Department at the Bentley Historical Library; *Michigan Daily; Michigan Alumnus; Detroit Free Press;* John U. Bacon, et al., *A Legacy of Champions: The Story of the Men Who Built University of Michigan Football* (1996); John Behee, *Hail to the Victors* (1974); and John Behee, *Fielding H. Yost's Legacy to the University of Michigan* (1970). Behee's latter book includes the quoted passage from Elton Weiman's letter to Herbert Wilson. Richard Lerner located the mention of Belford Lawson Jr. in the *Detroit Free Press*. Gregory Kinney of the Bentley Historical Library provided expert help on several points.

16: The Rise and Fall of J-Hop. The online archives of the *Michigan Daily* provided most of the sources for this story. The anecdote about Avery Hopwood is from Jack Sharrar, *Avery Hopwood: His Life and Plays* (1989).

17: The Negro-Caucasian Club. The papers of Oakley Johnson in the Joseph Labadie Collection, Special Collections, Harlan Hatcher Graduate Library; and Oakley Johnson, "The Negro-Caucasian Club: A History," *Michigan Quarterly Review* (Spring 1969).

18: Panty Raid, 1952. *Michigan Daily; Ann Arbor News; Detroit News; Life* magazine, and a U-M senior honors thesis in history, "The Dean's Last Stand: Deborah Bacon and the Student Politics of the Fifties" (2006), by Lindsey Helfman. I'm grateful to Jonathan Marwil, U-M lecturer in history and author of *A History of Ann Arbor* (1991), for suggesting a connection between the first panty raid and the student revolts of the 1960s.

19: Food Riot, 1956. The papers of the U-M Housing Division, Bentley Historical Library.

20: The End of Hours. *Michigan Daily* and the papers of the U-M Housing Division, Bentley Historical Library.

21: Earth Day Eve. Doug Scott's oral history, which includes his recollections of Michigan's Teach-In on the Environment, can be found online at the Sierra Club Oral History Series of the Bancroft Library, University of California at Berkeley. Also: Interview with Professor David Allan of U-M's School of Natural Resources and Environment; the papers of David Chudwin, Bentley Historical Library; and Adam Rome, *The Genius of Earth Day: How a 1970 Teach-In Unexpectedly Made the First Green Generation* (2013).

22: The BAM Strike. *The Michigan Daily*; President (University of Michigan) records, Bentley Historical Library; Henry Vance Davis, ed., *Sankofa: The University Since BAM: Twenty Years of Progress?* (1990); Robben W. Fleming, *Tempests into Rainbows: Managing Turbulence* (1996); Matthew Johnson, *Undermining Racial Justice: How One University Embraced Inclusion and Inequality* (2020); Alan Glenn, "Open It Up or Shut It Down," *Ann Arbor Chronicle*, 3/30/2010.

23: Remembering Michigamua. James Tobin, "Michigamua: Test of a Tradition," 11/30/1976, and "Michigamua: Pride or Prejudice?" 12/1/1976, *The Michigan Daily*; Papers of the Order of Angell/Michigamua, Bentley Historical Library; Robert F. Berkhofer, *The White Man's Indian: Images of the American Indian from Columbus to the Present* (1979); Philip J. Deloria, *Playing Indian* (1999).

Acknowledgments

It's a pleasure to express my thanks to people who helped these stories come into being.

Nearly all the stories were written for and shaped by three editors: John Lofy and Deborah Holdship, editors of *Michigan Today*; and Kim Clarke, leader of the online University of Michigan Heritage Project. I'm grateful for their ideas, guidance, support, and friendship.

At the Bentley Historical Library, these archivists in particular, all deeply knowledgeable about the University of Michigan's history, helped me in many ways—Karen Jania, Malgorzata Myc, Karen Wight, Brian Williams, Nancy Bartlett, Greg Kinney, and Diana Bachman. (This is not to forget Mary Jo Pugh, from whom I learned how to behave in an archive when I was a fledgling researcher.) These archivists worked under two estimable directors, Francis X. Blouin Jr. and Terrence J. McDonald, who have fortified the Bentley's standing as a great library.

At the University of Michigan Press, Scott Ham saw value in putting these stories between covers and helped me see how to make them something more than a mere collection. Then he shepherded them through the editorial process with a keen eye and a lot of patience. I'm grateful, too, to the Press for skillful copyediting.

Two friends with a strong interest in the University's history gave good advice along the way: John U. Bacon and Jonathan Marwil.

One cherished archivist deserves my thanks above all others: Leesa Erickson Tobin.